GRACE RANDOLPH'S
SUPURBIA ™

VOLUME FOUR
HARD
TRUTHS

⸻•◦ GRACE RANDOLPH'S ◦•⸻
SUPURBIA ™

ROSS RICHIE CEO & Founder • **JACK CUMMINS** President • **MARK SMYLIE** Founder of Archaia • **MATT GAGNON** Editor-in-Chief • **FILIP SABLIK** VP of Publishing & Marketing • **STEPHEN CHRISTY** VP of Development
LANCE KREITER VP of Licensing & Merchandising • **PHIL BARBARO** VP of Finance • **BRYCE CARLSON** Managing Editor • **MEL CAYLO** Marketing Manager • **SCOTT NEWMAN** Production Design Manager • **IRENE BRADISH** Operations Manager
DAFNA PLEBAN Editor • **SHANNON WATTERS** Editor • **ERIC HARBURN** Editor • **REBECCA TAYLOR** Editor • **IAN BRILL** Editor • **CHRIS ROSA** Assistant Editor • **ALEX GALER** Assistant Editor • **WHITNEY LEOPARD** Assistant Editor
JASMINE AMIRI Assistant Editor • **CAMERON CHITTOCK** Assistant Editor • **HANNAH NANCE PARTLOW** Production Designer • **KELSEY DIETERICH** Production Designer • **EMI YONEMURA BROWN** Production Designer
DEVIN FUNCHES E-Commerce & Inventory Coordinator • **ANDY LIEGL** Event Coordinator • **BRIANNA HART** Executive Assistant • **AARON FERRARA** Operations Assistant • **JOSÉ MEZA** Sales Assistant • **ELIZABETH LOUGHRIDGE** Accounting Assistant

A catalog record of this book is available from OCLC and from the BOOM! Studios website, www.boom-studios.com, on the Librarians Page.

BOOM! Studios, 5670 Wilshire Boulevard, Suite 450, Los Angeles, CA 90036-5679. Printed in South Korea. First Printing.
ISBN: 978-1-60886-394-5, eISBN: 978-1-61398-248-8

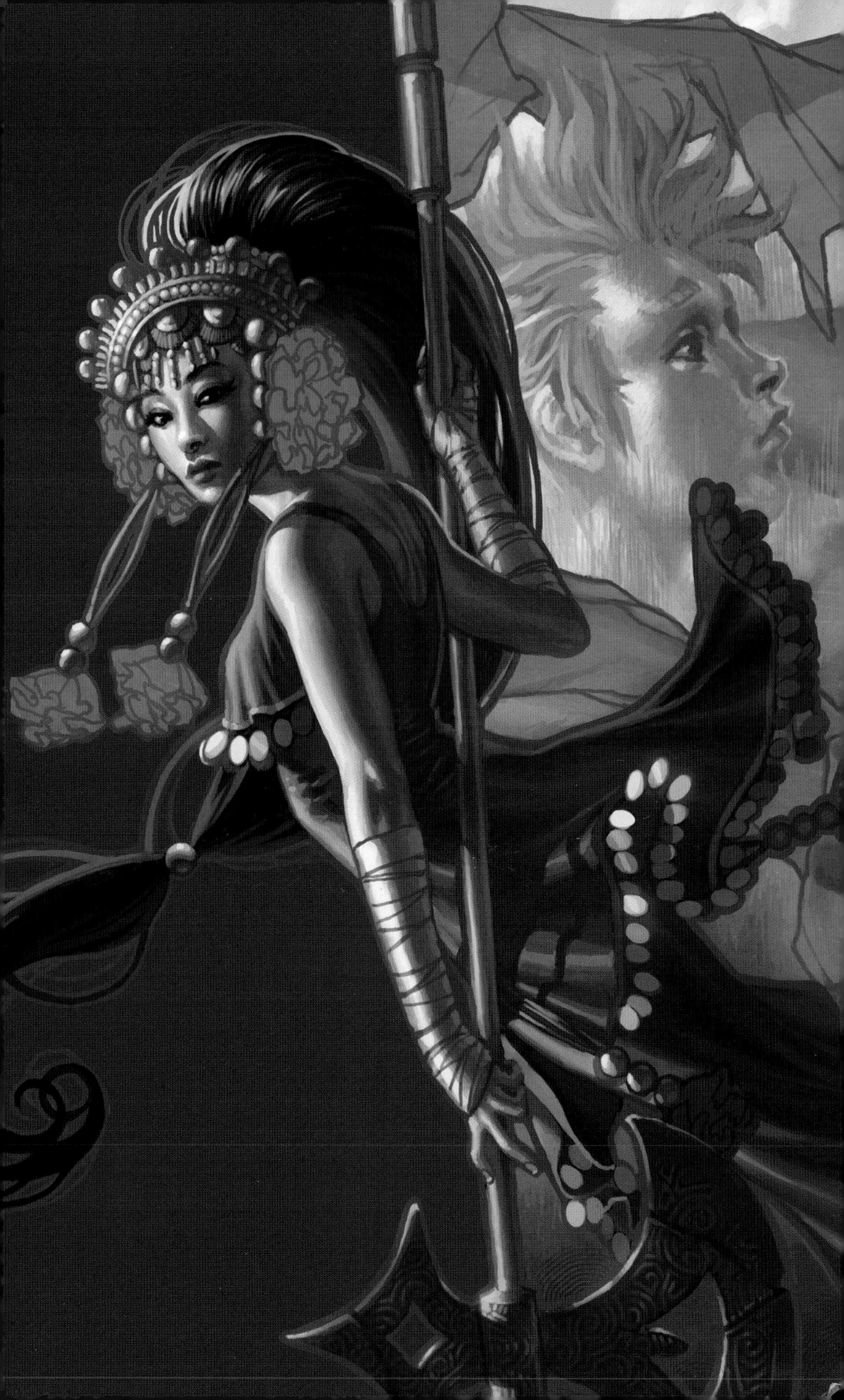

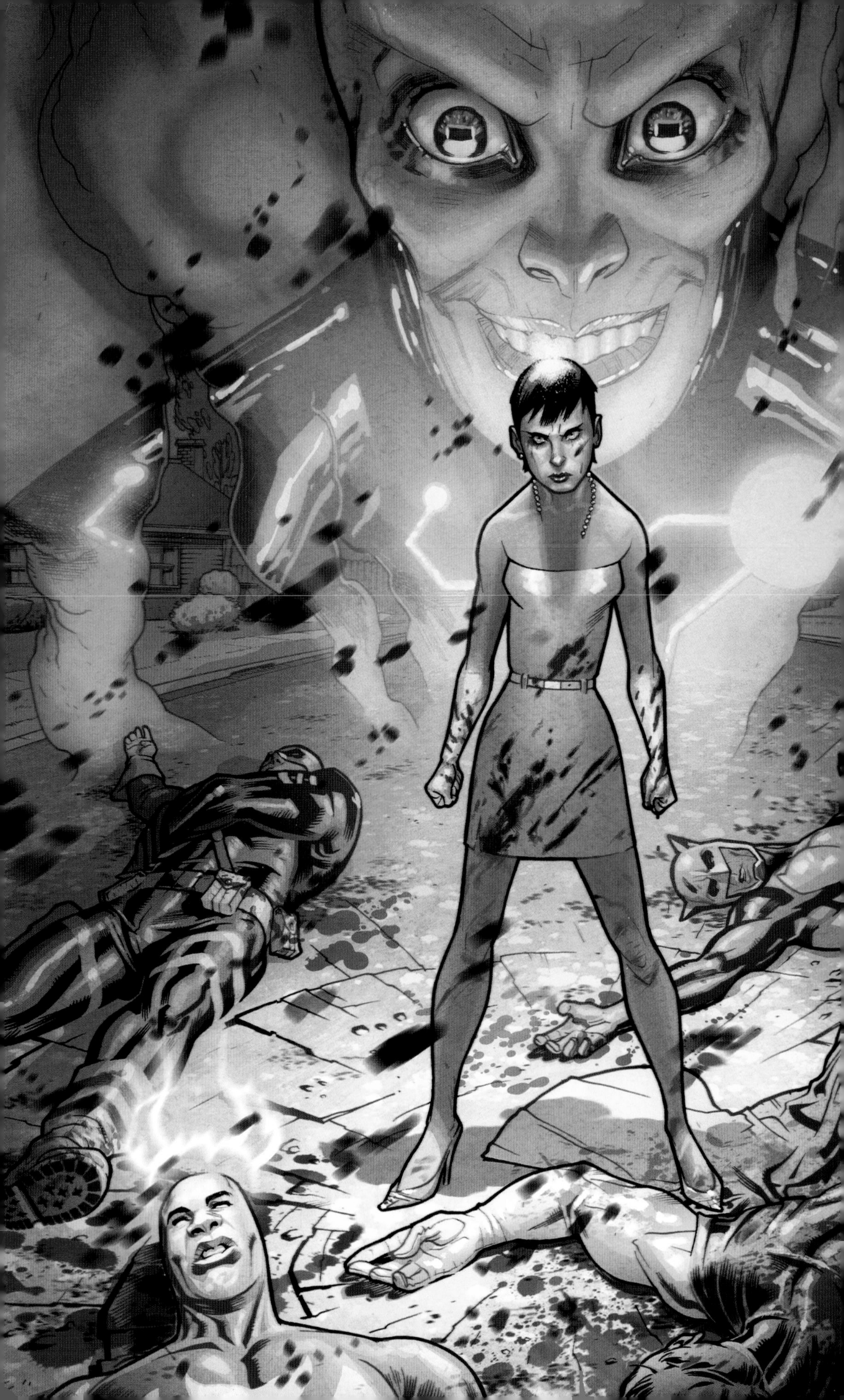

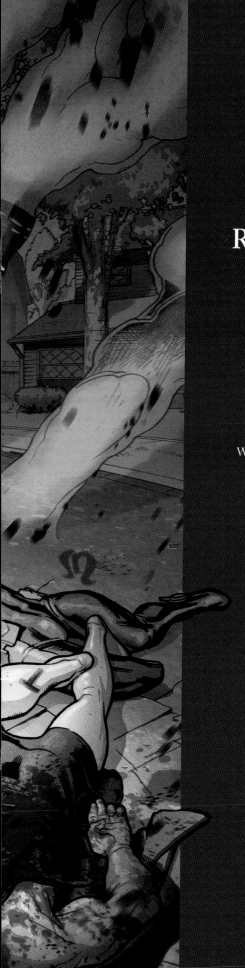

CREATED AND WRITTEN BY
GRACE RANDOLPH
ART BY
RUSSELL DAUTERMAN

COLORS BY
GABRIEL CASSATA
LETTERS BY
STEVE WANDS

COVER BY
RUSSELL DAUTERMAN
WITH COLORS BY **GABRIEL CASSATA**

TRADE DESIGNER
KELSEY DIETERICH

EDITOR
ERIC HARBURN

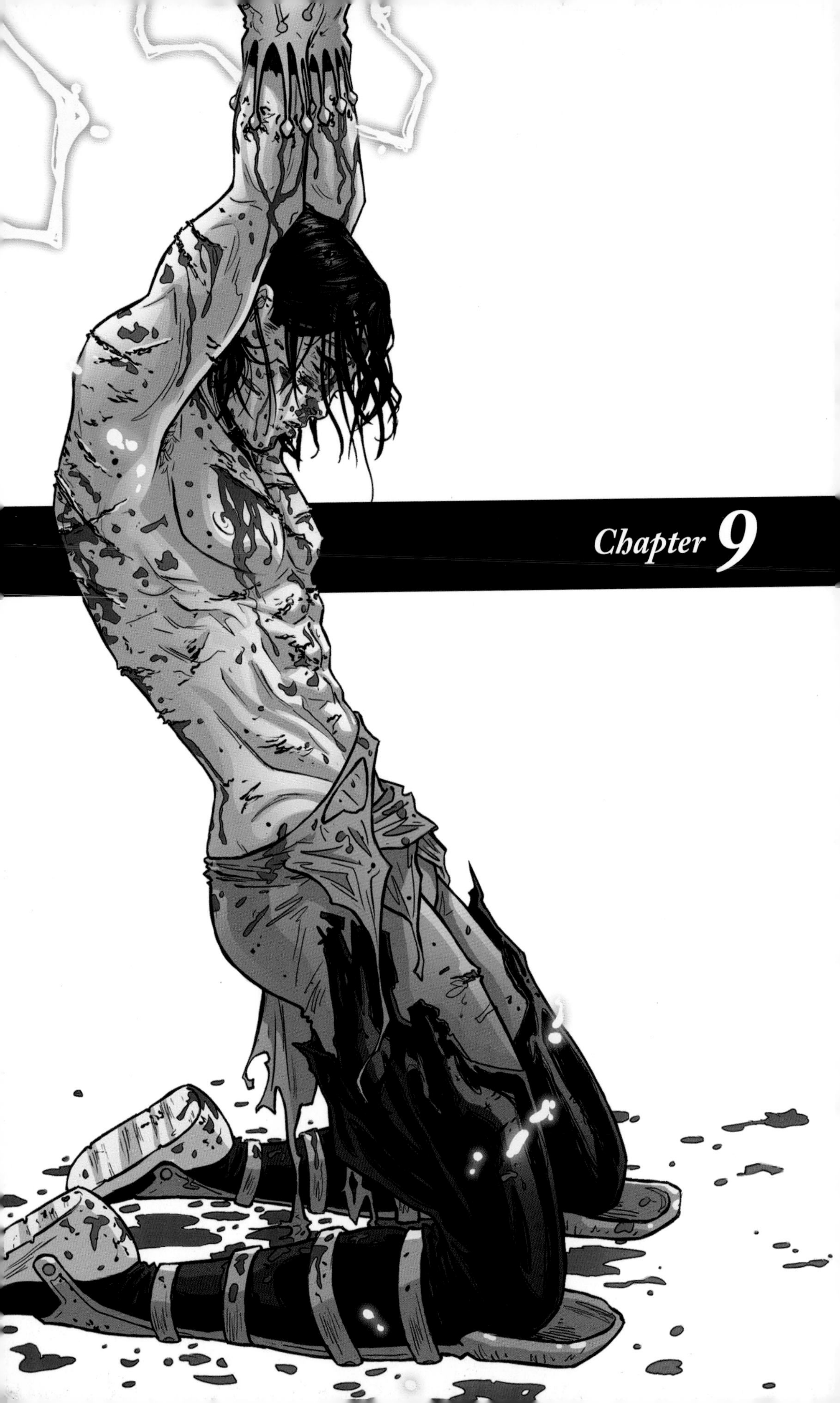

Chapter 9

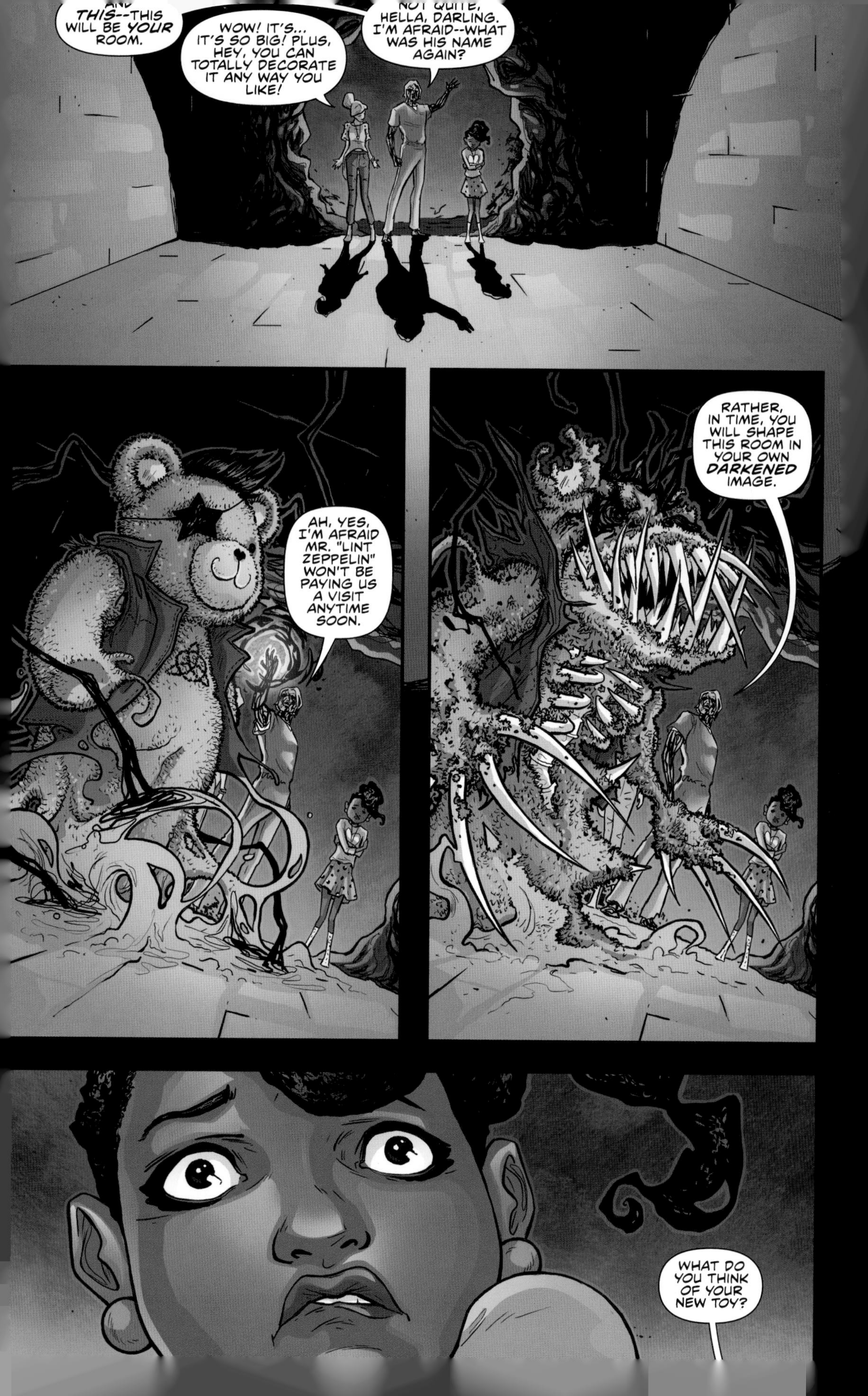
AND THIS--THIS WILL BE YOUR ROOM.
WOW! IT'S... IT'S SO BIG! PLUS, HEY, YOU CAN TOTALLY DECORATE IT ANY WAY YOU LIKE!
NOT QUITE, HELLA, DARLING. I'M AFRAID--WHAT WAS HIS NAME AGAIN?
AH, YES, I'M AFRAID MR. "LINT ZEPPELIN" WON'T BE PAYING US A VISIT ANYTIME SOON.
RATHER, IN TIME, YOU WILL SHAPE THIS ROOM IN YOUR OWN DARKENED IMAGE.
WHAT DO YOU THINK OF YOUR NEW TOY?

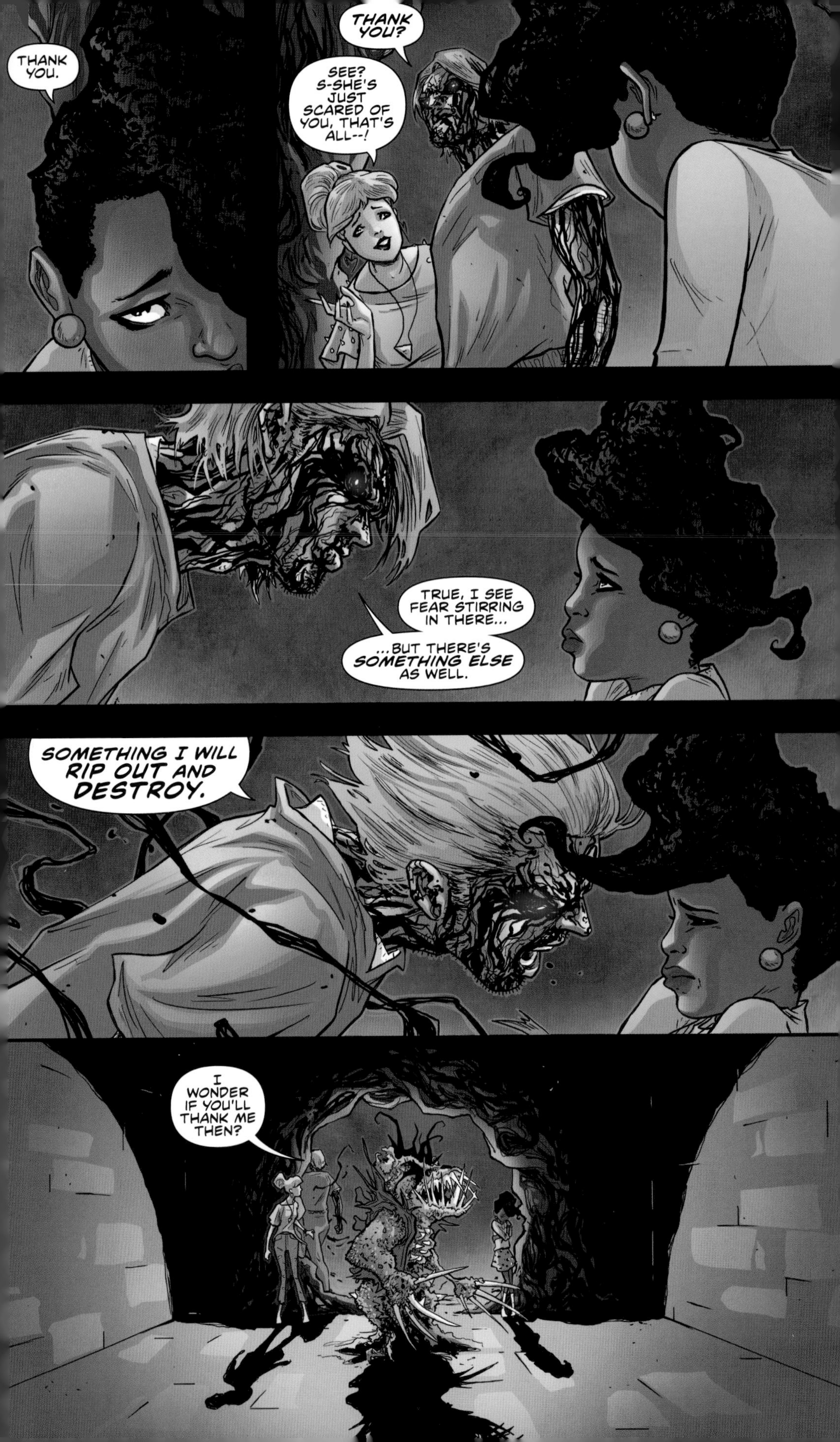
THANK YOU.
THANK YOU?
SEE? S-SHE'S JUST SCARED OF YOU, THAT'S ALL--!
TRUE, I SEE FEAR STIRRING IN THERE...
...BUT THERE'S SOMETHING ELSE AS WELL.
SOMETHING I WILL RIP OUT AND DESTROY.
I WONDER IF YOU'LL THANK ME THEN?

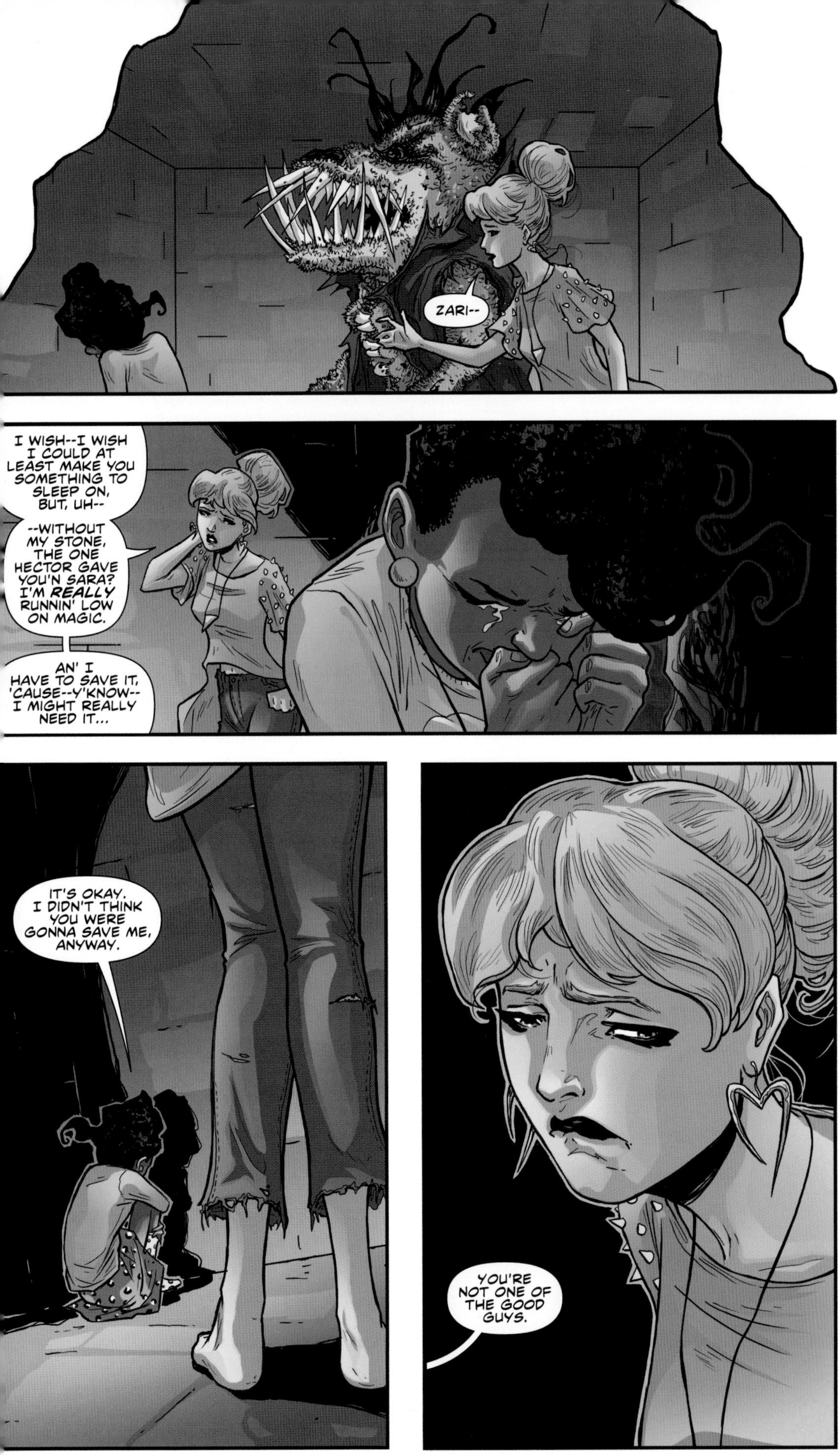
ZARI--
I WISH--I WISH I COULD AT LEAST MAKE YOU SOMETHING TO SLEEP ON, BUT, UH--
--WITHOUT MY STONE, THE ONE HECTOR GAVE YOU'N SARA? I'M **REALLY** RUNNIN' LOW ON MAGIC.
AN' I HAVE TO SAVE IT, 'CAUSE--Y'KNOW-- I MIGHT REALLY NEED IT...
IT'S OKAY. I DIDN'T THINK YOU WERE GONNA SAVE ME, ANYWAY.
YOU'RE NOT ONE OF THE GOOD GUYS.

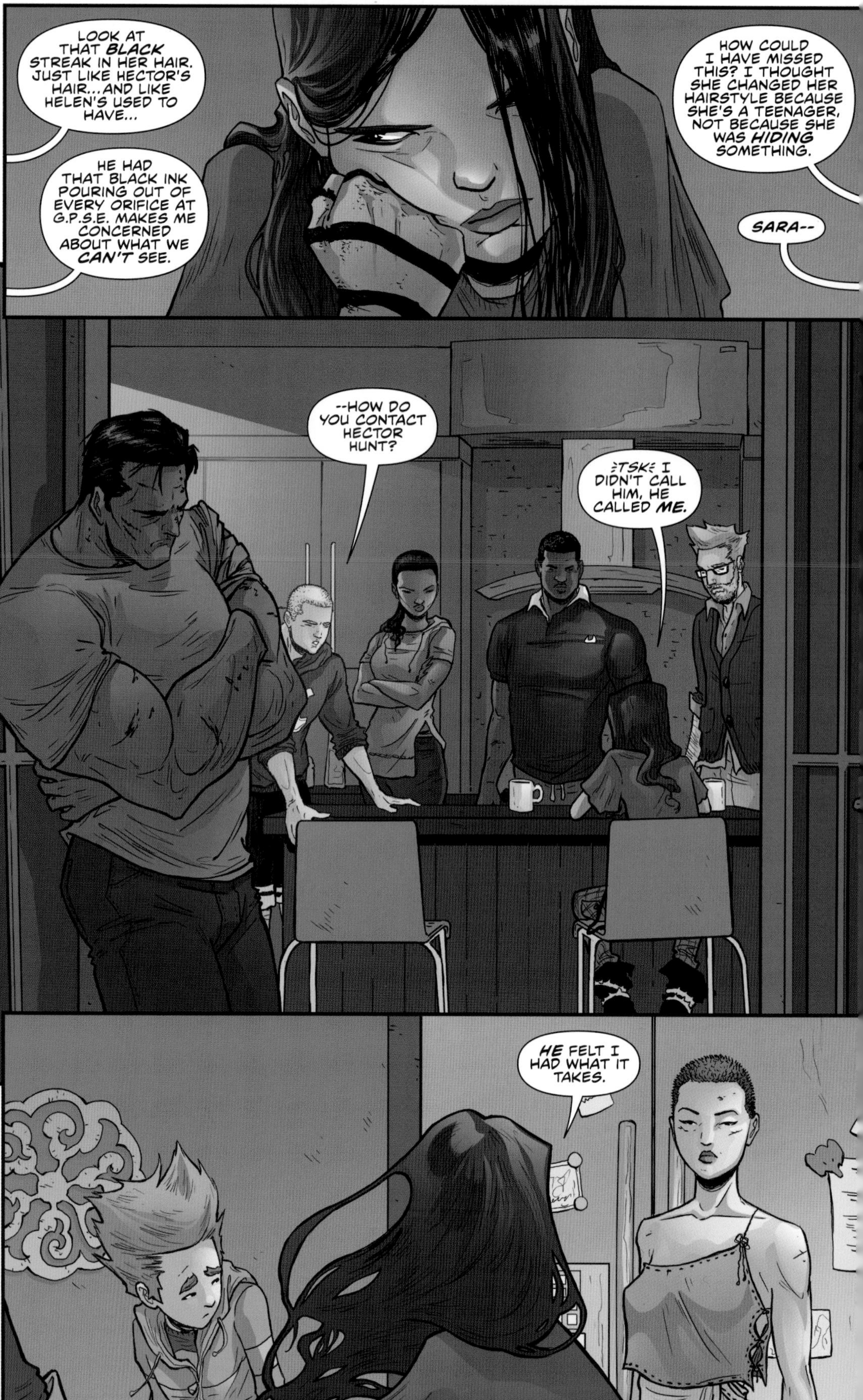

LOOK AT THAT BLACK STREAK IN HER HAIR. JUST LIKE HECTOR'S HAIR...AND LIKE HELEN'S USED TO HAVE...
HE HAD THAT BLACK INK POURING OUT OF EVERY ORIFICE AT G.P.S.E. MAKES ME CONCERNED ABOUT WHAT WE CAN'T SEE.
HOW COULD I HAVE MISSED THIS? I THOUGHT SHE CHANGED HER HAIRSTYLE BECAUSE SHE'S A TEENAGER, NOT BECAUSE SHE WAS HIDING SOMETHING.
SARA--
--HOW DO YOU CONTACT HECTOR HUNT?
TSK I DIDN'T CALL HIM, HE CALLED ME.
HE FELT I HAD WHAT IT TAKES.

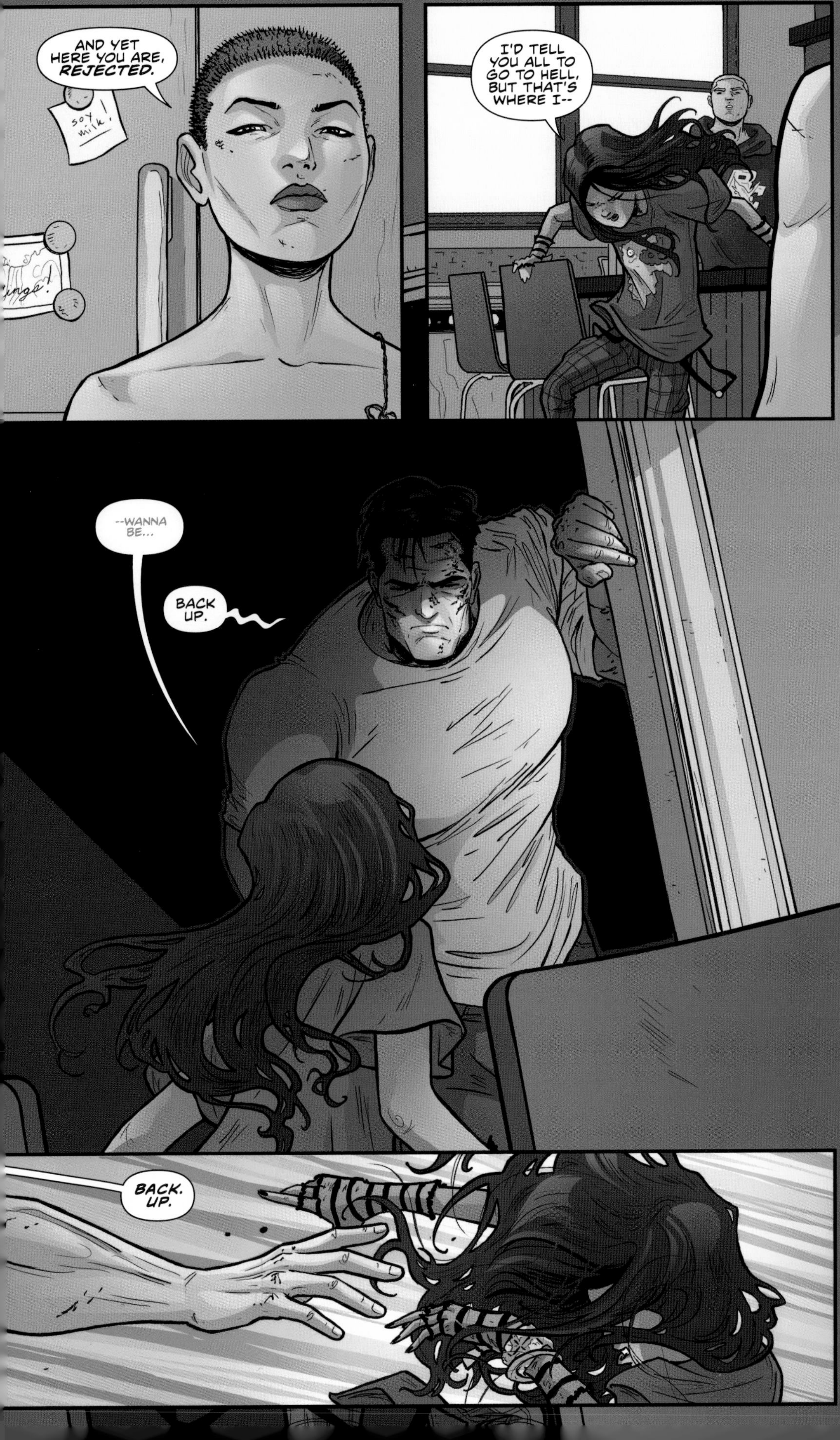
AND YET HERE YOU ARE, *REJECTED.*
soy milk!
I'D TELL YOU ALL TO GO TO HELL, BUT THAT'S WHERE I--
--WANNA BE...
BACK UP.
BACK. UP.

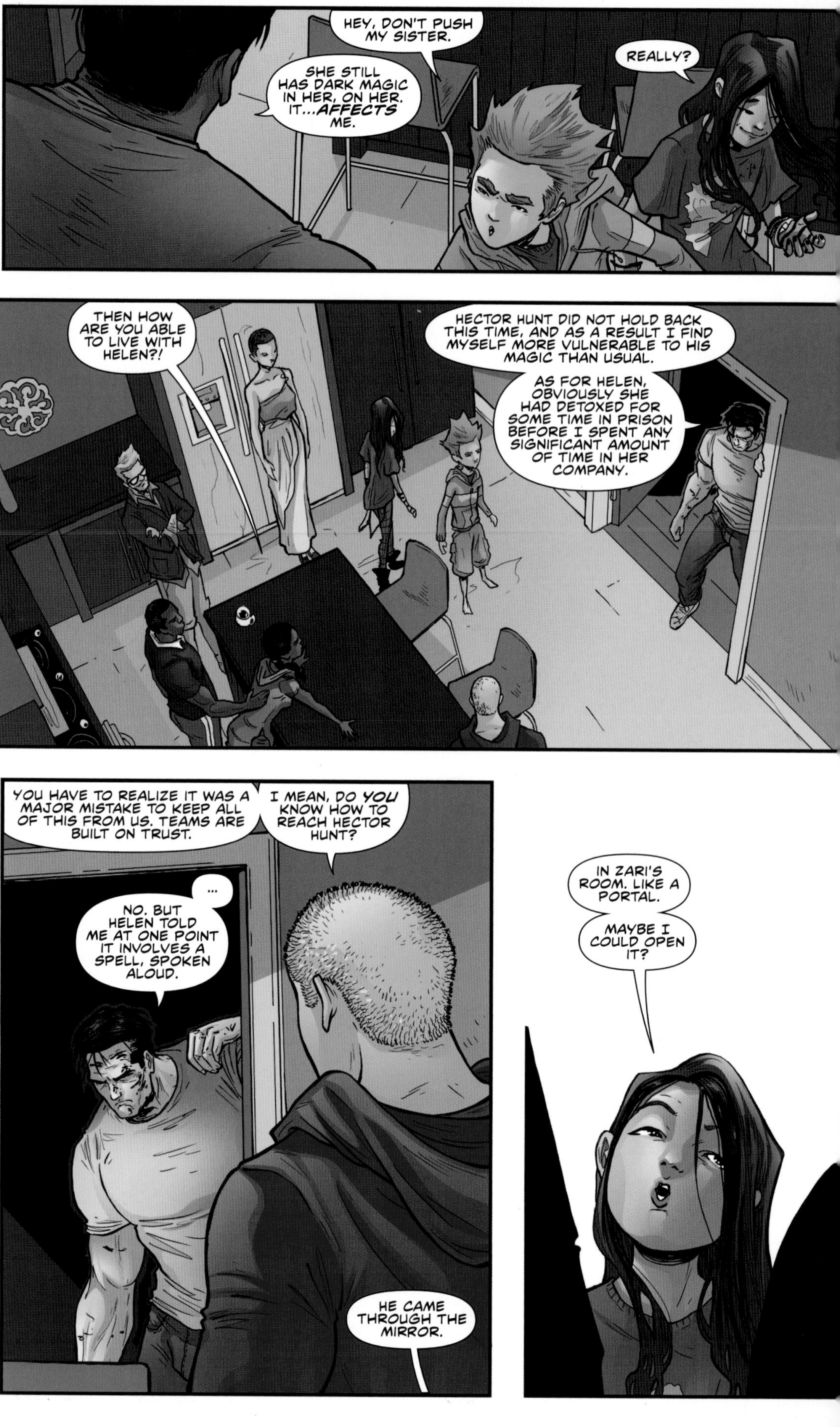
HEY, DON'T PUSH MY SISTER.
SHE STILL HAS DARK MAGIC IN HER, ON HER. IT...AFFECTS ME.
REALLY?
THEN HOW ARE YOU ABLE TO LIVE WITH HELEN?!
HECTOR HUNT DID NOT HOLD BACK THIS TIME, AND AS A RESULT I FIND MYSELF MORE VULNERABLE TO HIS MAGIC THAN USUAL.
AS FOR HELEN, OBVIOUSLY SHE HAD DETOXED FOR SOME TIME IN PRISON BEFORE I SPENT ANY SIGNIFICANT AMOUNT OF TIME IN HER COMPANY.
YOU HAVE TO REALIZE IT WAS A MAJOR MISTAKE TO KEEP ALL OF THIS FROM US. TEAMS ARE BUILT ON TRUST.
I MEAN, DO YOU KNOW HOW TO REACH HECTOR HUNT?
...
NO. BUT HELEN TOLD ME AT ONE POINT IT INVOLVES A SPELL, SPOKEN ALOUD.
HE CAME THROUGH THE MIRROR.
IN ZARI'S ROOM. LIKE A PORTAL.
MAYBE I COULD OPEN IT?

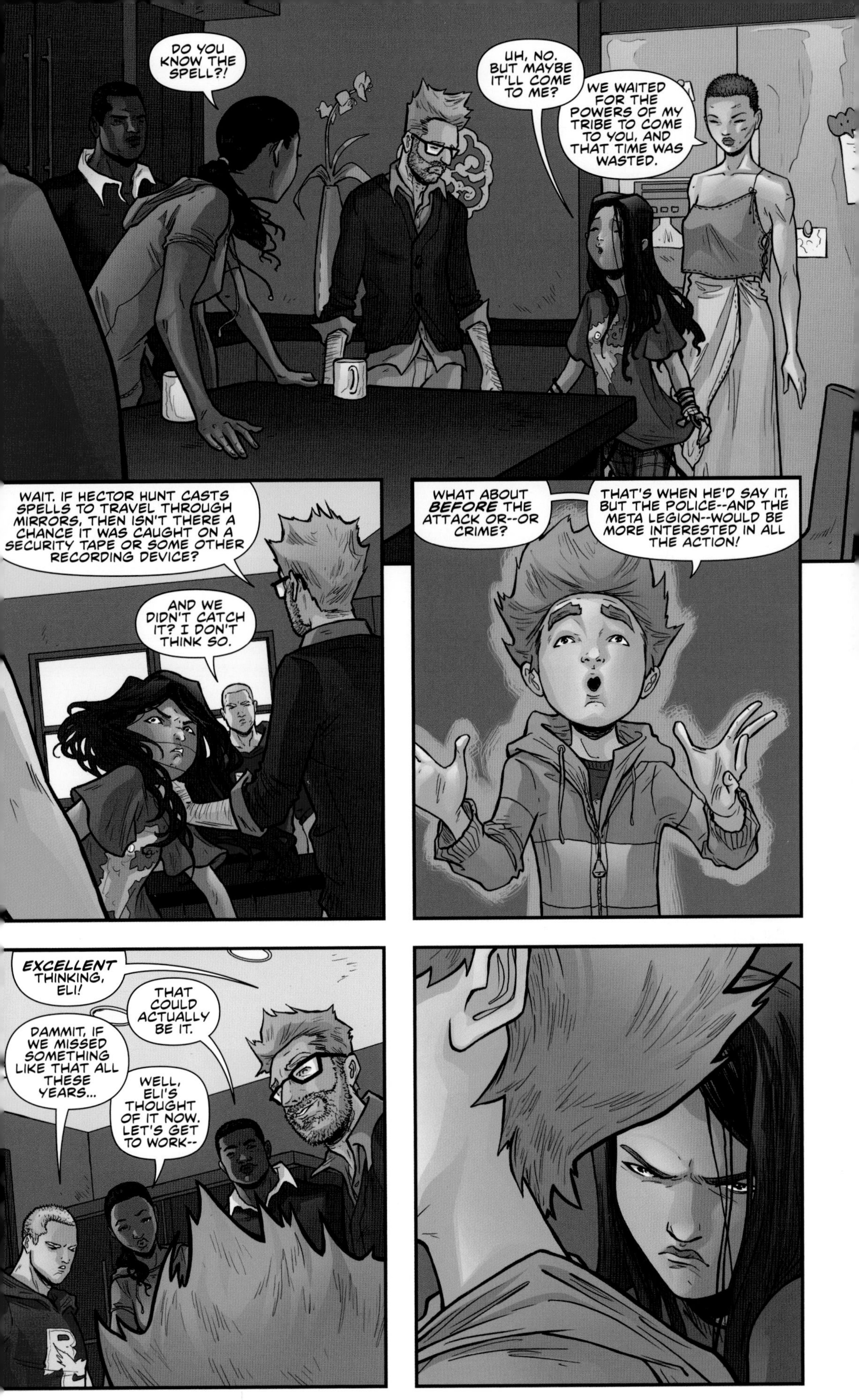
DO YOU KNOW THE SPELL?!
UH, NO. BUT MAYBE IT'LL COME TO ME?
WE WAITED FOR THE POWERS OF MY TRIBE TO COME TO YOU, AND THAT TIME WAS WASTED.
WAIT. IF HECTOR HUNT CASTS SPELLS TO TRAVEL THROUGH MIRRORS, THEN ISN'T THERE A CHANCE IT WAS CAUGHT ON A SECURITY TAPE OR SOME OTHER RECORDING DEVICE?
AND WE DIDN'T CATCH IT? I DON'T THINK SO.
WHAT ABOUT *BEFORE* THE ATTACK OR--OR CRIME?
THAT'S WHEN HE'D SAY IT, BUT THE POLICE--AND THE META LEGION--WOULD BE MORE INTERESTED IN ALL THE ACTION!
EXCELLENT THINKING, ELI!
THAT COULD ACTUALLY BE IT.
DAMMIT, IF WE MISSED SOMETHING LIKE THAT ALL THESE YEARS...
WELL, ELI'S THOUGHT OF IT NOW. LET'S GET TO WORK--

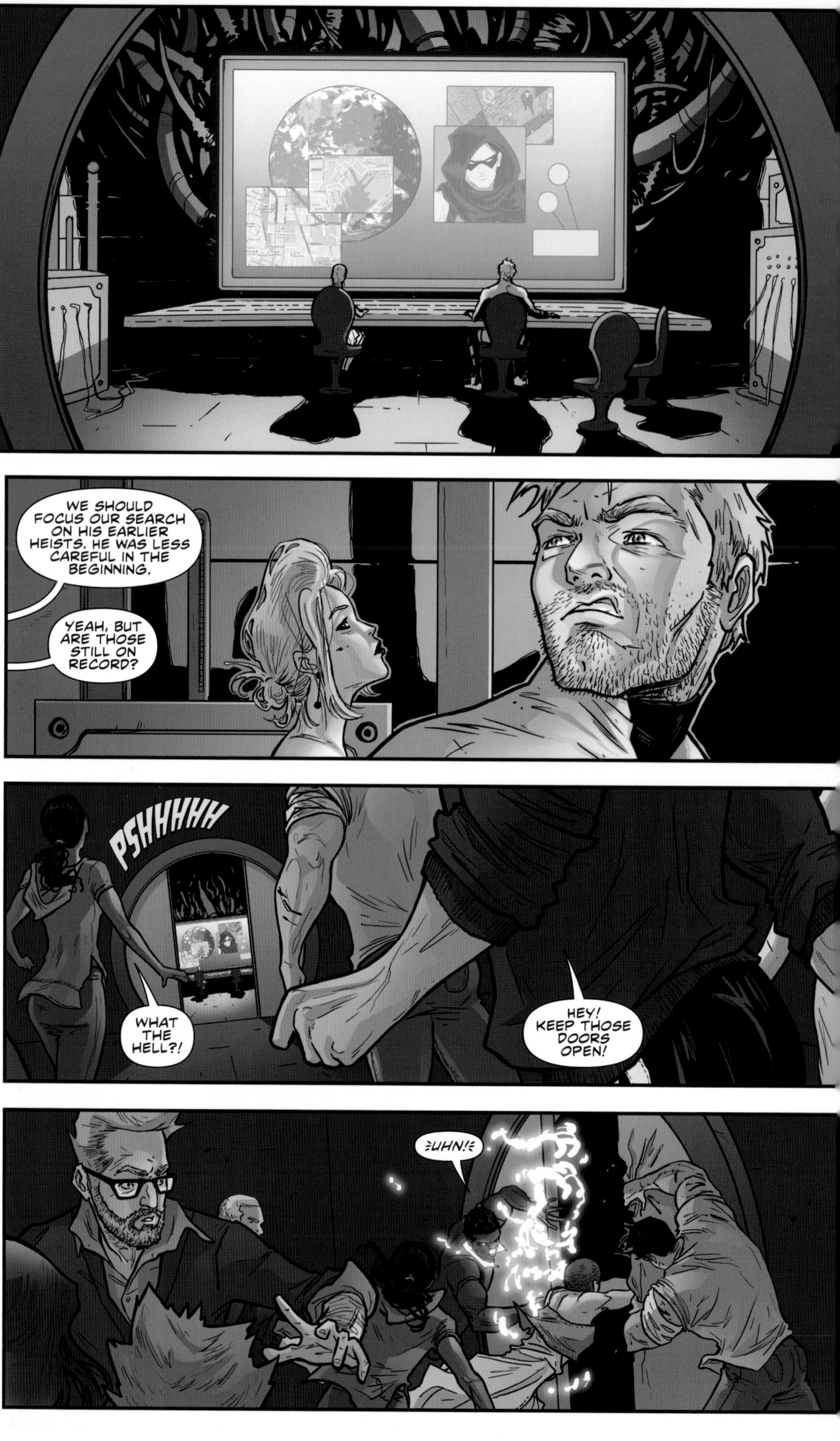
WE SHOULD FOCUS OUR SEARCH ON HIS EARLIER HEISTS. HE WAS LESS CAREFUL IN THE BEGINNING.
YEAH, BUT ARE THOSE STILL ON RECORD?
PSHHHHH
WHAT THE HELL?!
HEY! KEEP THOSE DOORS OPEN!
UHN!

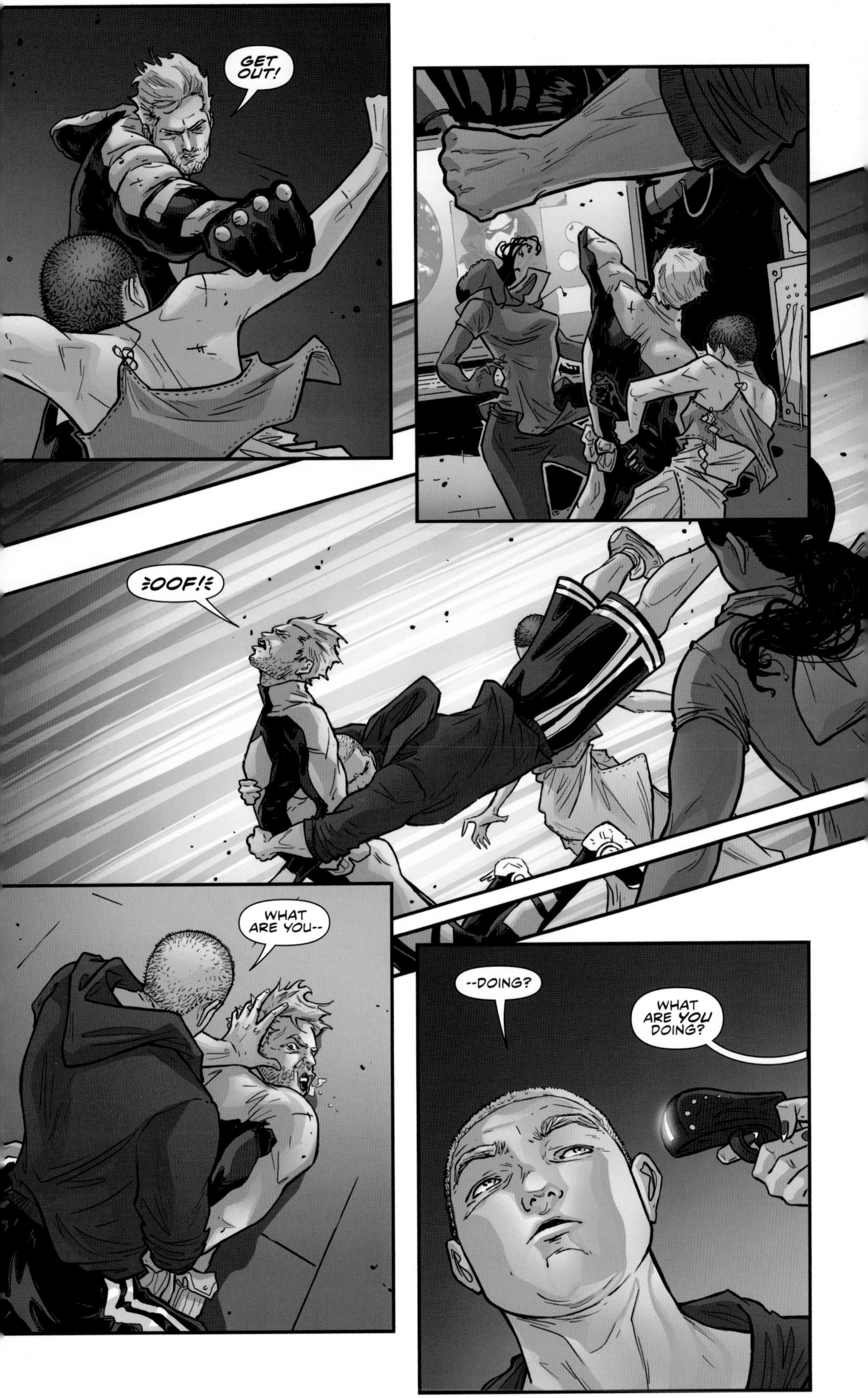
GET OUT!
OOF!
WHAT ARE YOU--
--DOING?
WHAT ARE YOU DOING?

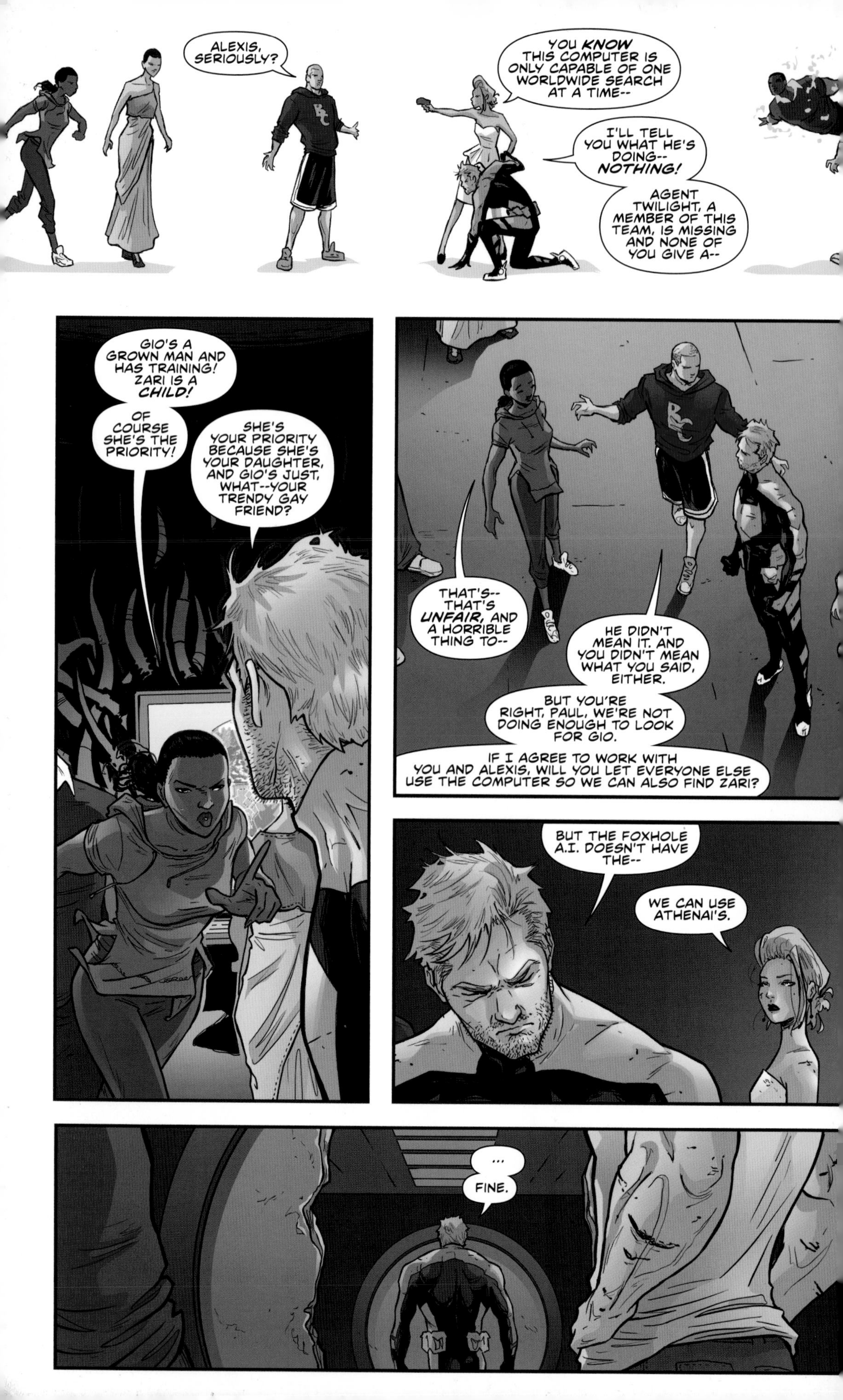
ALEXIS, SERIOUSLY?
YOU KNOW THIS COMPUTER IS ONLY CAPABLE OF ONE WORLDWIDE SEARCH AT A TIME--
I'LL TELL YOU WHAT HE'S DOING-- NOTHING!
AGENT TWILIGHT, A MEMBER OF THIS TEAM, IS MISSING AND NONE OF YOU GIVE A--
GIO'S A GROWN MAN AND HAS TRAINING! ZARI IS A CHILD!
OF COURSE SHE'S THE PRIORITY!
SHE'S YOUR PRIORITY BECAUSE SHE'S YOUR DAUGHTER, AND GIO'S JUST, WHAT--YOUR TRENDY GAY FRIEND?
THAT'S-- THAT'S UNFAIR, AND A HORRIBLE THING TO--
HE DIDN'T MEAN IT. AND YOU DIDN'T MEAN WHAT YOU SAID, EITHER.
BUT YOU'RE RIGHT, PAUL, WE'RE NOT DOING ENOUGH TO LOOK FOR GIO.
IF I AGREE TO WORK WITH YOU AND ALEXIS, WILL YOU LET EVERYONE ELSE USE THE COMPUTER SO WE CAN ALSO FIND ZARI?
BUT THE FOXHOLE A.I. DOESN'T HAVE THE--
WE CAN USE ATHENAI'S.
...
FINE.

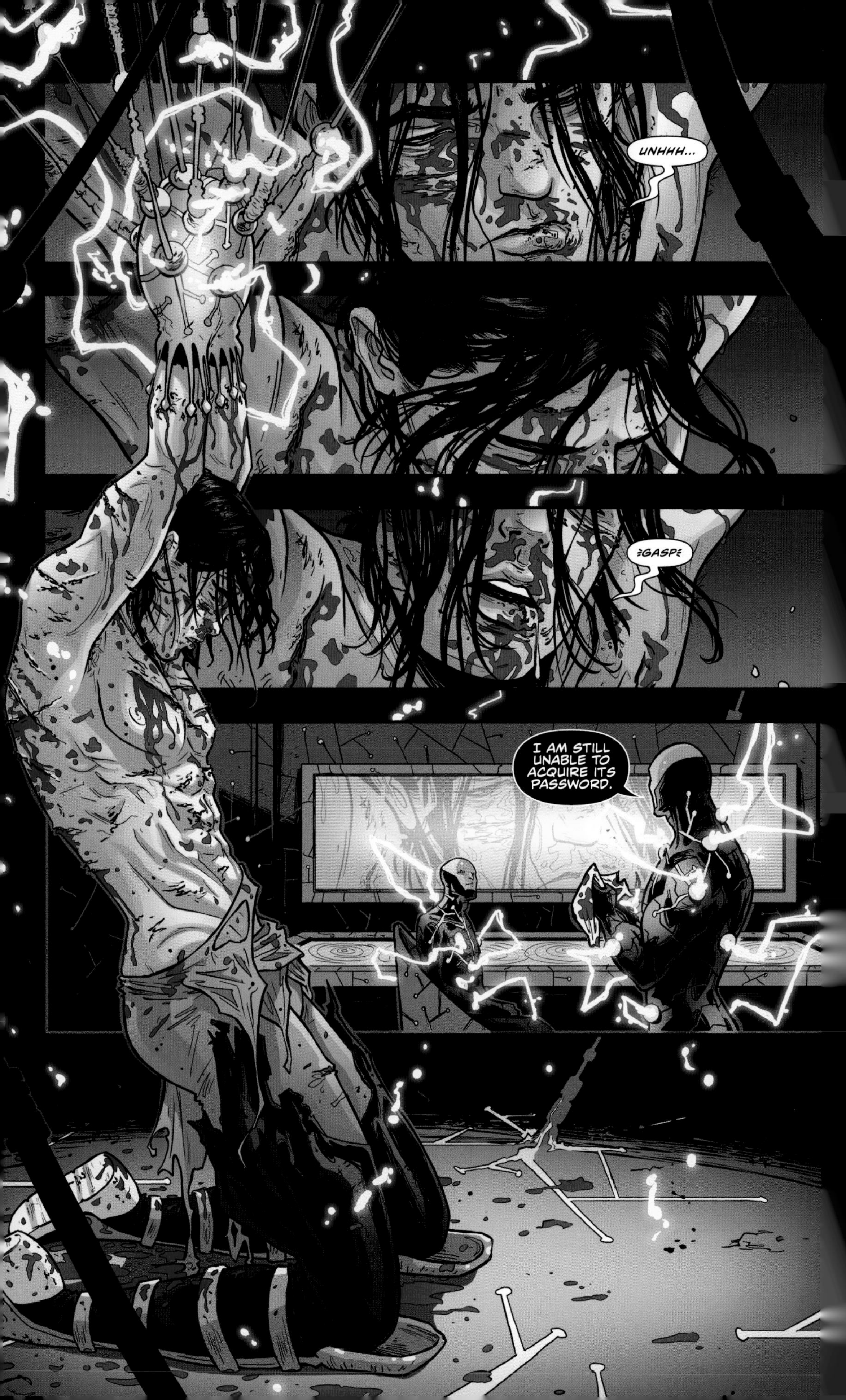
UNHHH...
GASP
I AM STILL UNABLE TO ACQUIRE ITS PASSWORD.

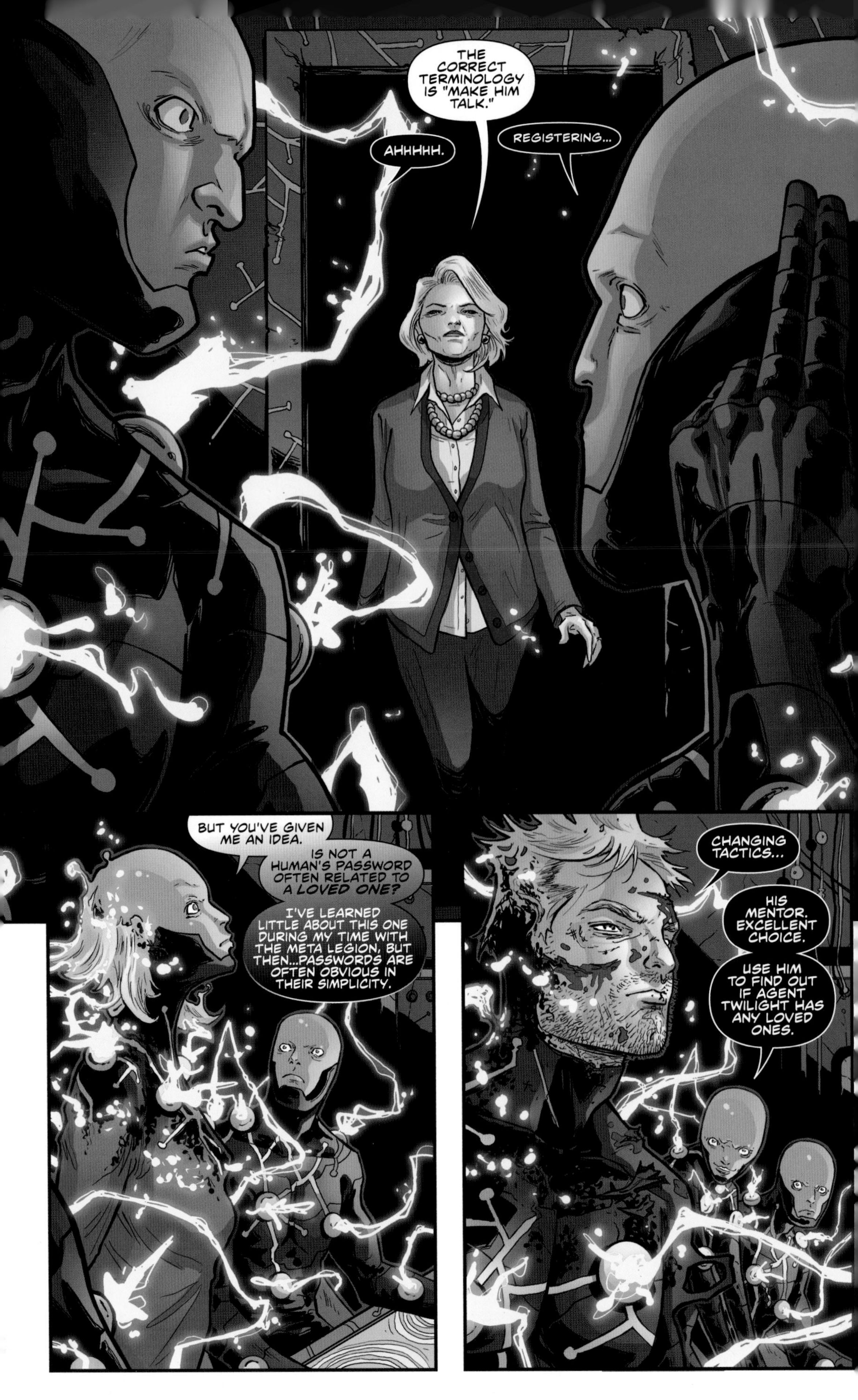

THE CORRECT TERMINOLOGY IS "MAKE HIM TALK."
AHHHHH.
REGISTERING...
BUT YOU'VE GIVEN ME AN IDEA.
IS NOT A HUMAN'S PASSWORD OFTEN RELATED TO A LOVED ONE?
I'VE LEARNED LITTLE ABOUT THIS ONE DURING MY TIME WITH THE META LEGION, BUT THEN...PASSWORDS ARE OFTEN OBVIOUS IN THEIR SIMPLICITY.
CHANGING TACTICS...
HIS MENTOR. EXCELLENT CHOICE.
USE HIM TO FIND OUT IF AGENT TWILIGHT HAS ANY LOVED ONES.

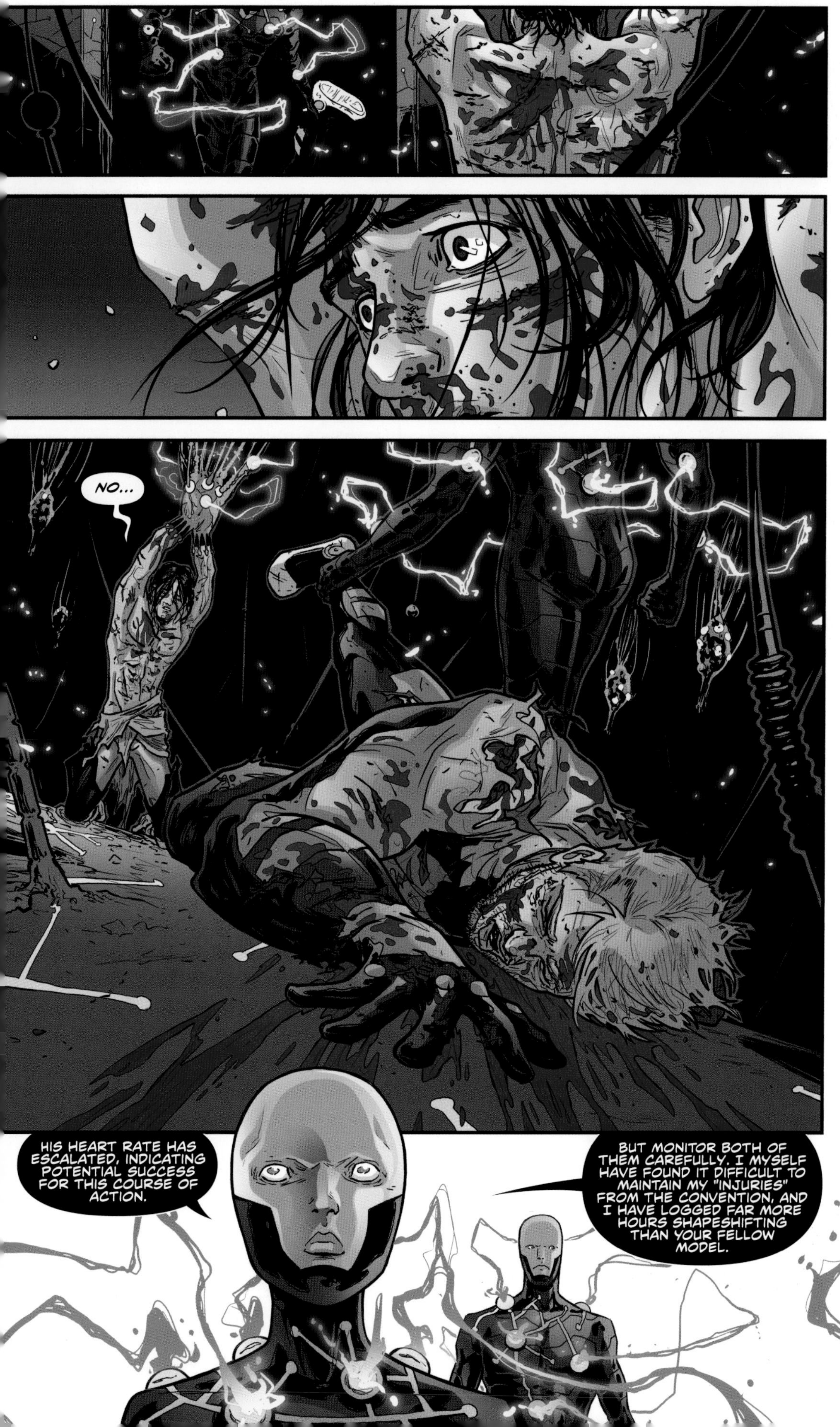
NO...
HIS HEART RATE HAS ESCALATED, INDICATING POTENTIAL SUCCESS FOR THIS COURSE OF ACTION.
BUT MONITOR BOTH OF THEM CAREFULLY. I MYSELF HAVE FOUND IT DIFFICULT TO MAINTAIN MY "INJURIES" FROM THE CONVENTION, AND I HAVE LOGGED FAR MORE HOURS SHAPESHIFTING THAN YOUR FELLOW MODEL.

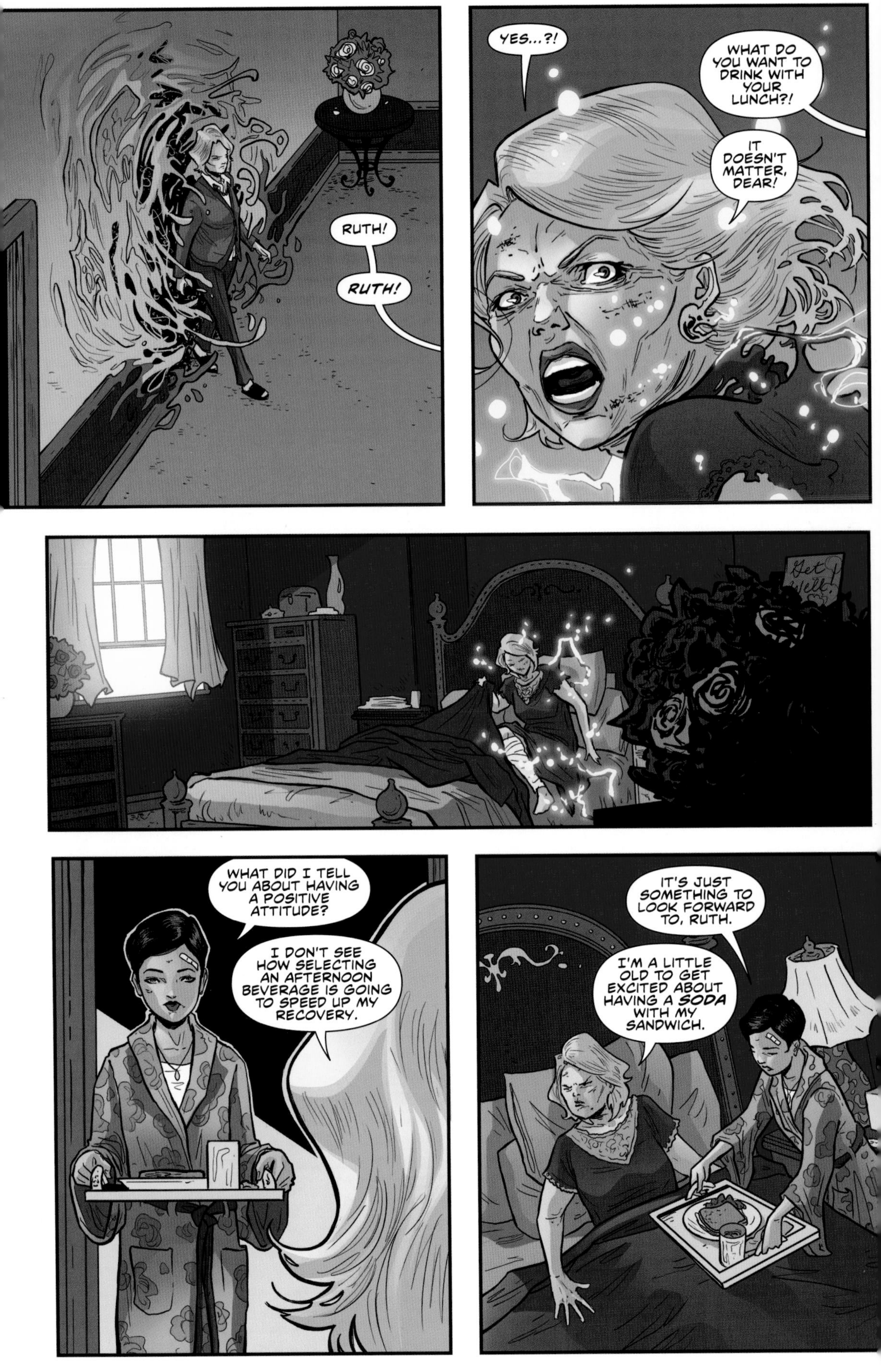
RUTH!
RUTH!
YES...?!
WHAT DO YOU WANT TO DRINK WITH YOUR LUNCH?!
IT DOESN'T MATTER, DEAR!
Get Well
WHAT DID I TELL YOU ABOUT HAVING A POSITIVE ATTITUDE?
I DON'T SEE HOW SELECTING AN AFTERNOON BEVERAGE IS GOING TO SPEED UP MY RECOVERY.
IT'S JUST SOMETHING TO LOOK FORWARD TO, RUTH.
I'M A LITTLE OLD TO GET EXCITED ABOUT HAVING A SODA WITH MY SANDWICH.

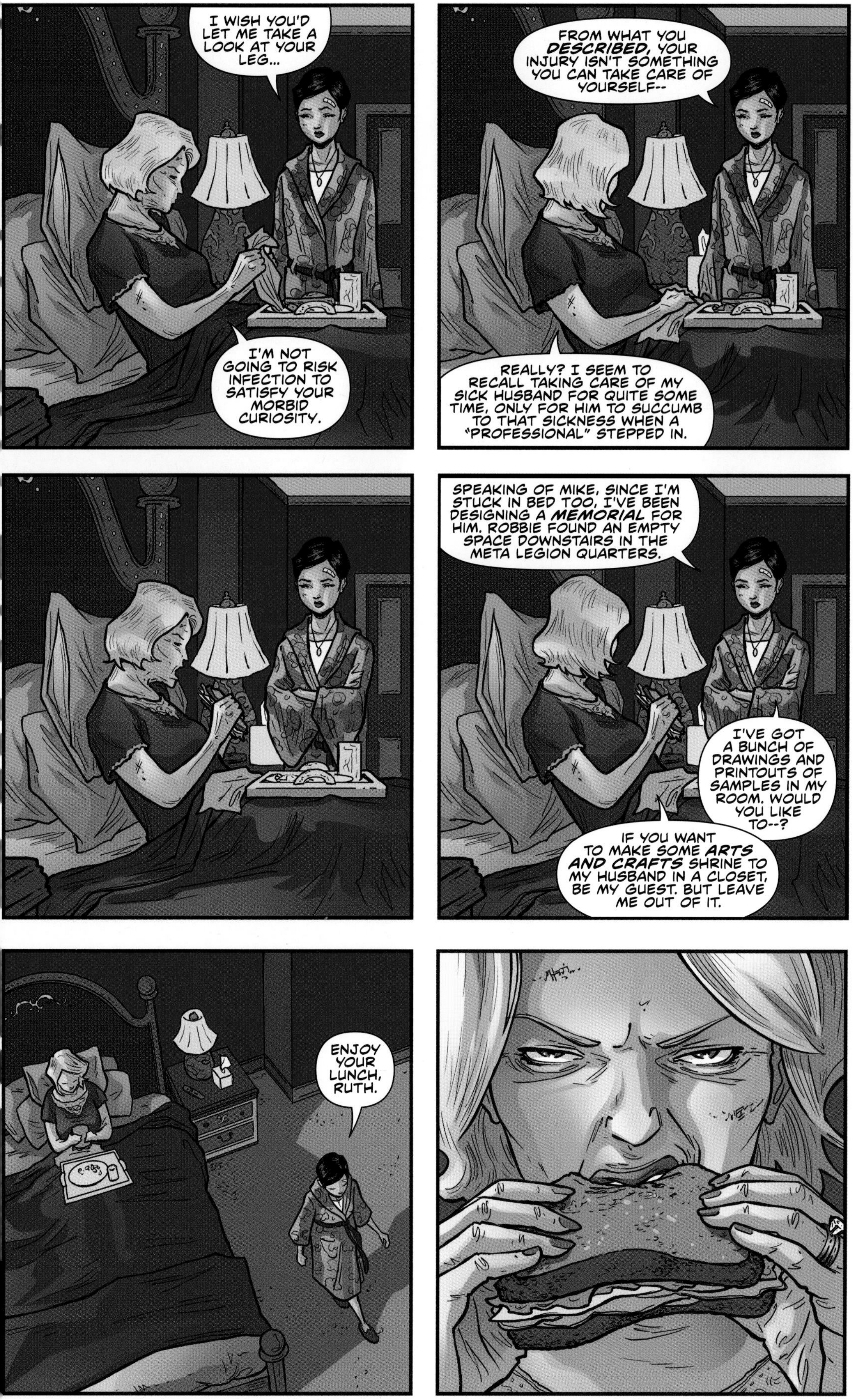
I WISH YOU'D LET ME TAKE A LOOK AT YOUR LEG...
I'M NOT GOING TO RISK INFECTION TO SATISFY YOUR MORBID CURIOSITY.
FROM WHAT YOU DESCRIBED, YOUR INJURY ISN'T SOMETHING YOU CAN TAKE CARE OF YOURSELF--
REALLY? I SEEM TO RECALL TAKING CARE OF MY SICK HUSBAND FOR QUITE SOME TIME, ONLY FOR HIM TO SUCCUMB TO THAT SICKNESS WHEN A "PROFESSIONAL" STEPPED IN.
SPEAKING OF MIKE, SINCE I'M STUCK IN BED TOO, I'VE BEEN DESIGNING A MEMORIAL FOR HIM. ROBBIE FOUND AN EMPTY SPACE DOWNSTAIRS IN THE META LEGION QUARTERS.
I'VE GOT A BUNCH OF DRAWINGS AND PRINTOUTS OF SAMPLES IN MY ROOM. WOULD YOU LIKE TO--?
IF YOU WANT TO MAKE SOME ARTS AND CRAFTS SHRINE TO MY HUSBAND IN A CLOSET, BE MY GUEST. BUT LEAVE ME OUT OF IT.
ENJOY YOUR LUNCH, RUTH.

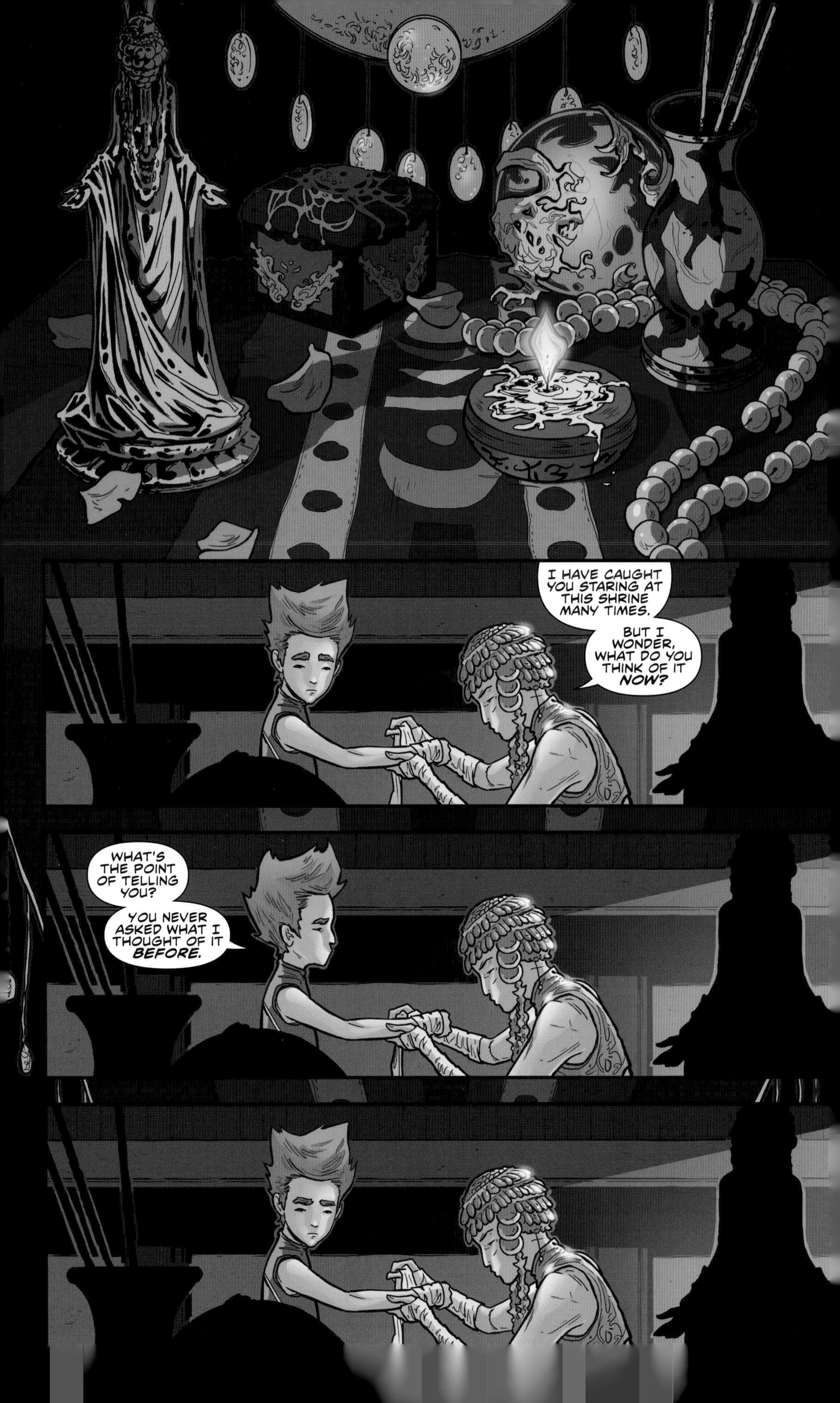
I HAVE CAUGHT YOU STARING AT THIS SHRINE MANY TIMES.
BUT I WONDER, WHAT DO YOU THINK OF IT NOW?
WHAT'S THE POINT OF TELLING YOU?
YOU NEVER ASKED WHAT I THOUGHT OF IT BEFORE.

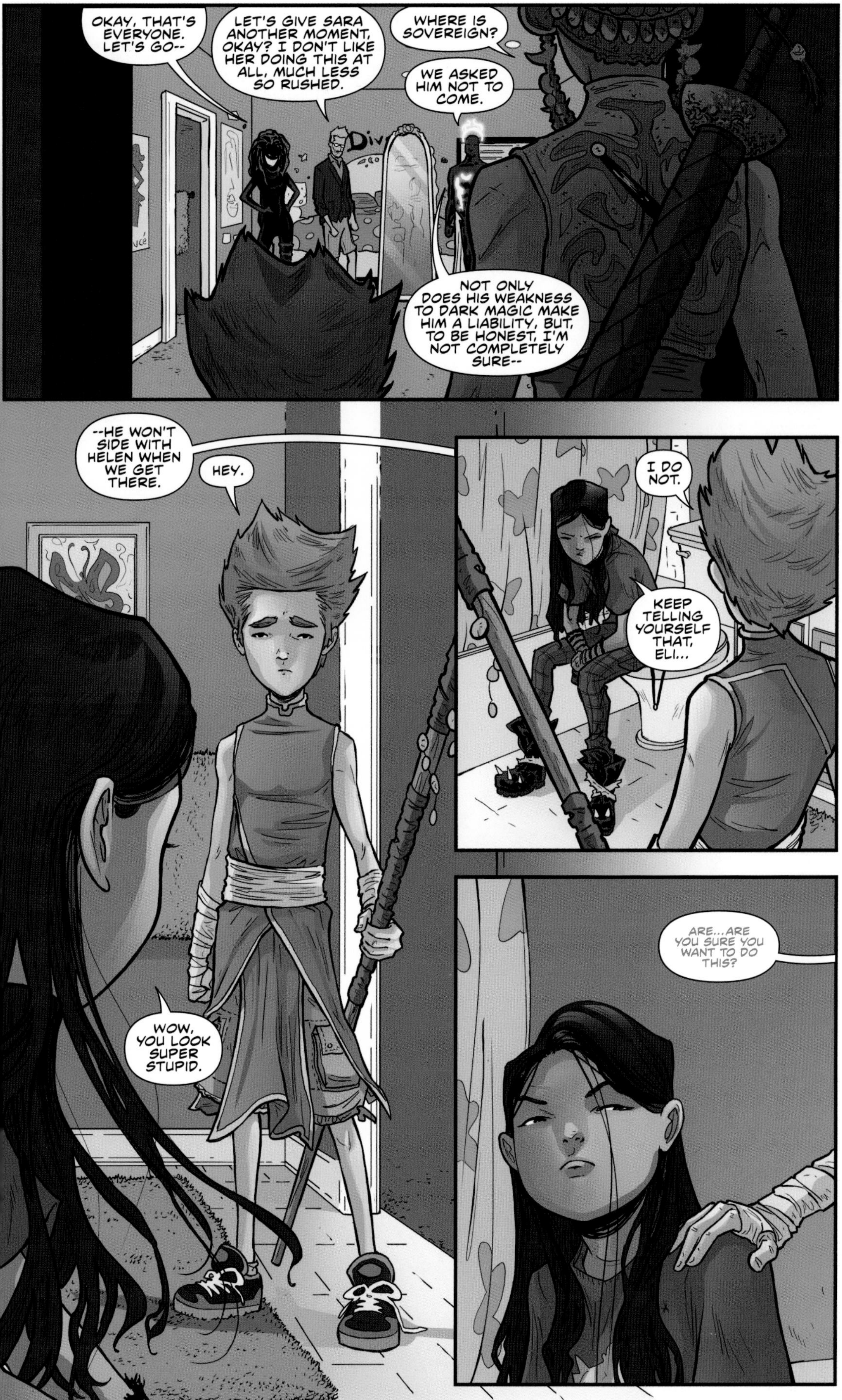

OKAY, THAT'S EVERYONE. LET'S GO--
LET'S GIVE SARA ANOTHER MOMENT, OKAY? I DON'T LIKE HER DOING THIS AT ALL, MUCH LESS SO RUSHED.
WHERE IS SOVEREIGN?
WE ASKED HIM NOT TO COME.
NOT ONLY DOES HIS WEAKNESS TO DARK MAGIC MAKE HIM A LIABILITY, BUT, TO BE HONEST, I'M NOT COMPLETELY SURE--
--HE WON'T SIDE WITH HELEN WHEN WE GET THERE.
HEY.
WOW, YOU LOOK SUPER STUPID.
I DO NOT.
KEEP TELLING YOURSELF THAT, ELI...
ARE...ARE YOU SURE YOU WANT TO DO THIS?

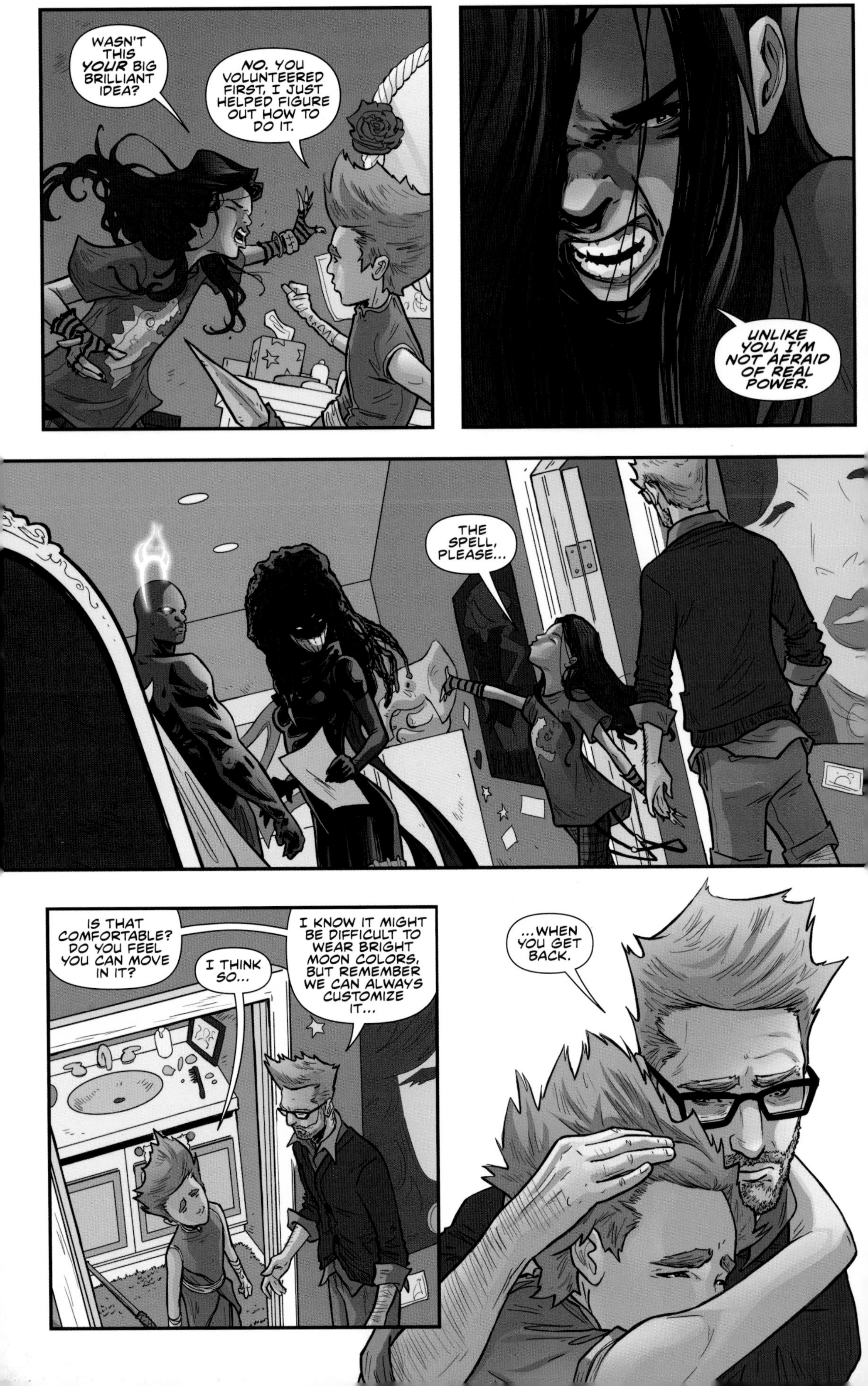
WASN'T THIS YOUR BIG BRILLIANT IDEA?
NO. YOU VOLUNTEERED FIRST, I JUST HELPED FIGURE OUT HOW TO DO IT.
UNLIKE YOU, I'M NOT AFRAID OF REAL POWER.
THE SPELL, PLEASE...
IS THAT COMFORTABLE? DO YOU FEEL YOU CAN MOVE IN IT?
I THINK SO...
I KNOW IT MIGHT BE DIFFICULT TO WEAR BRIGHT MOON COLORS, BUT REMEMBER WE CAN ALWAYS CUSTOMIZE IT...
...WHEN YOU GET BACK.

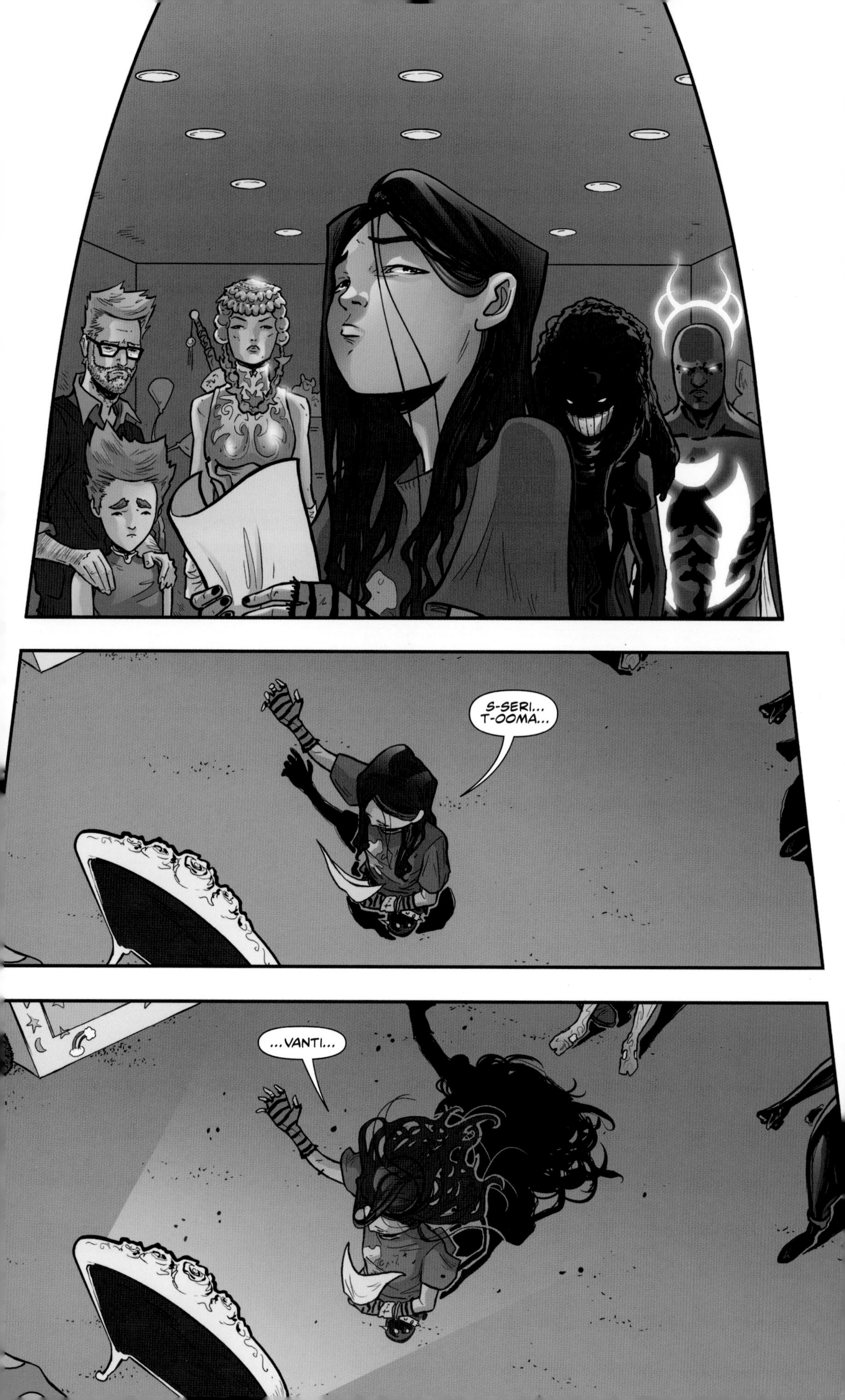
S-SERI...
T-OOMA...
...VANTI...

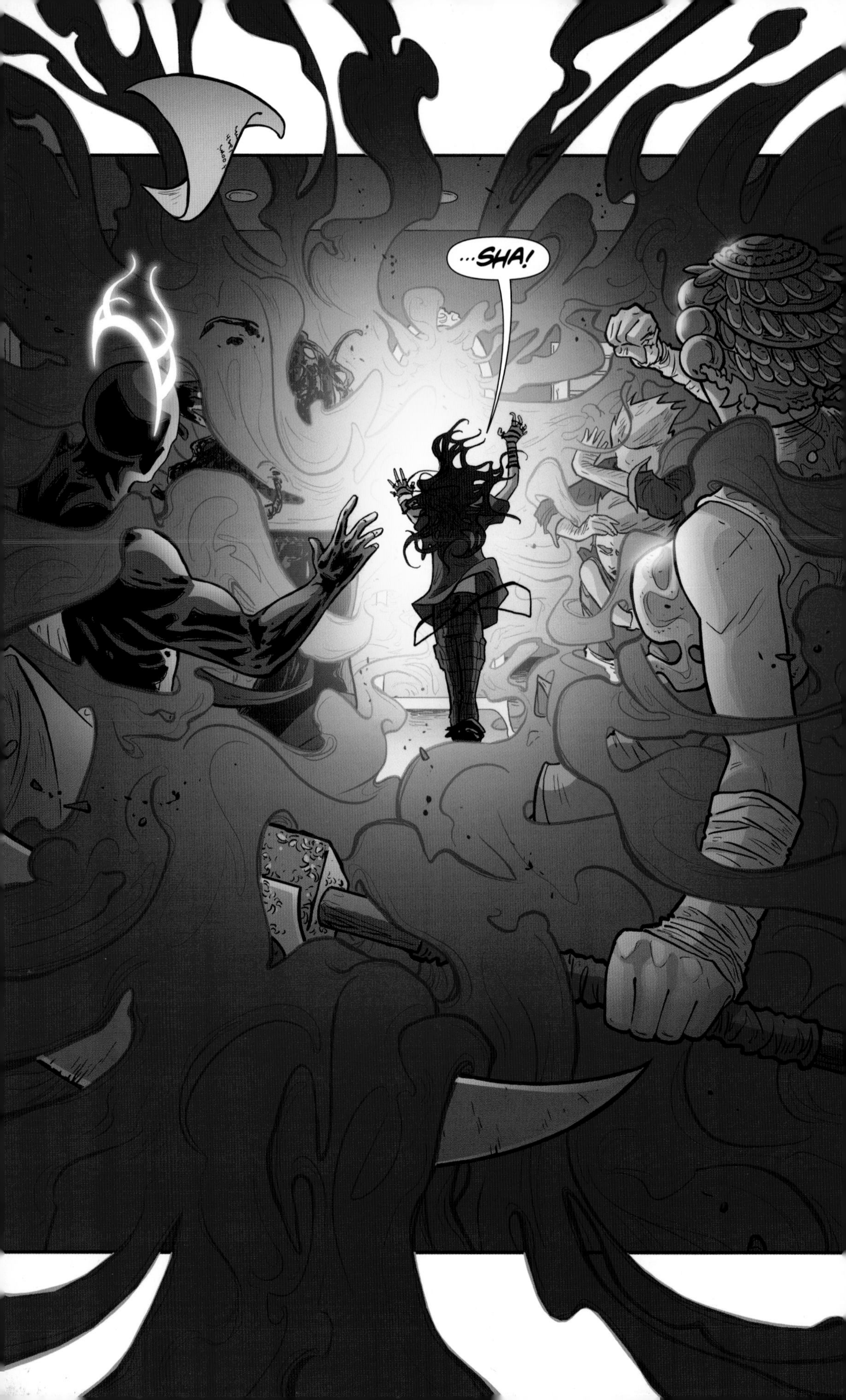
...SHA!

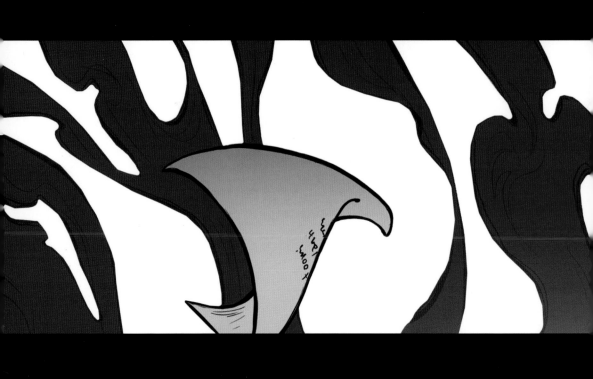

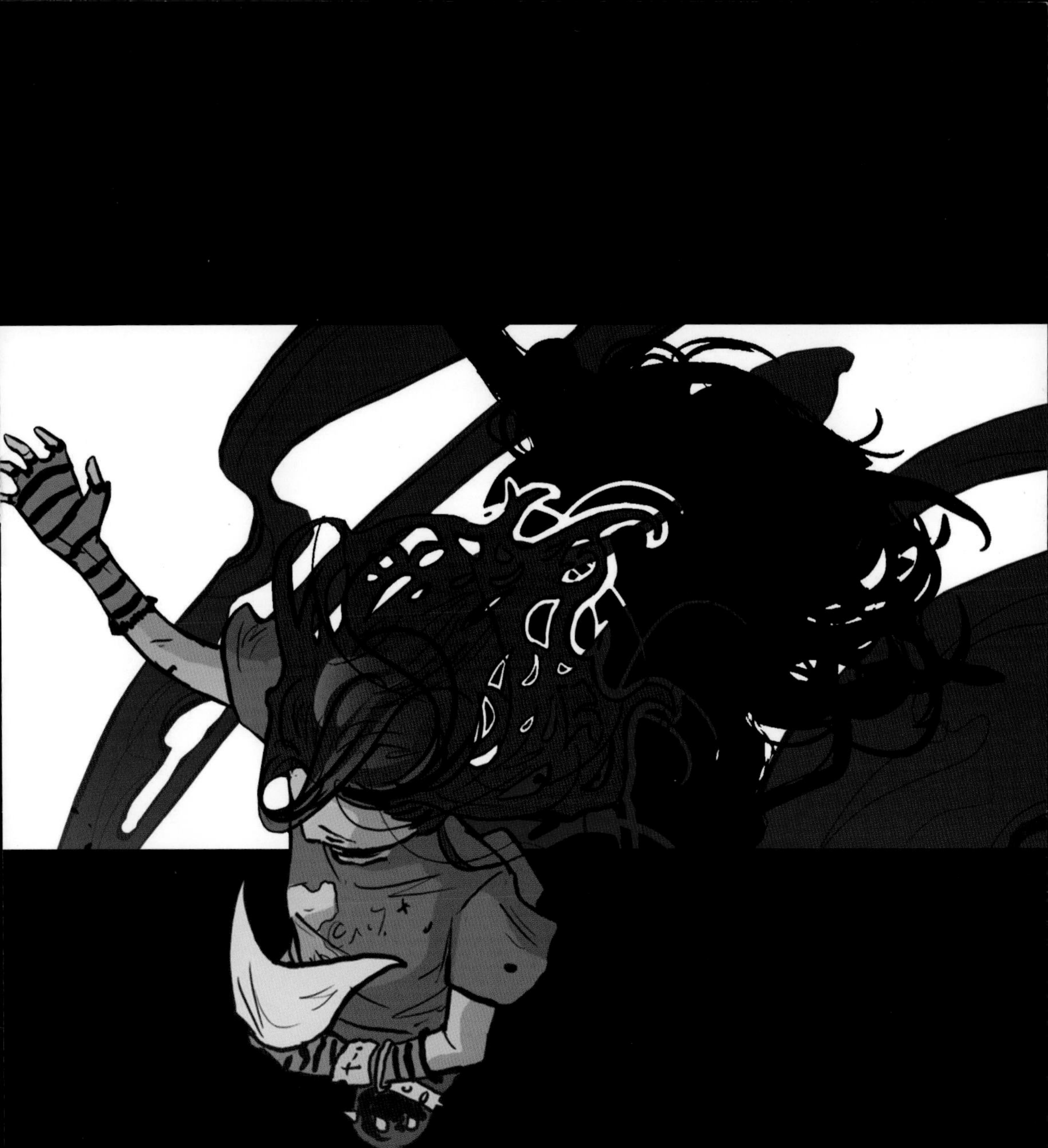

Chapter 10

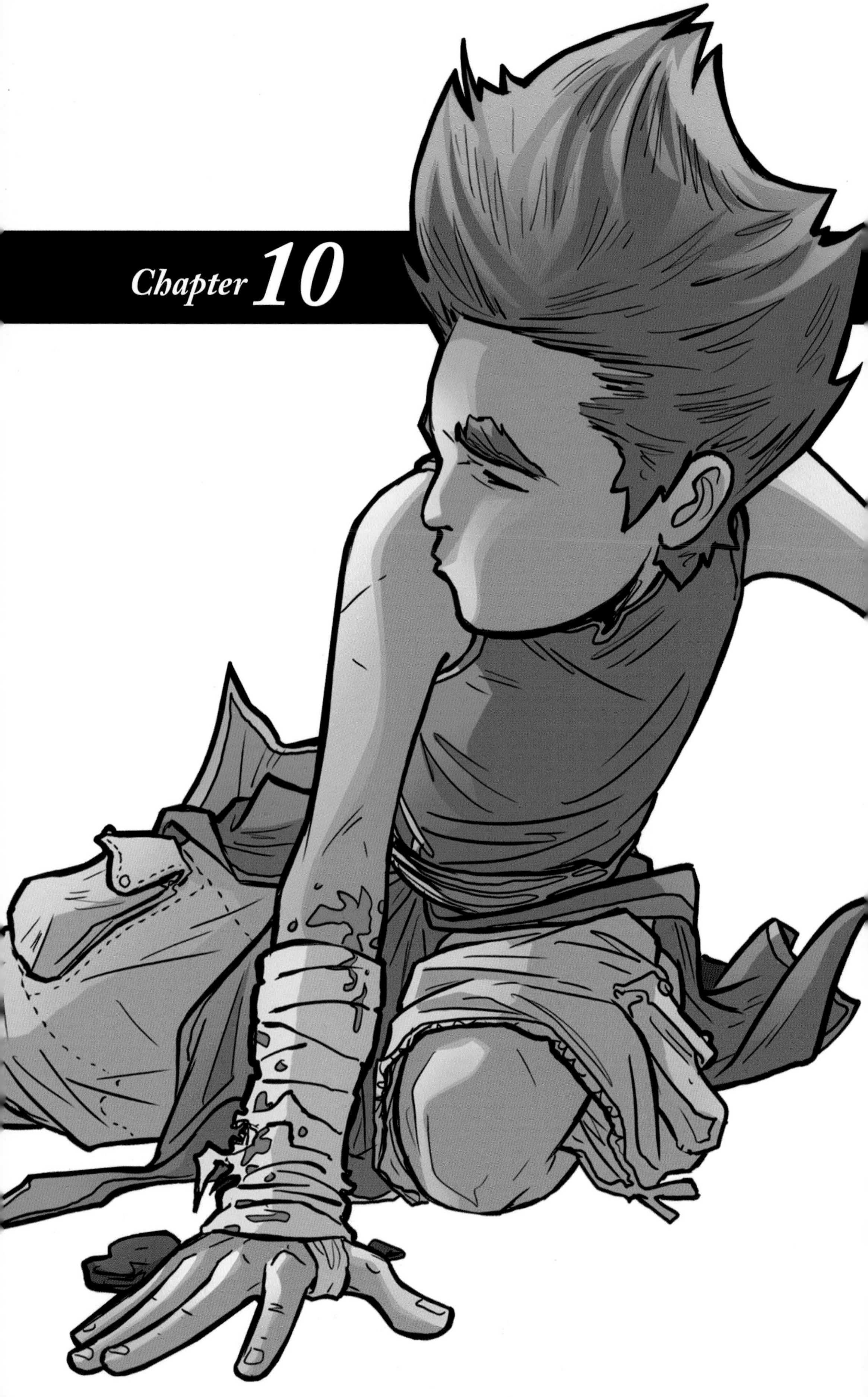

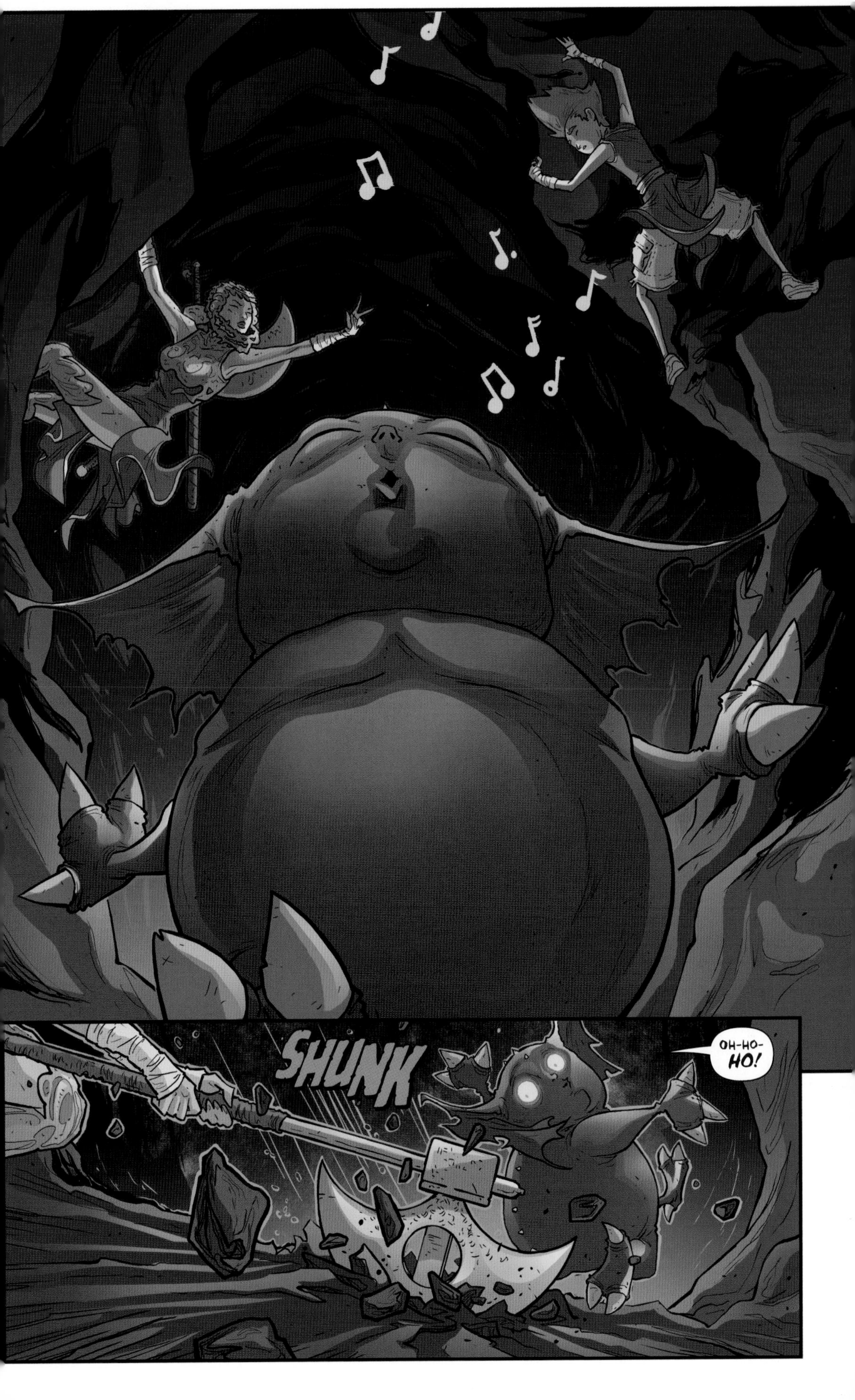
SHUNK
OH-HO-HO!

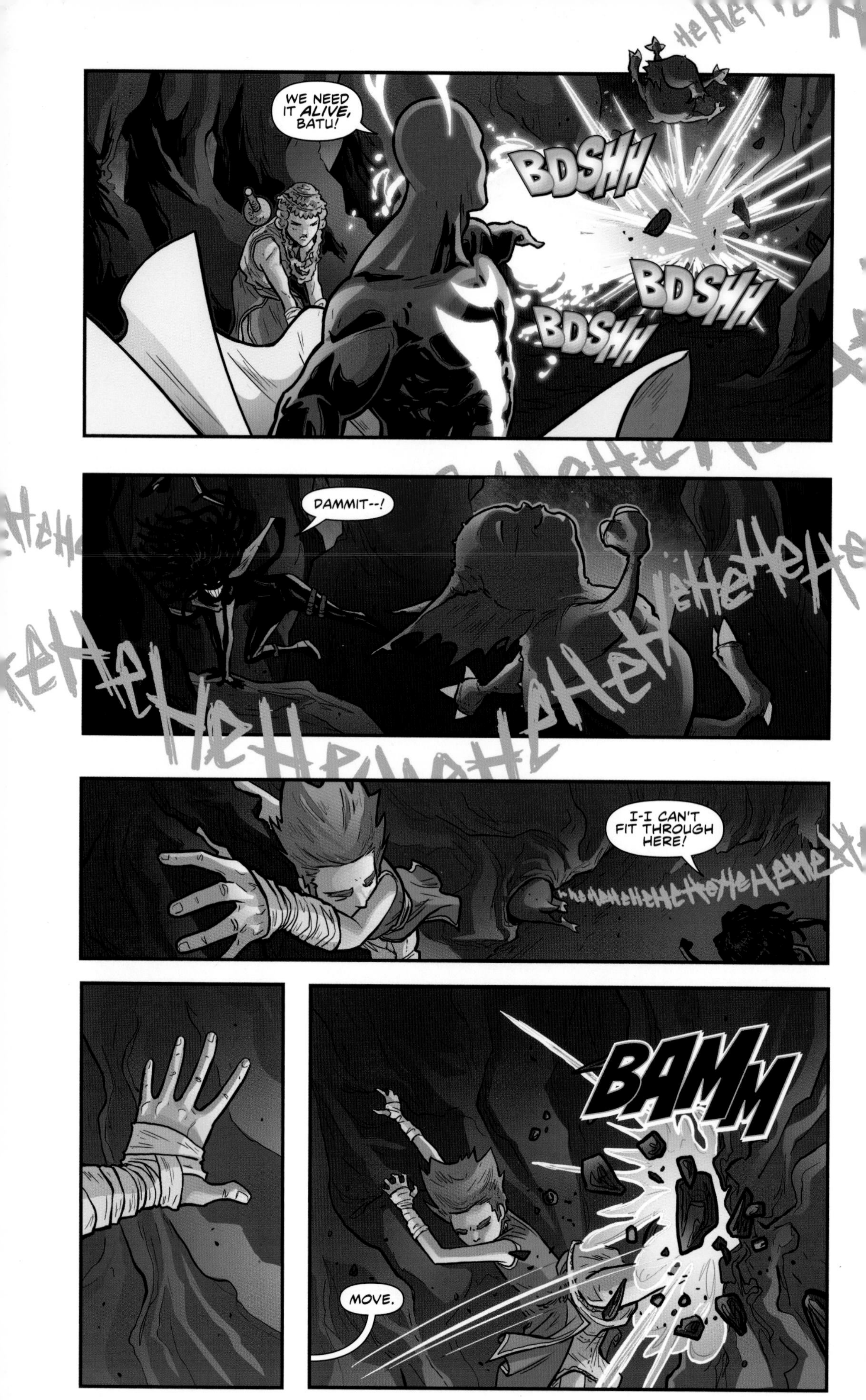
WE NEED IT ALIVE, BATU!
BDSHH
BDSHH
BDSHH
DAMMIT--!
I-I CAN'T FIT THROUGH HERE!
BAMM
MOVE.

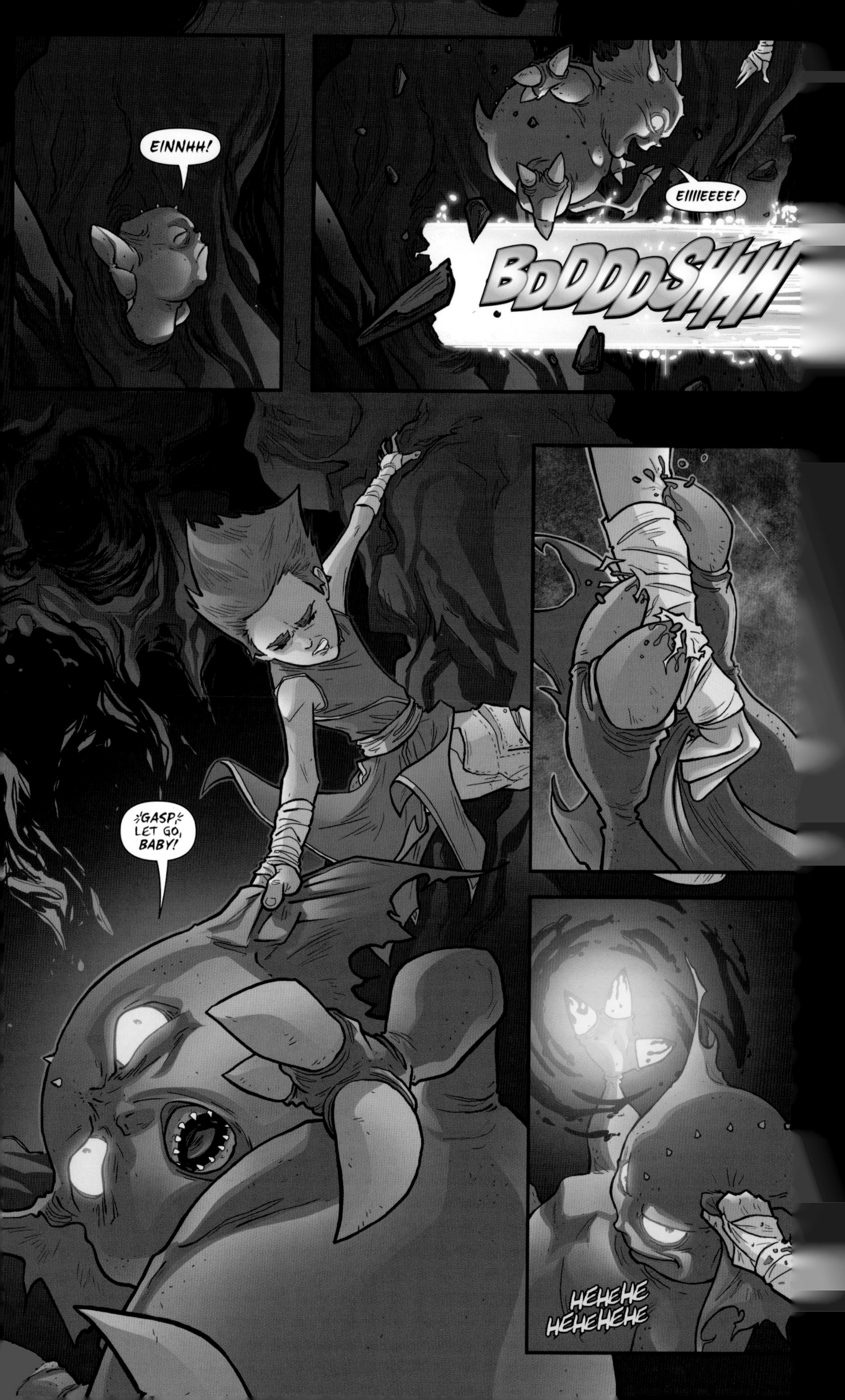
EINNHH!
EIIIIEEEE!
BDDDDSHH
GASP LET GO, BABY!
HEHEHE HEHEHEHE

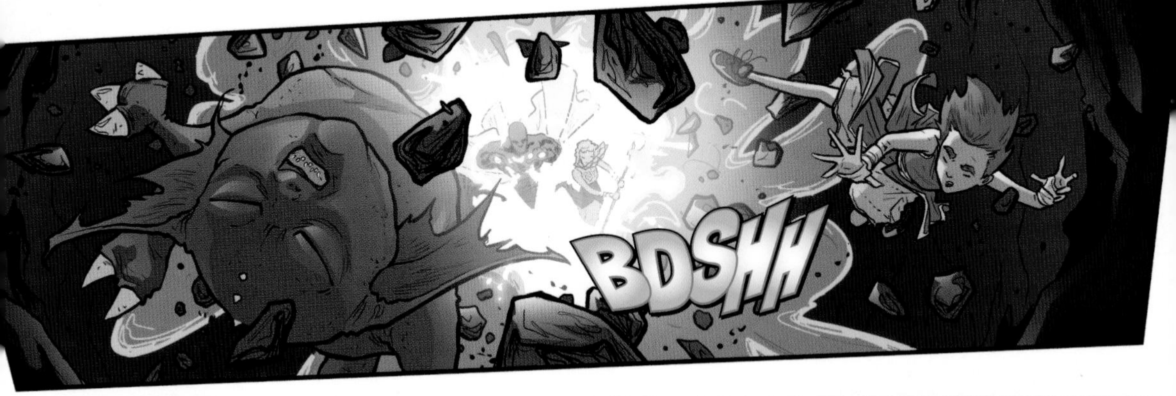
BDSHH

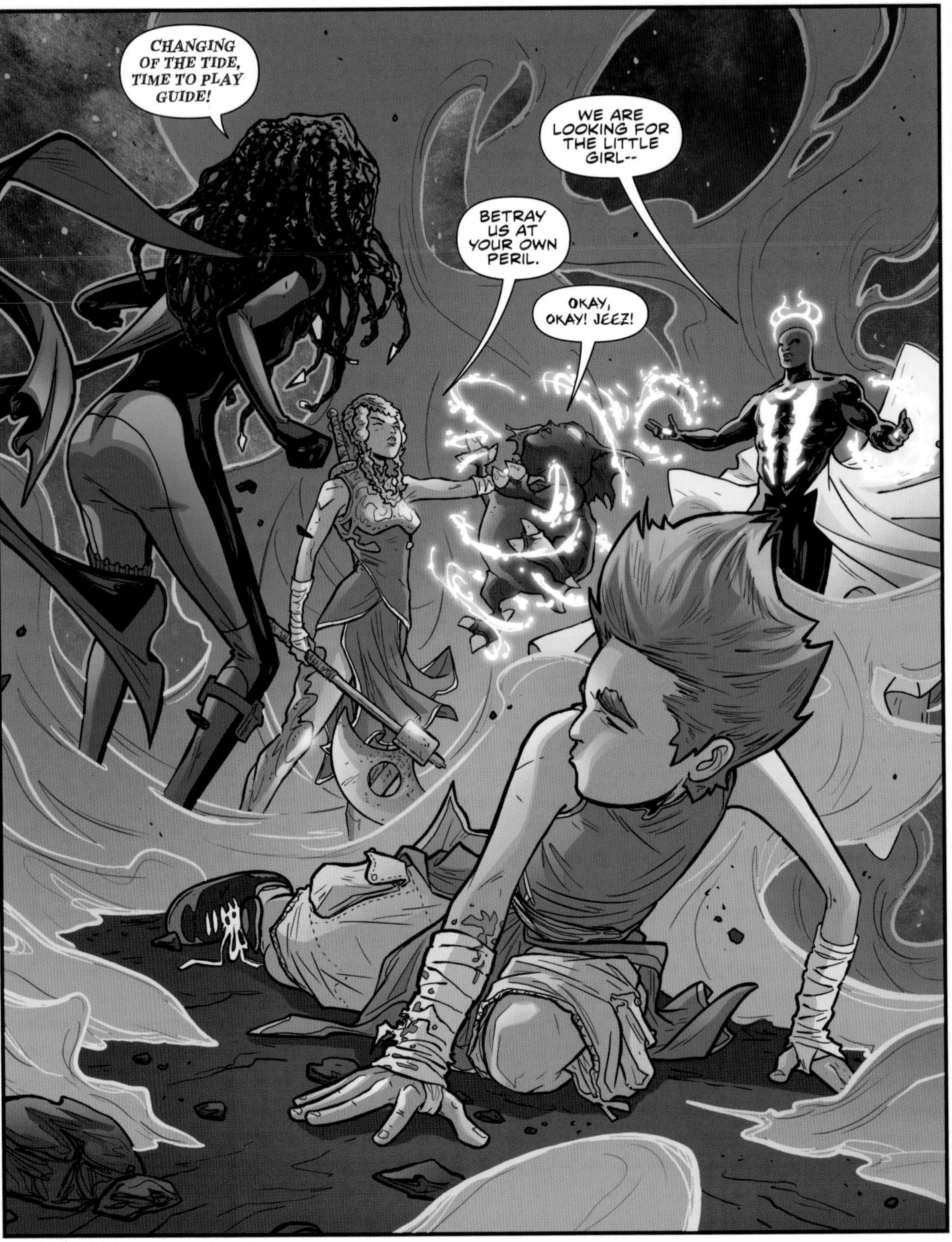
CHANGING OF THE TIDE, TIME TO PLAY GUIDE!
WE ARE LOOKING FOR THE LITTLE GIRL--
BETRAY US AT YOUR OWN PERIL.
OKAY, OKAY! JEEZ!

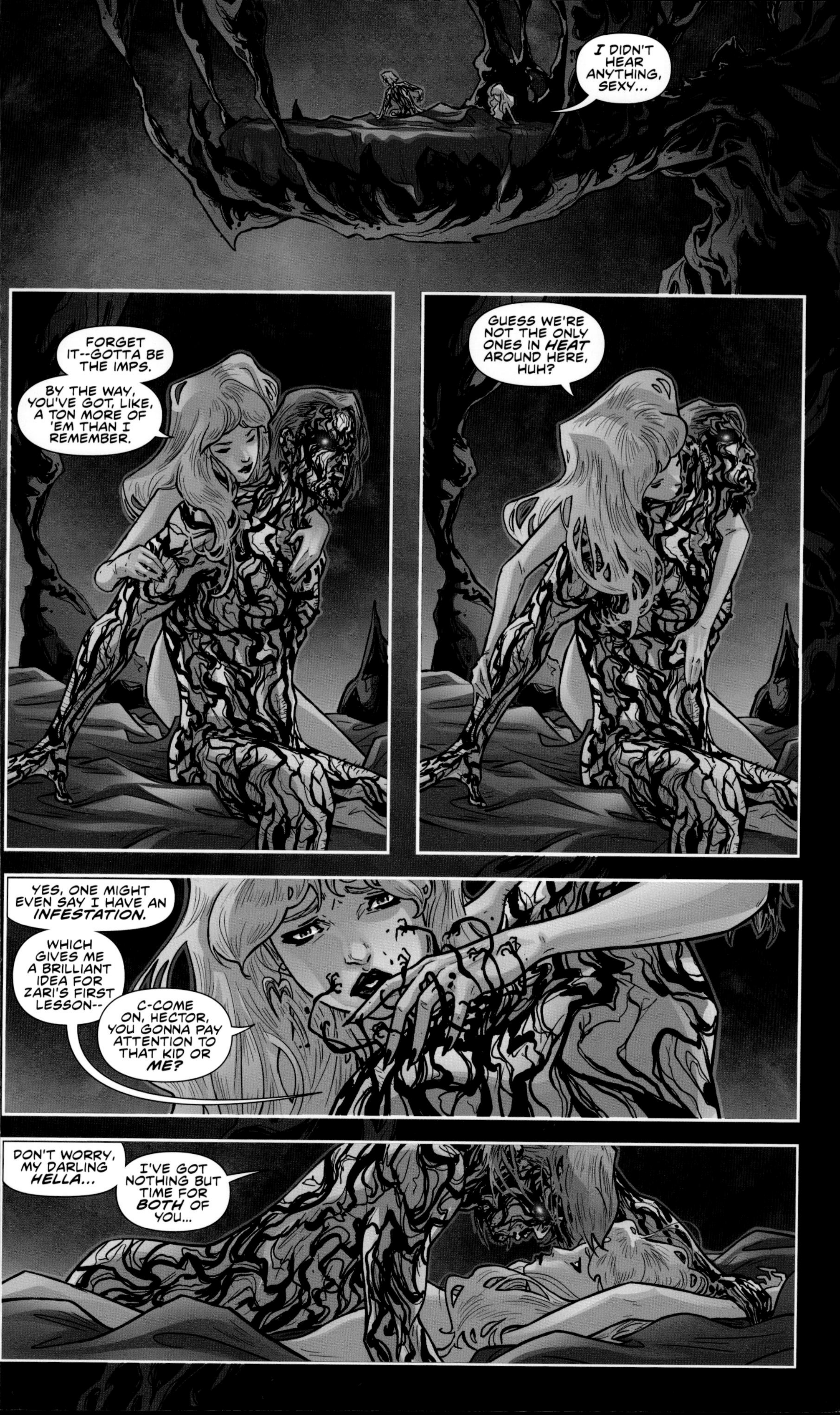
I DIDN'T HEAR ANYTHING, SEXY...
FORGET IT--GOTTA BE THE IMPS.
BY THE WAY, YOU'VE GOT, LIKE, A TON MORE OF 'EM THAN I REMEMBER.
GUESS WE'RE NOT THE ONLY ONES IN HEAT AROUND HERE, HUH?
YES, ONE MIGHT EVEN SAY I HAVE AN INFESTATION.
WHICH GIVES ME A BRILLIANT IDEA FOR ZARI'S FIRST LESSON--
C-COME ON, HECTOR, YOU GONNA PAY ATTENTION TO THAT KID OR ME?
DON'T WORRY, MY DARLING HELLA...
I'VE GOT NOTHING BUT TIME FOR BOTH OF YOU...

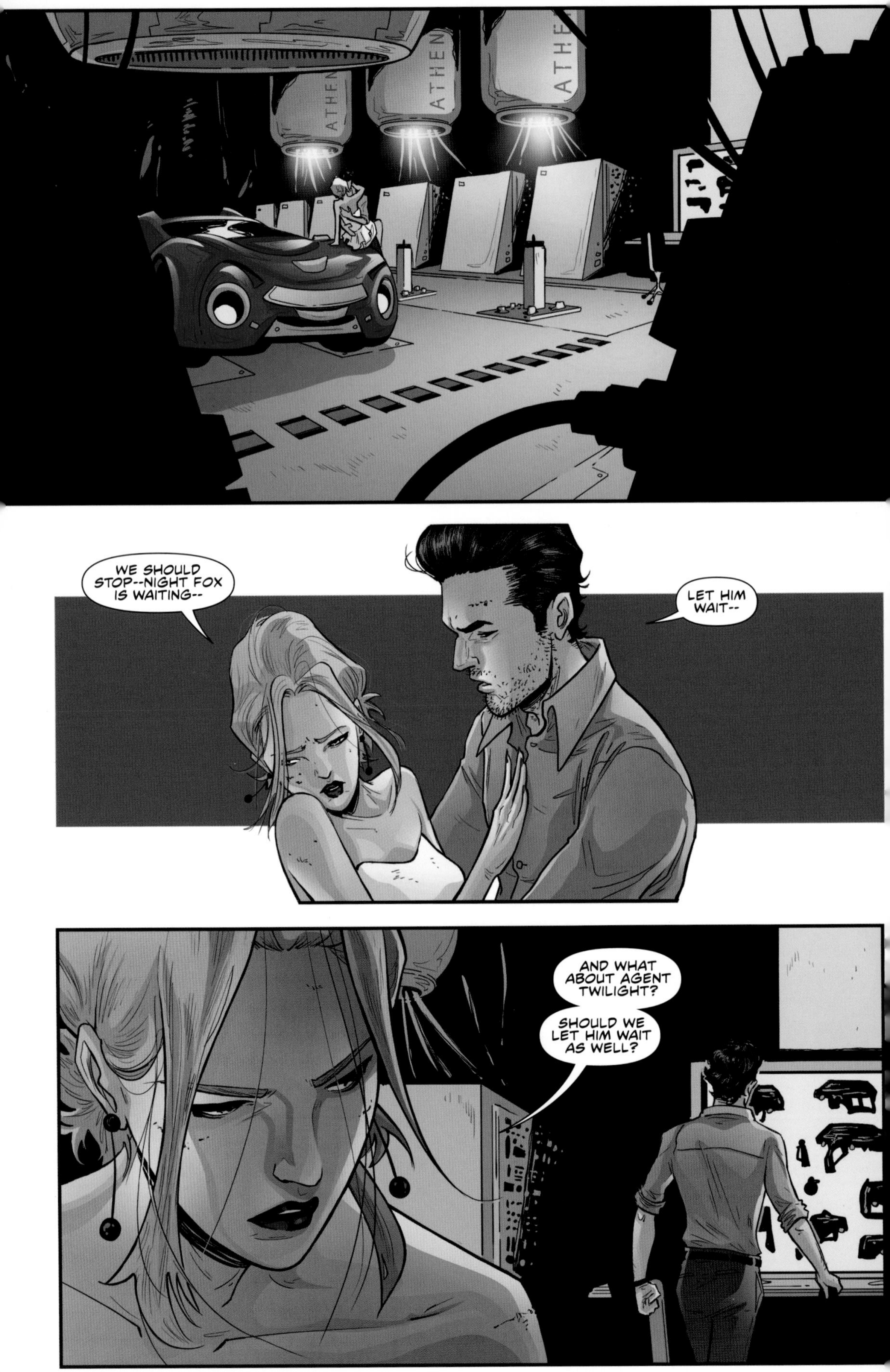

WE SHOULD STOP--NIGHT FOX IS WAITING--
LET HIM WAIT--
AND WHAT ABOUT AGENT TWILIGHT?
SHOULD WE LET HIM WAIT AS WELL?

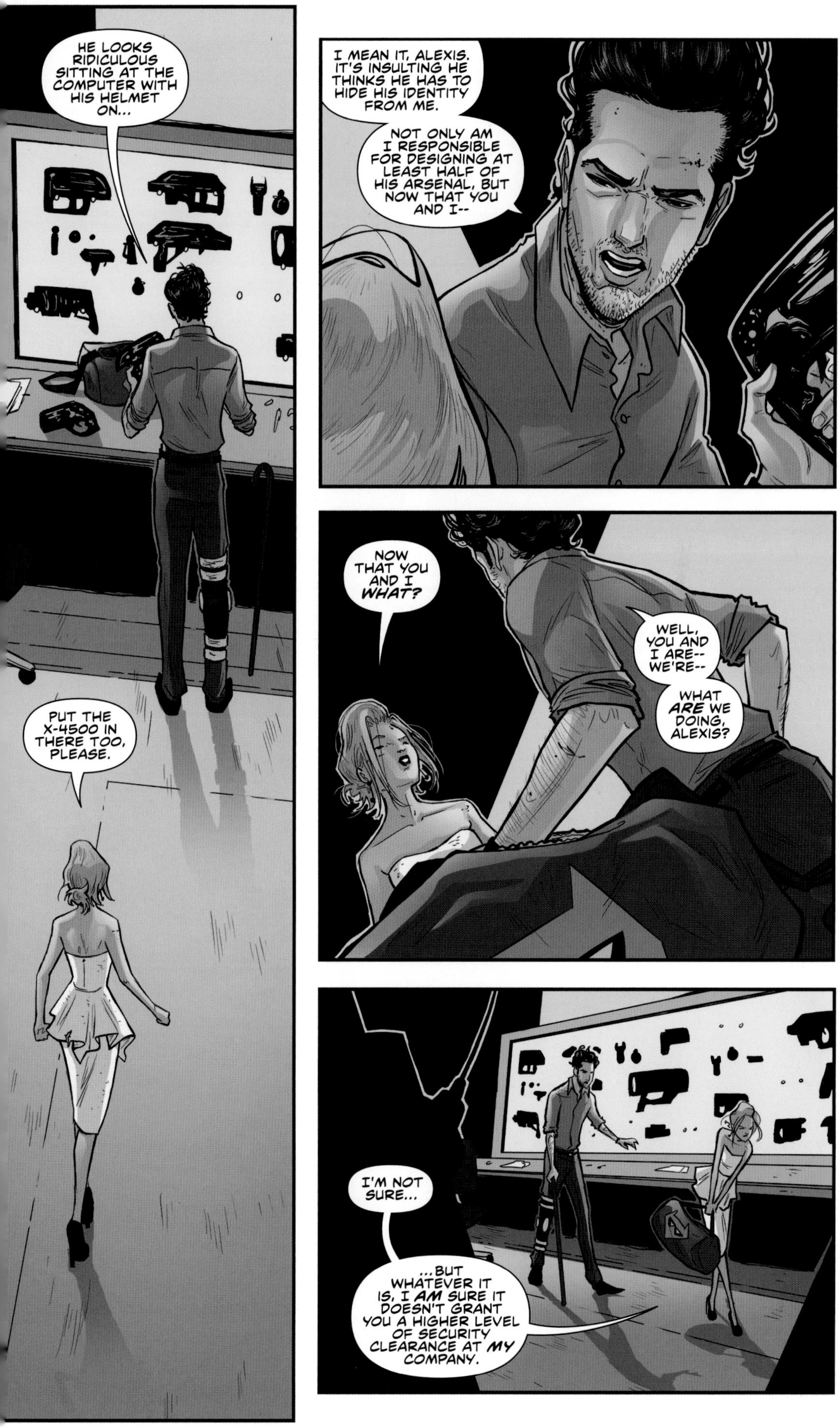
HE LOOKS RIDICULOUS SITTING AT THE COMPUTER WITH HIS HELMET ON...
PUT THE X-4500 IN THERE TOO, PLEASE.
I MEAN IT, ALEXIS. IT'S INSULTING HE THINKS HE HAS TO HIDE HIS IDENTITY FROM ME.
NOT ONLY AM I RESPONSIBLE FOR DESIGNING AT LEAST HALF OF HIS ARSENAL, BUT NOW THAT YOU AND I--
NOW THAT YOU AND I *WHAT?*
WELL, YOU AND I ARE-- WE'RE--
WHAT *ARE* WE DOING, ALEXIS?
I'M NOT SURE...
...BUT WHATEVER IT IS, I *AM* SURE IT DOESN'T GRANT YOU A HIGHER LEVEL OF SECURITY CLEARANCE AT *MY* COMPANY.

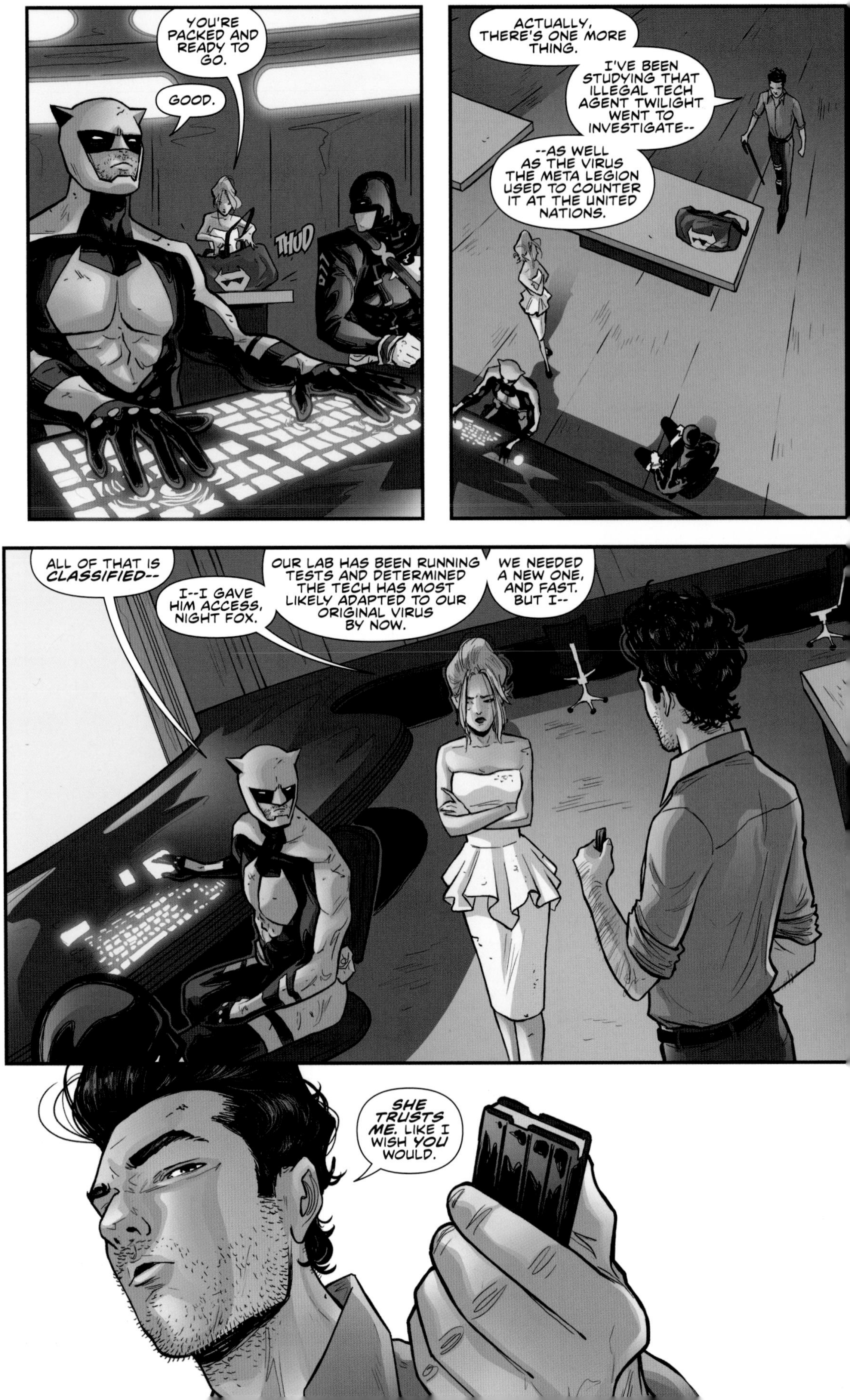
YOU'RE PACKED AND READY TO GO.
GOOD.
THUD
ACTUALLY, THERE'S ONE MORE THING.
I'VE BEEN STUDYING THAT ILLEGAL TECH AGENT TWILIGHT WENT TO INVESTIGATE--
--AS WELL AS THE VIRUS THE META LEGION USED TO COUNTER IT AT THE UNITED NATIONS.
ALL OF THAT IS *CLASSIFIED*--
I--I GAVE HIM ACCESS, NIGHT FOX.
OUR LAB HAS BEEN RUNNING TESTS AND DETERMINED THE TECH HAS MOST LIKELY ADAPTED TO OUR ORIGINAL VIRUS BY NOW.
WE NEEDED A NEW ONE, AND FAST. BUT I--
SHE TRUSTS ME. LIKE I WISH *YOU* WOULD.

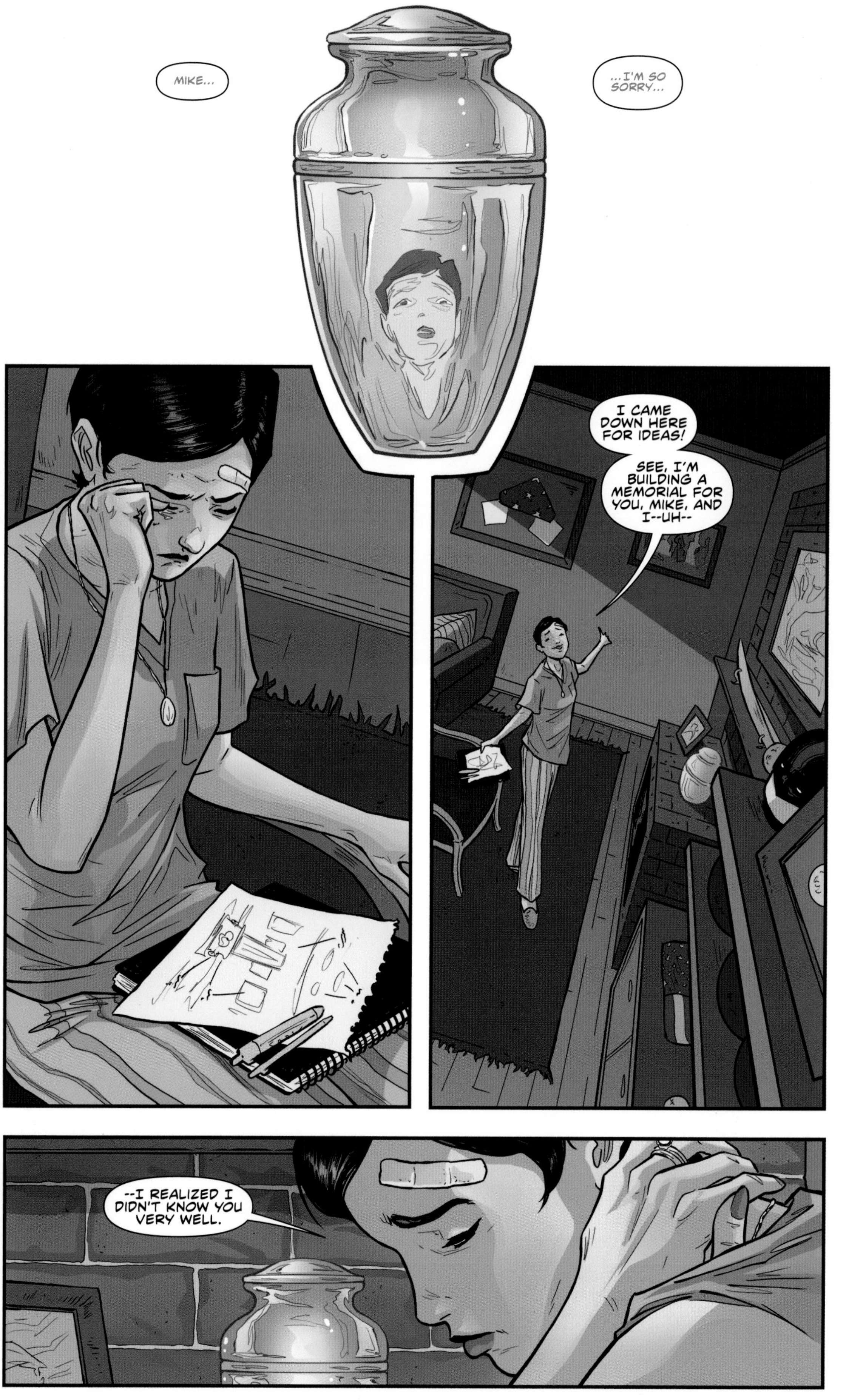

MIKE...
...I'M SO SORRY...
I CAME DOWN HERE FOR IDEAS!
SEE, I'M BUILDING A MEMORIAL FOR YOU, MIKE, AND I--UH--
--I REALIZED I DIDN'T KNOW YOU VERY WELL.

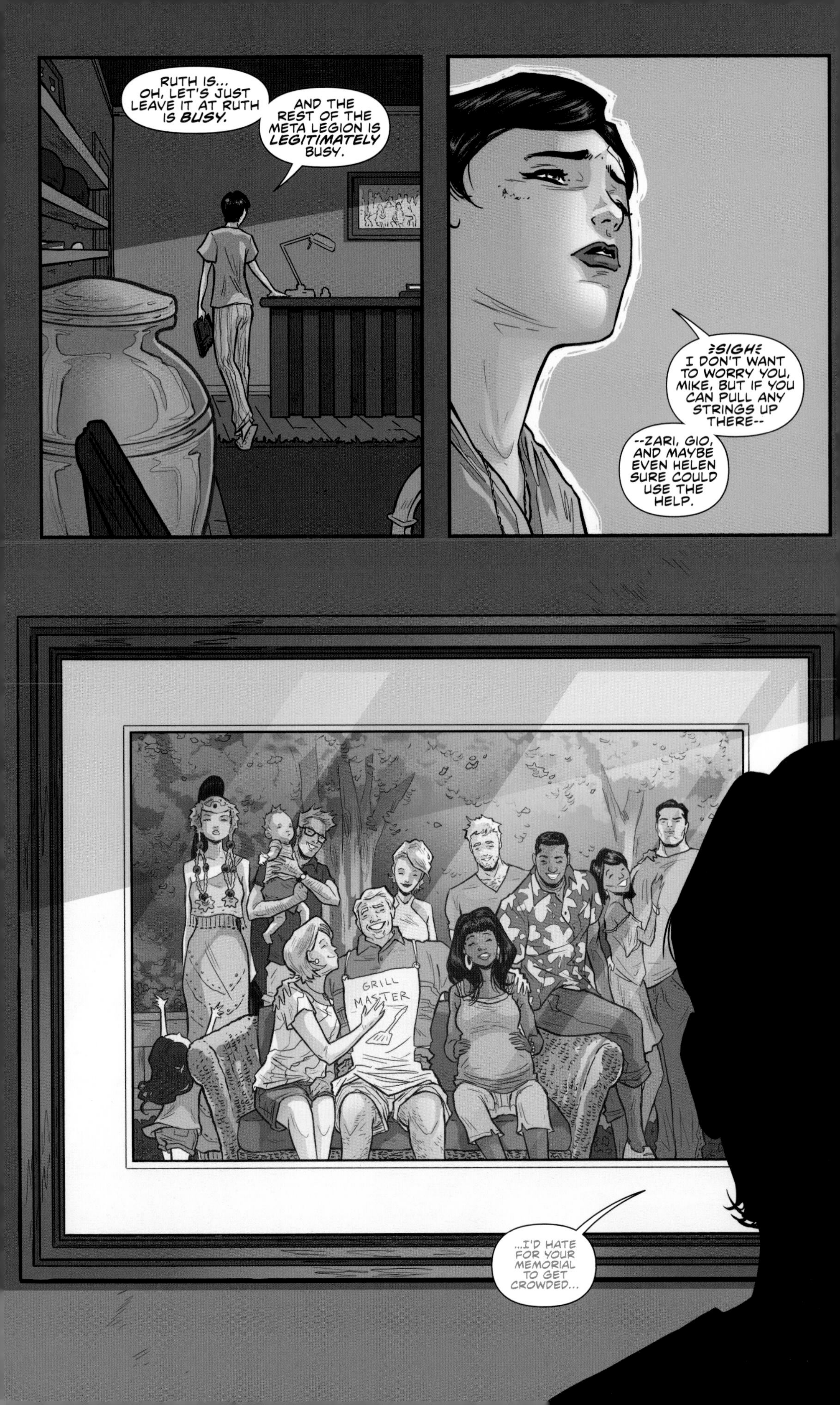
RUTH IS... OH, LET'S JUST LEAVE IT AT RUTH IS *BUSY.*
AND THE REST OF THE META LEGION IS *LEGITIMATELY* BUSY.
SIGH I DON'T WANT TO WORRY YOU, MIKE, BUT IF YOU CAN PULL ANY STRINGS UP THERE--
--ZARI, GIO, AND MAYBE EVEN HELEN SURE COULD USE THE HELP.
GRILL MASTER
...I'D HATE FOR YOUR MEMORIAL TO GET CROWDED...

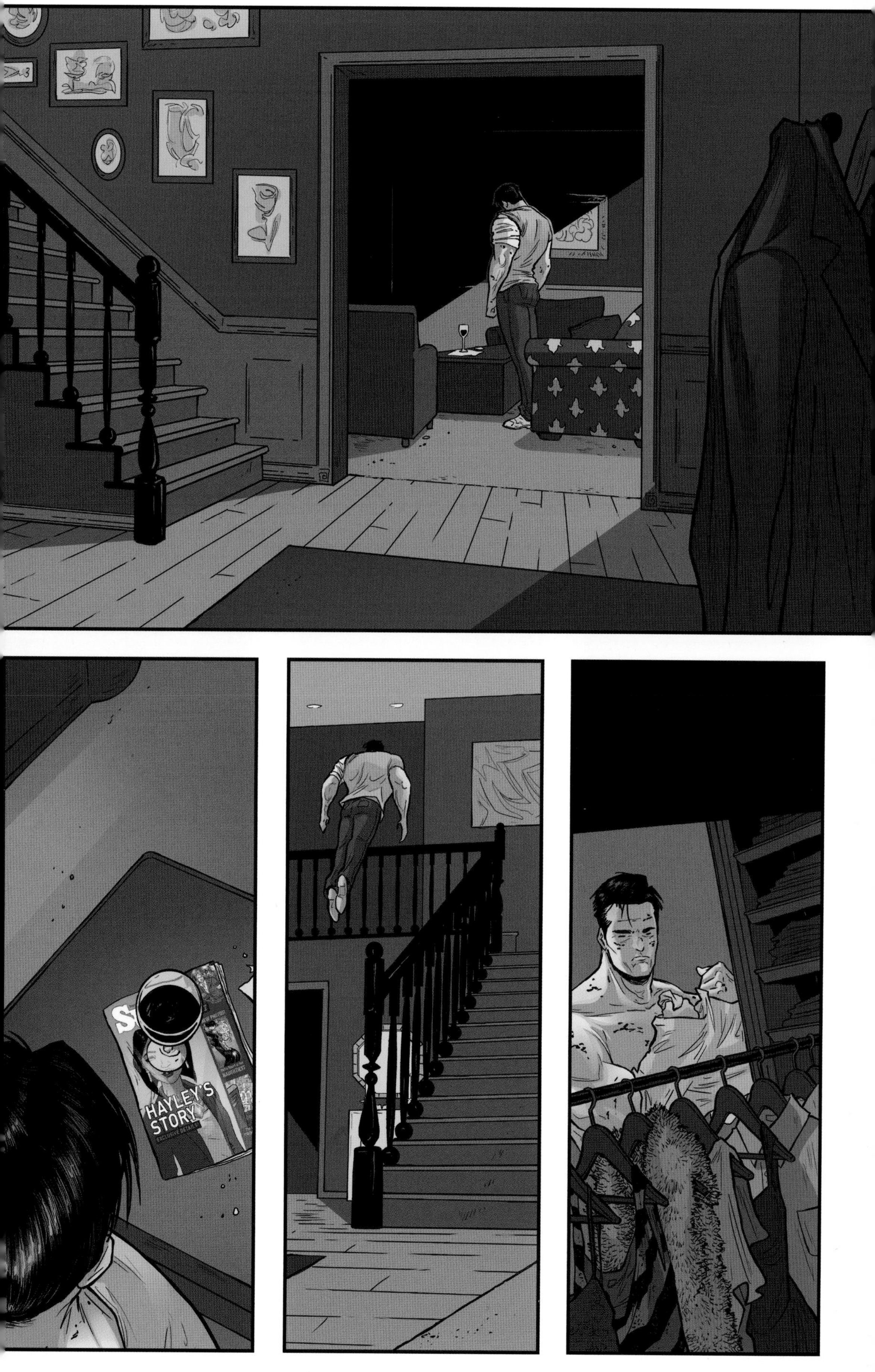
HAYLEY'S STORY
EXCLUSIVE DETAILS!
NEW PHOTOS
NAUGHTIEST

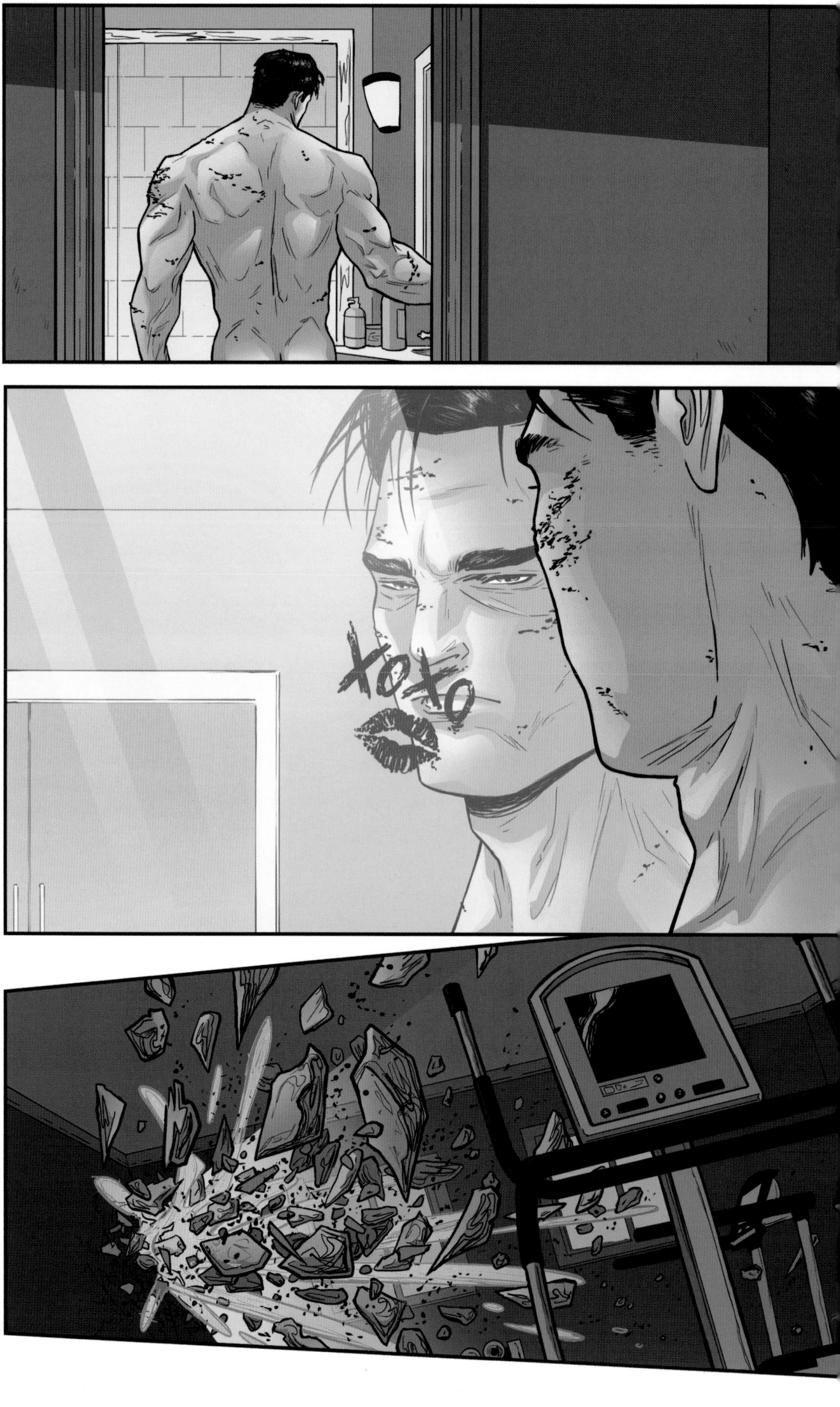
xoxo

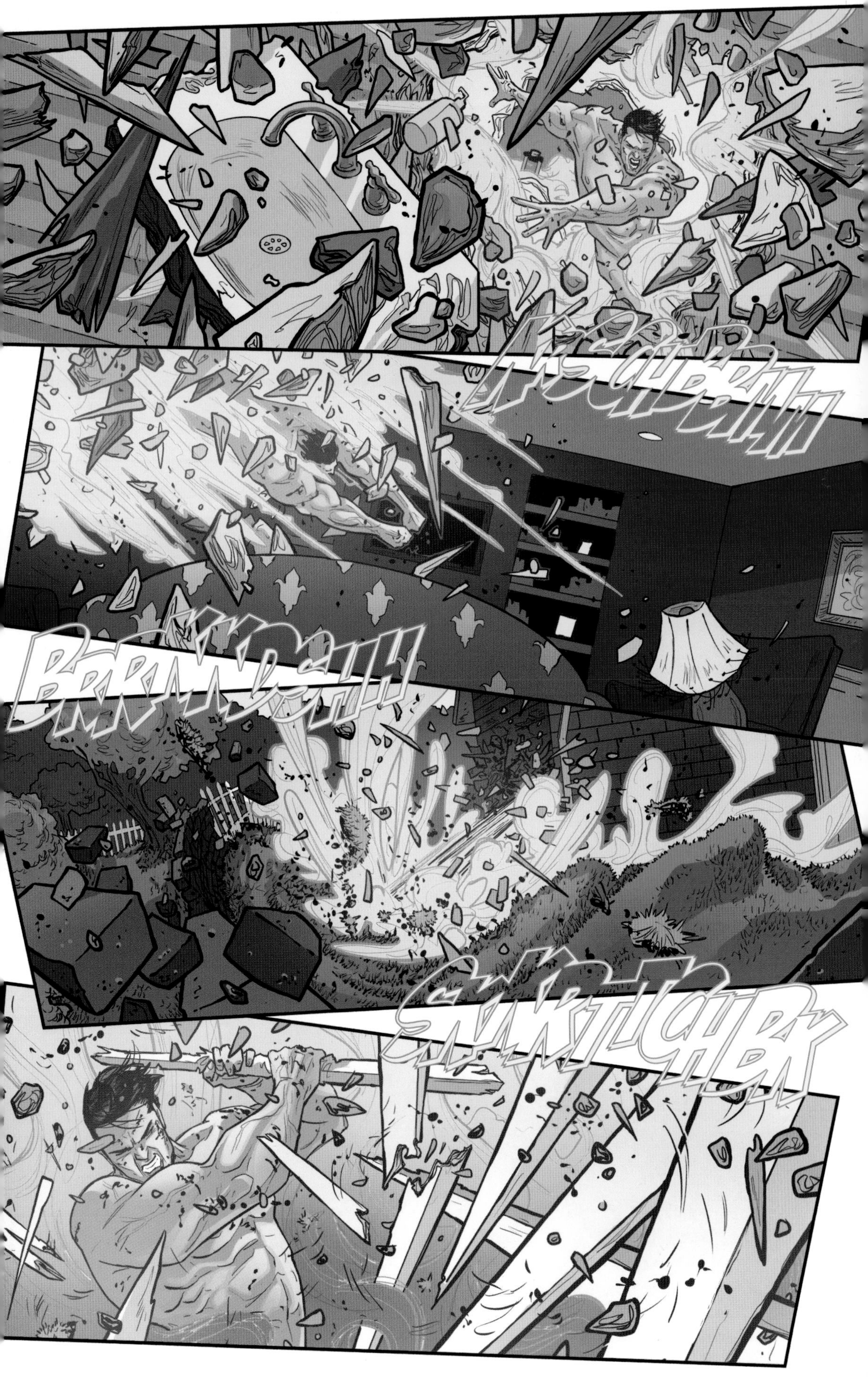

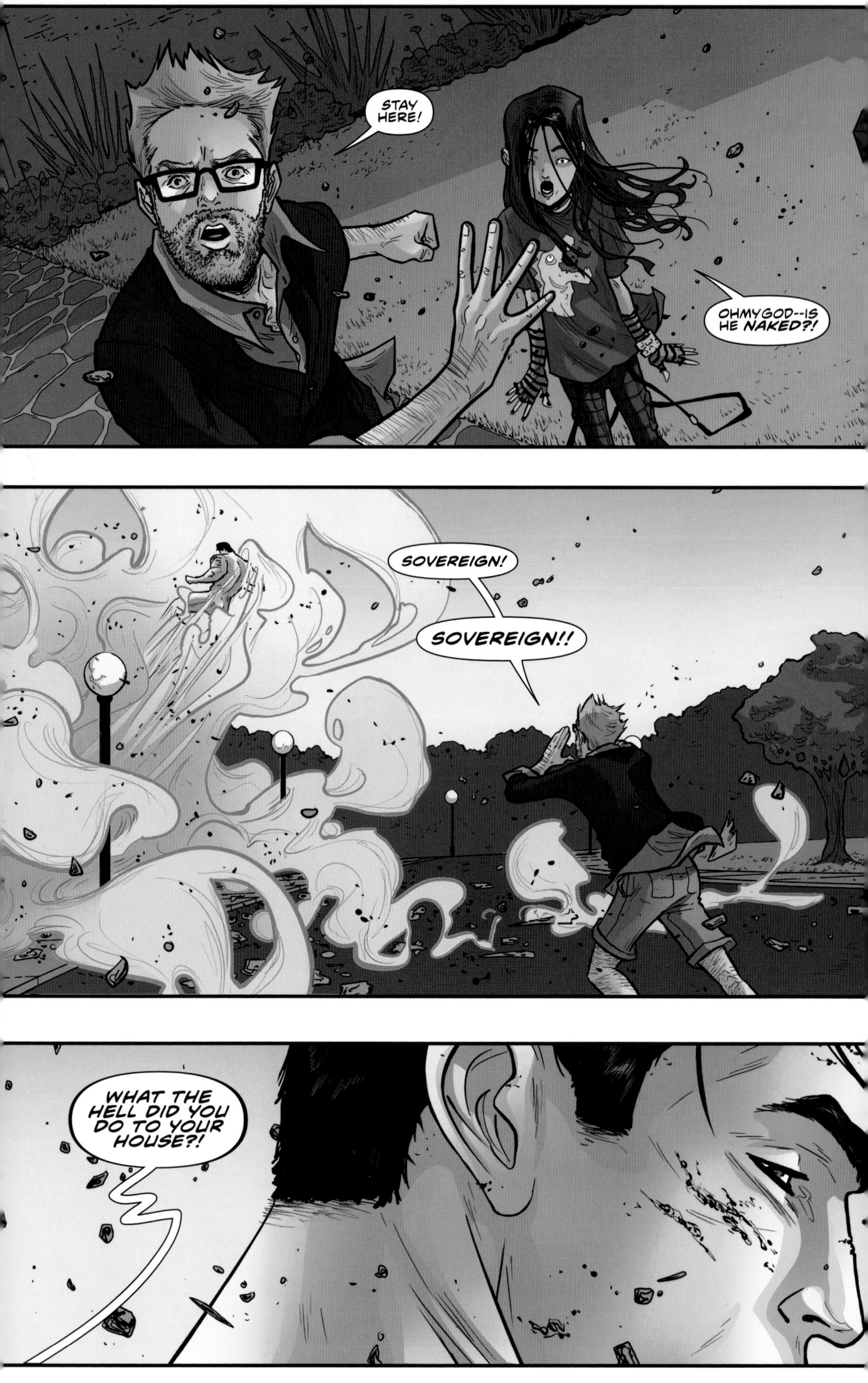
STAY HERE!
OHMYGOD--IS HE NAKED?!
SOVEREIGN!
SOVEREIGN!!
WHAT THE HELL DID YOU DO TO YOUR HOUSE?!

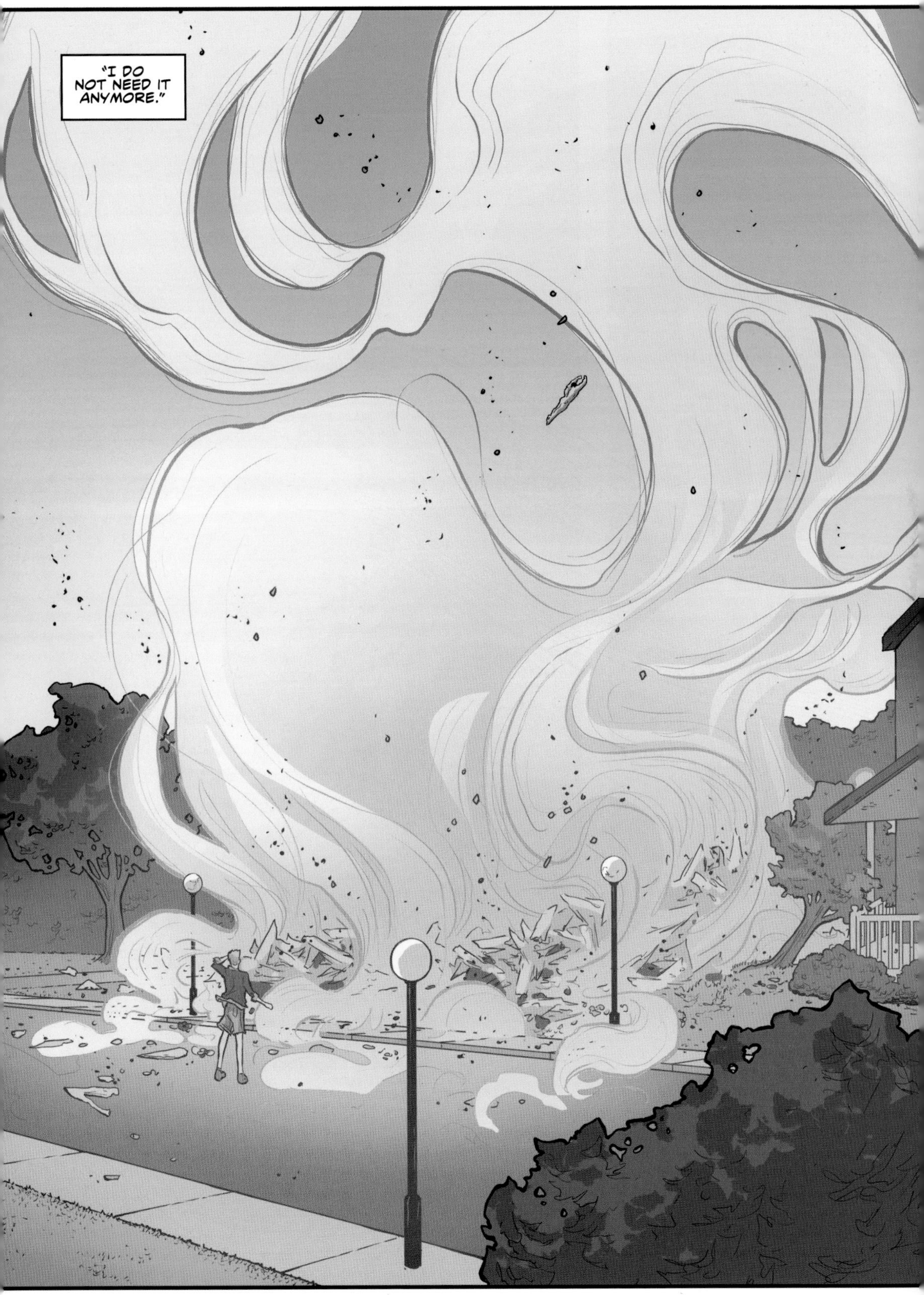
"I DO NOT NEED IT ANYMORE."

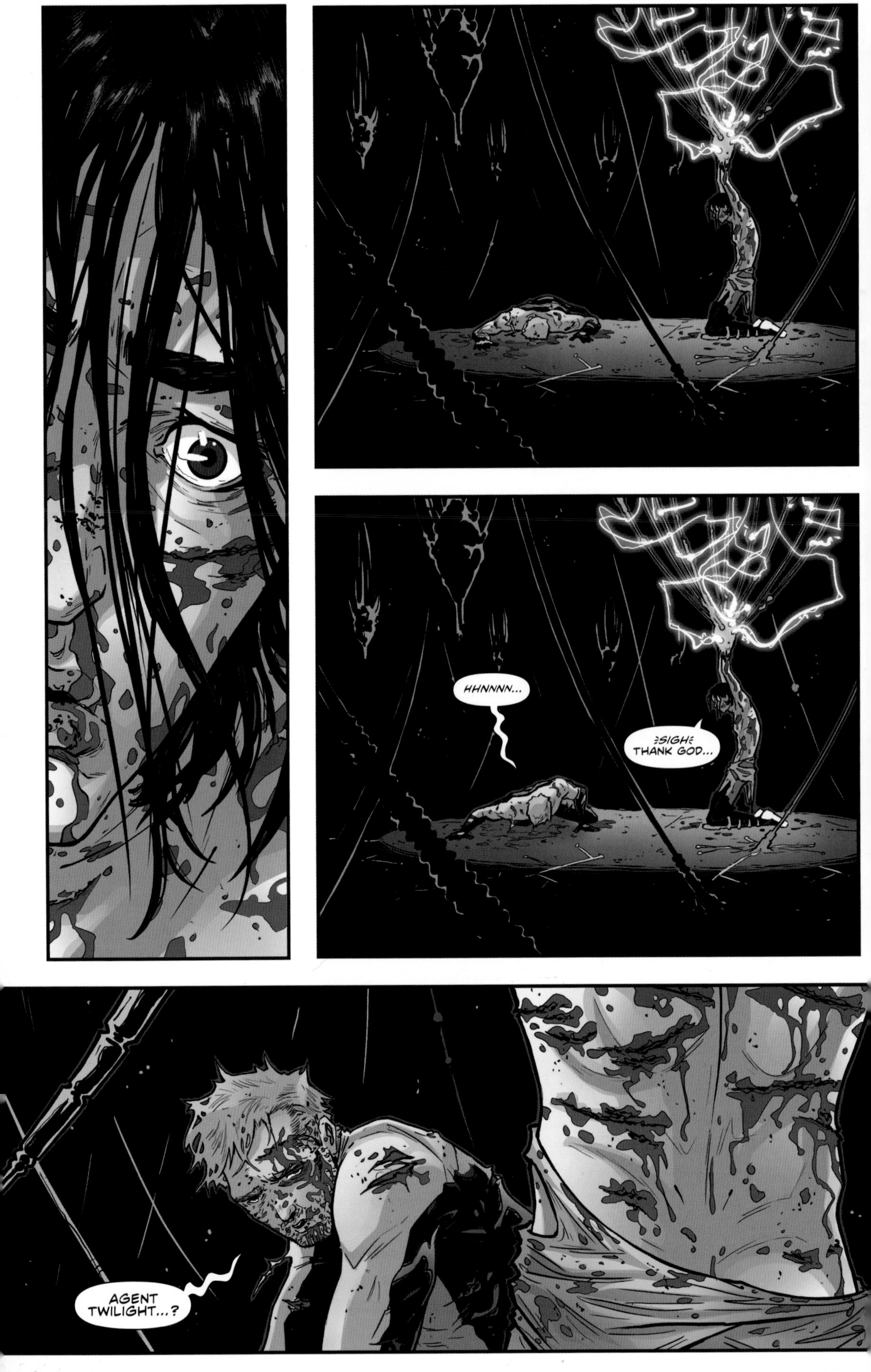
HHNNNN...
≷SIGH≶
THANK GOD...
AGENT
TWILIGHT...?

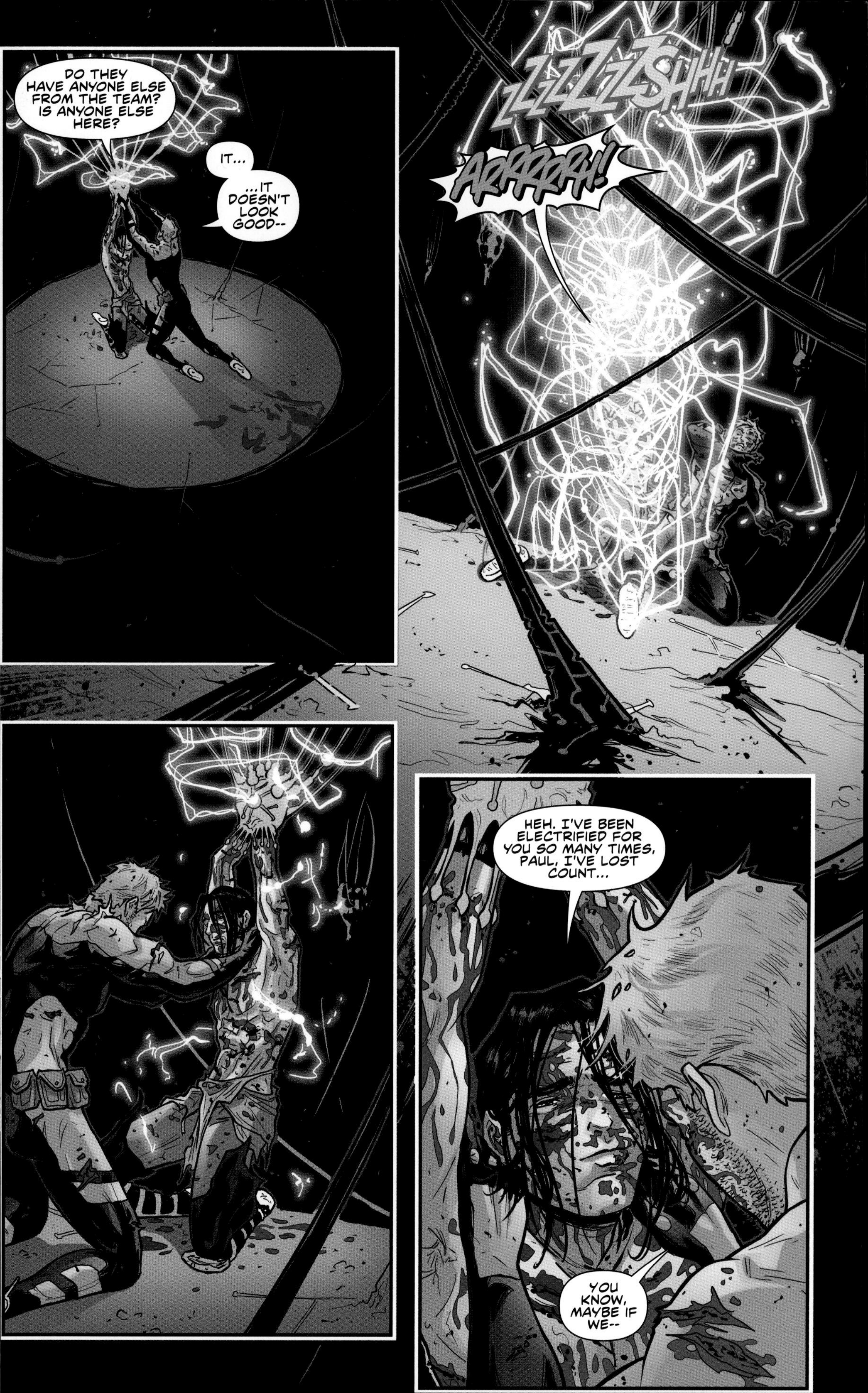
DO THEY HAVE ANYONE ELSE FROM THE TEAM? IS ANYONE ELSE HERE?
IT...
...IT DOESN'T LOOK GOOD--
ZZZZZZSHHH
ARRRRRH!!
HEH. I'VE BEEN ELECTRIFIED FOR YOU SO MANY TIMES, PAUL, I'VE LOST COUNT...
YOU KNOW, MAYBE IF WE--

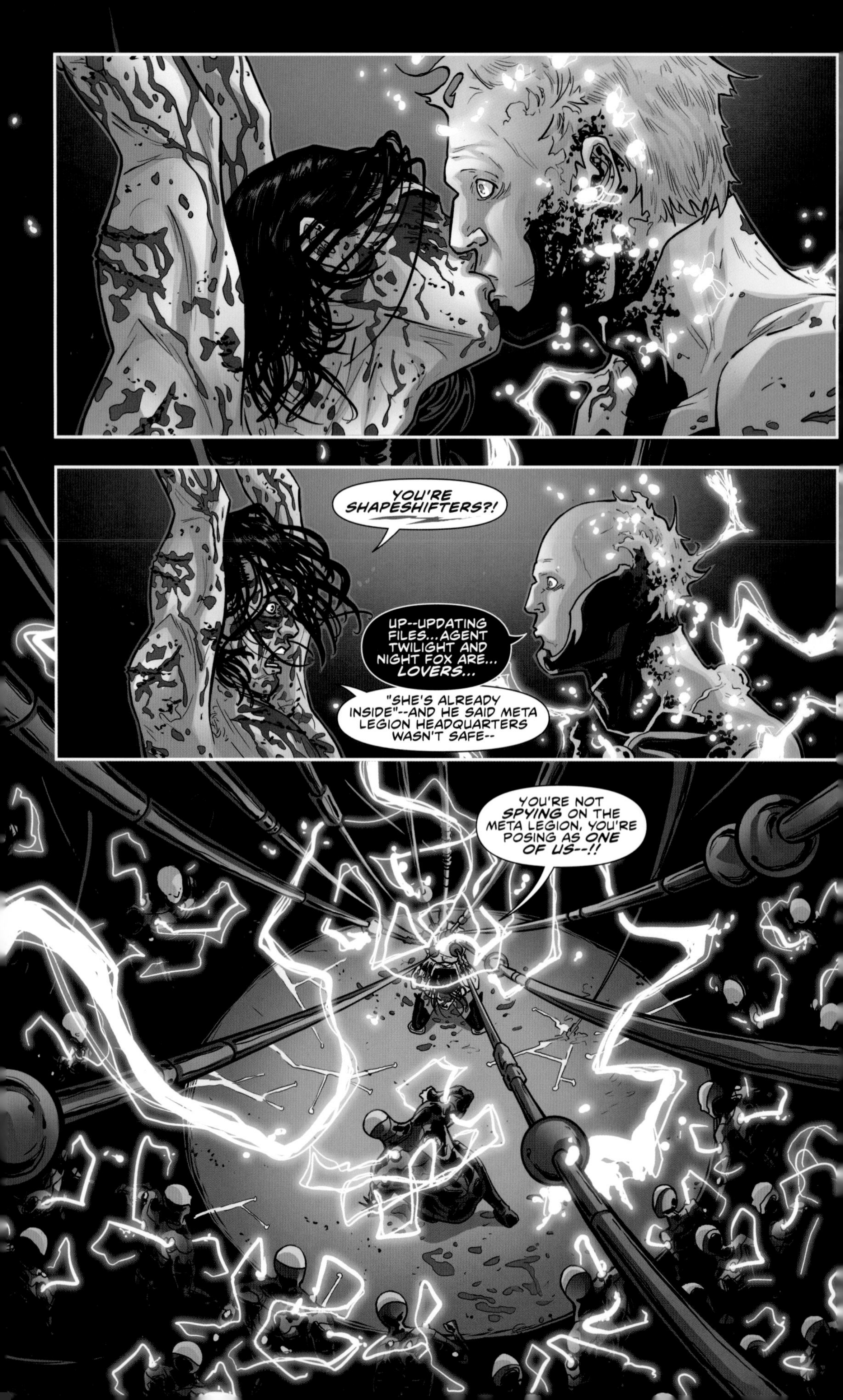
YOU'RE SHAPESHIFTERS?!
UP--UPDATING FILES...AGENT TWILIGHT AND NIGHT FOX ARE... LOVERS...
"SHE'S ALREADY INSIDE"--AND HE SAID META LEGION HEADQUARTERS WASN'T SAFE--
YOU'RE NOT SPYING ON THE META LEGION, YOU'RE POSING AS ONE OF US--!!

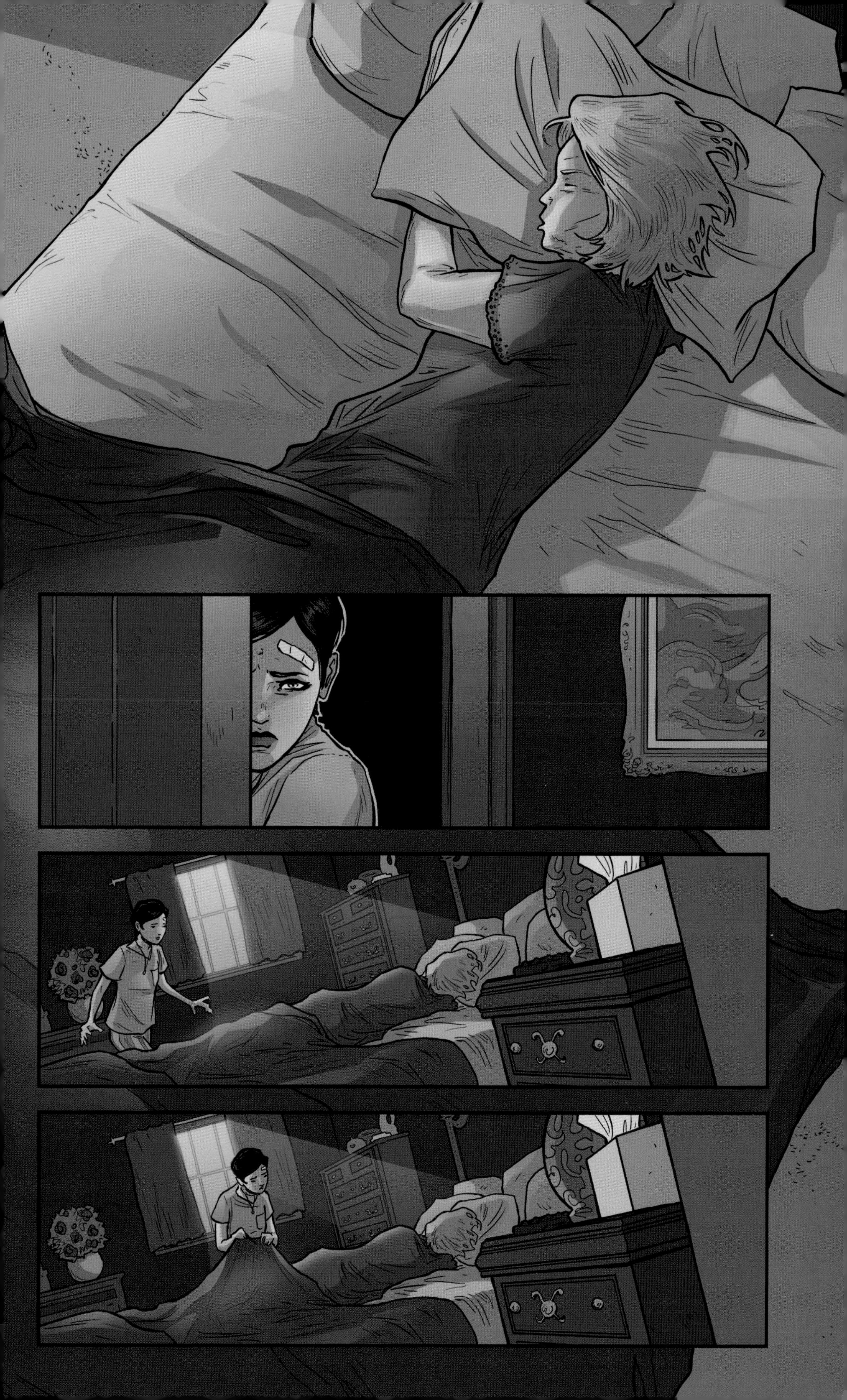

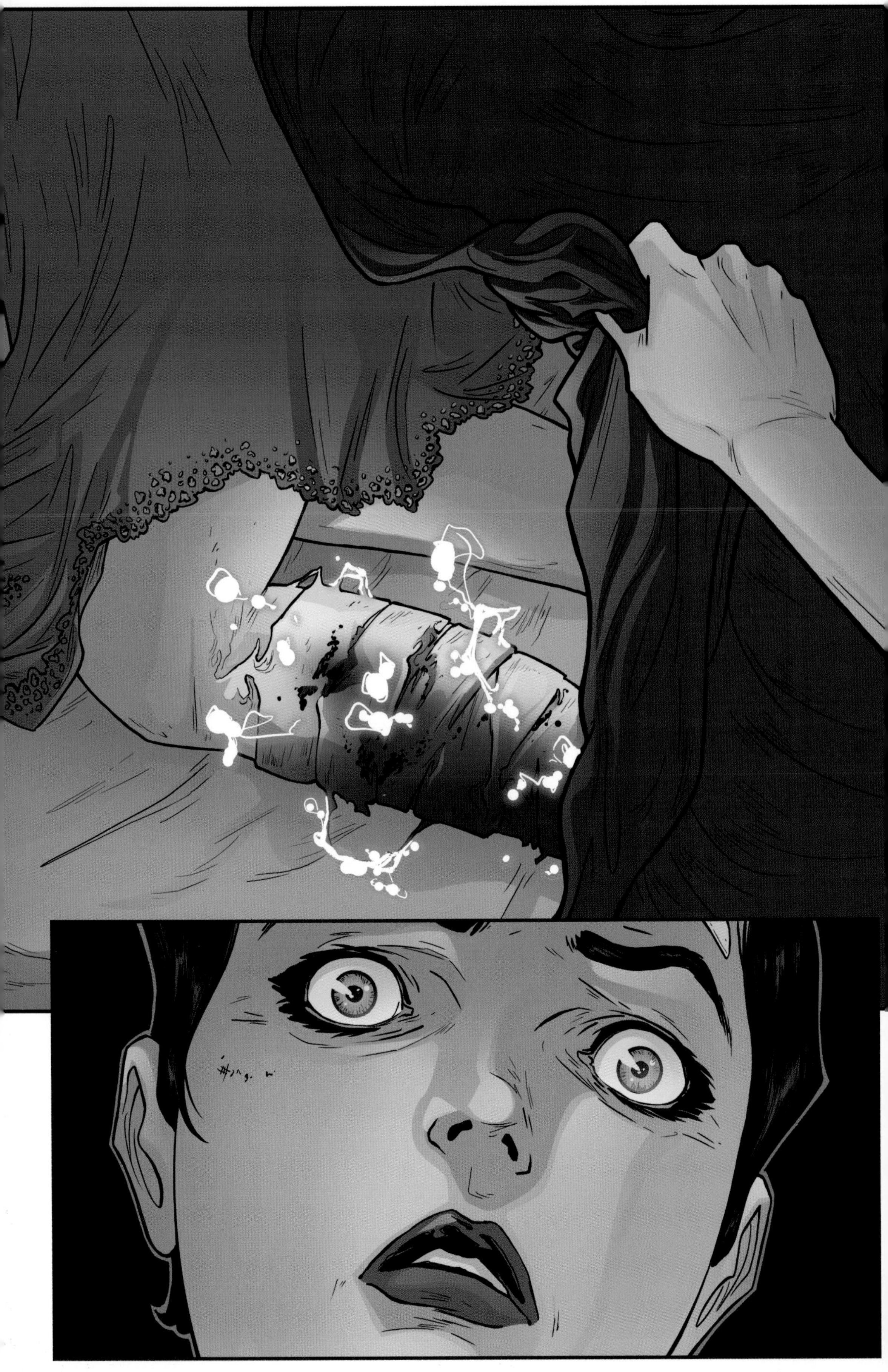

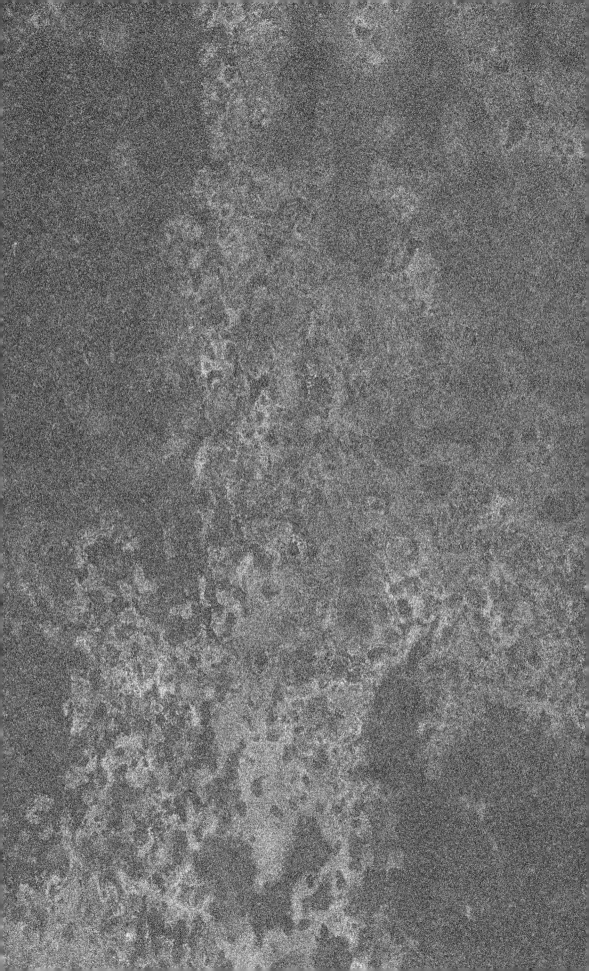

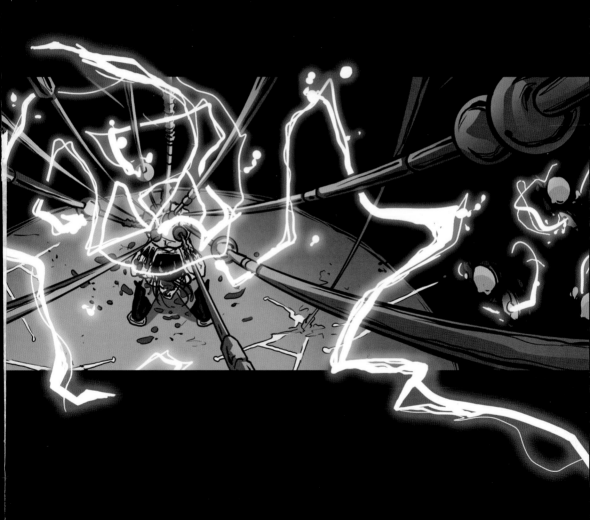

Chapter 11

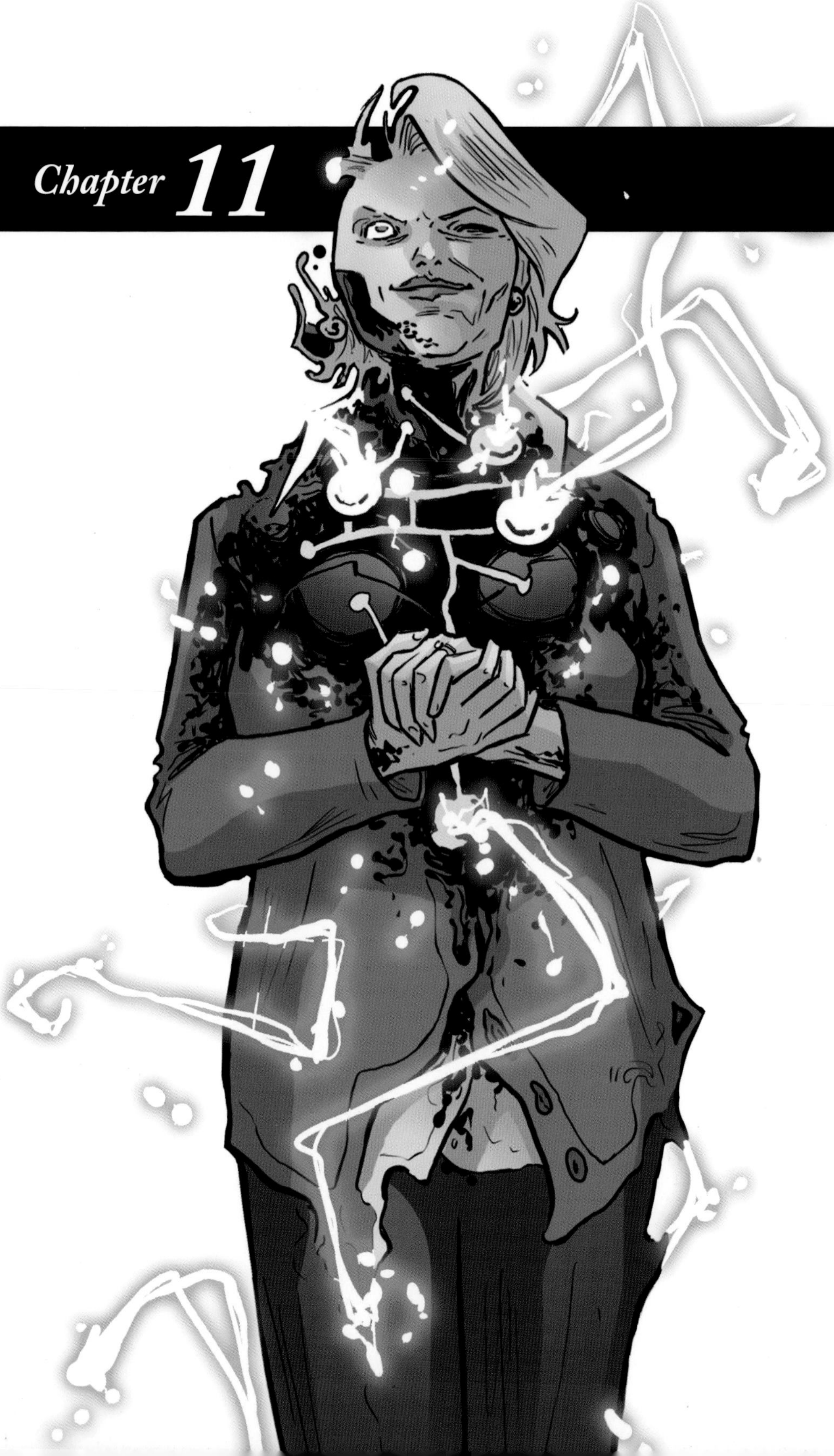

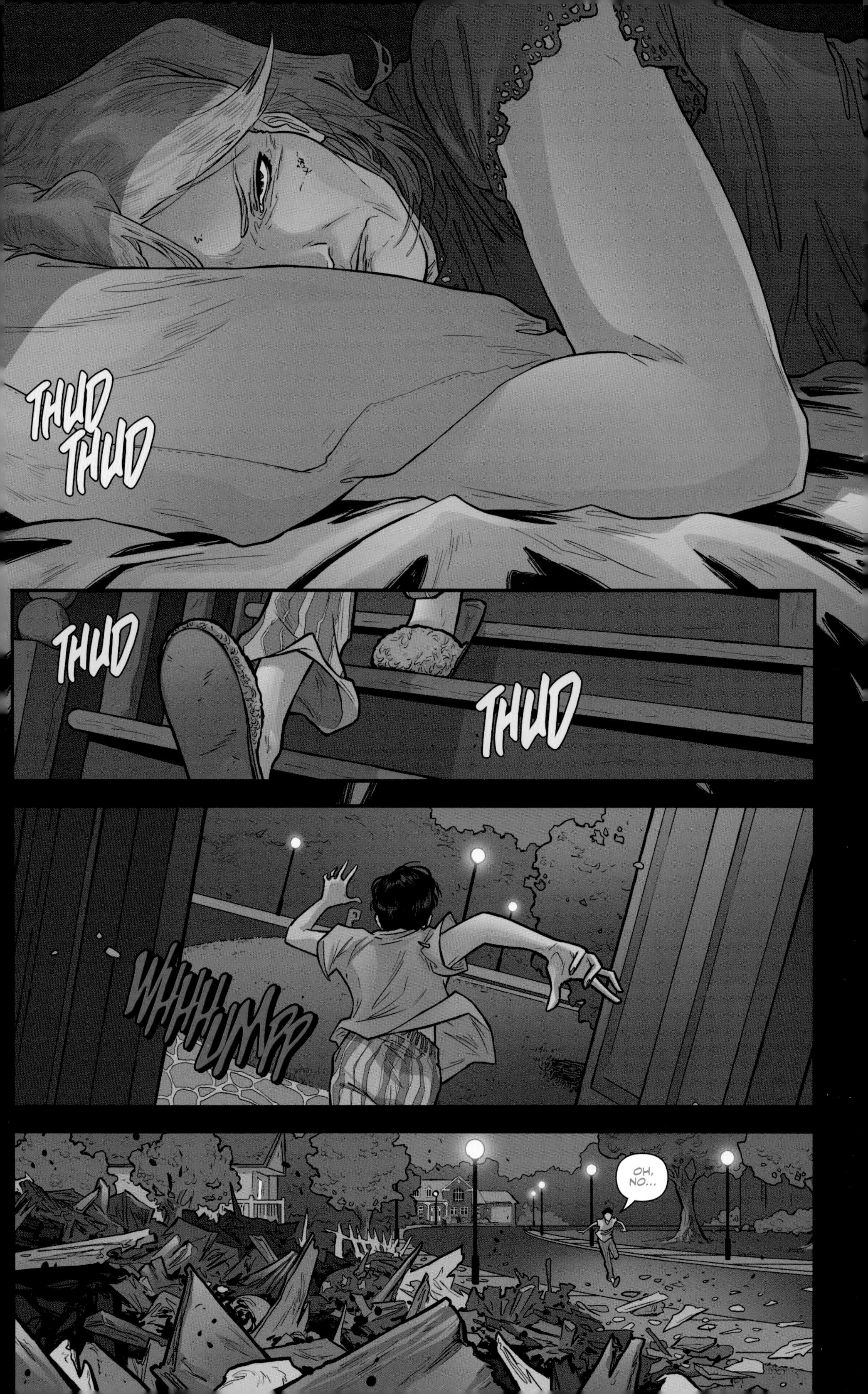
THUD THUD
THUD
THUD
WHHUMP
OH, NO...

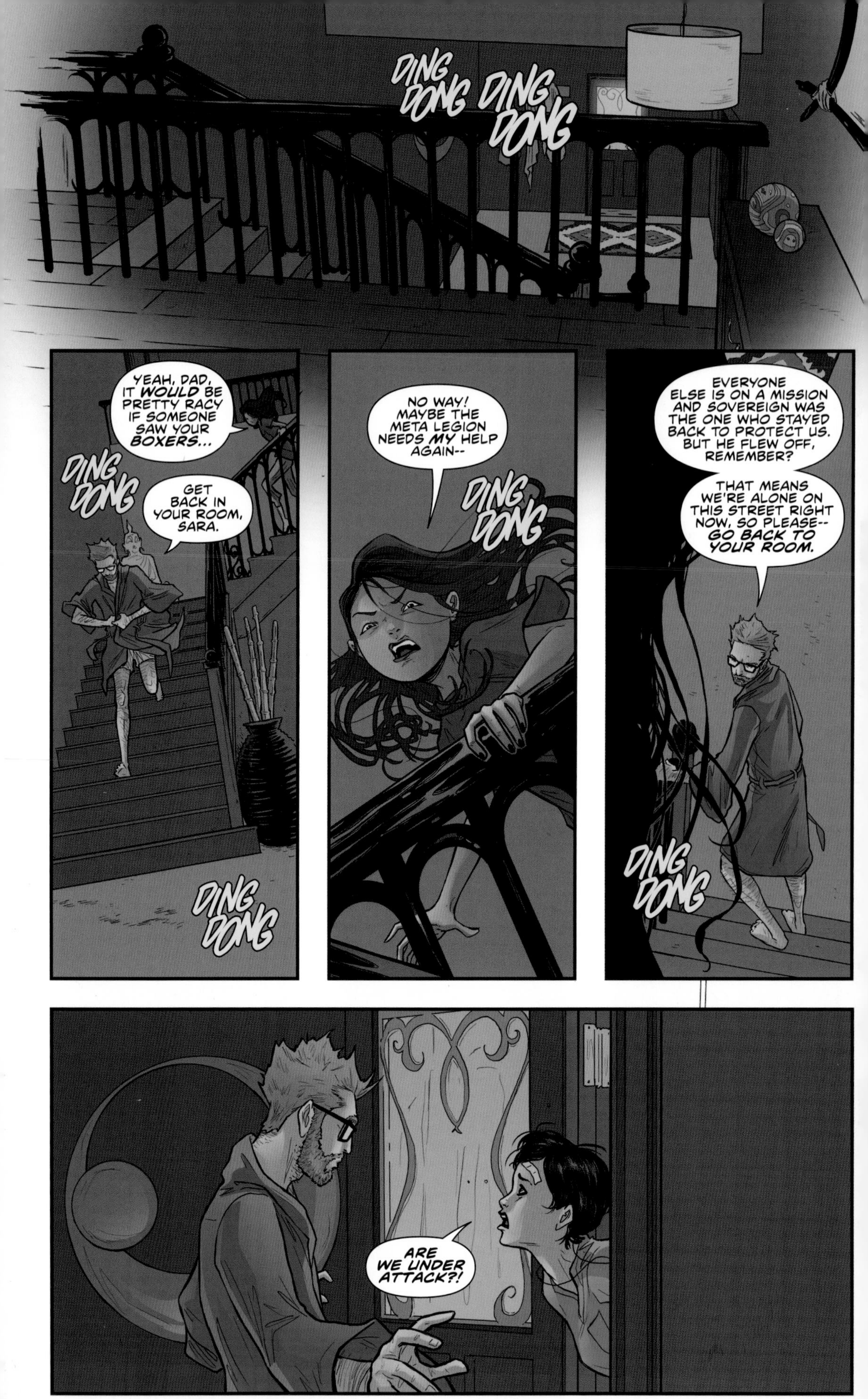
DING DONG DING DONG
YEAH, DAD, IT WOULD BE PRETTY RACY IF SOMEONE SAW YOUR BOXERS...
DING DONG
GET BACK IN YOUR ROOM, SARA.
DING DONG
NO WAY! MAYBE THE META LEGION NEEDS MY HELP AGAIN--
DING DONG
EVERYONE ELSE IS ON A MISSION AND SOVEREIGN WAS THE ONE WHO STAYED BACK TO PROTECT US. BUT HE FLEW OFF, REMEMBER?
THAT MEANS WE'RE ALONE ON THIS STREET RIGHT NOW, SO PLEASE-- GO BACK TO YOUR ROOM.
DING DONG
ARE WE UNDER ATTACK?!

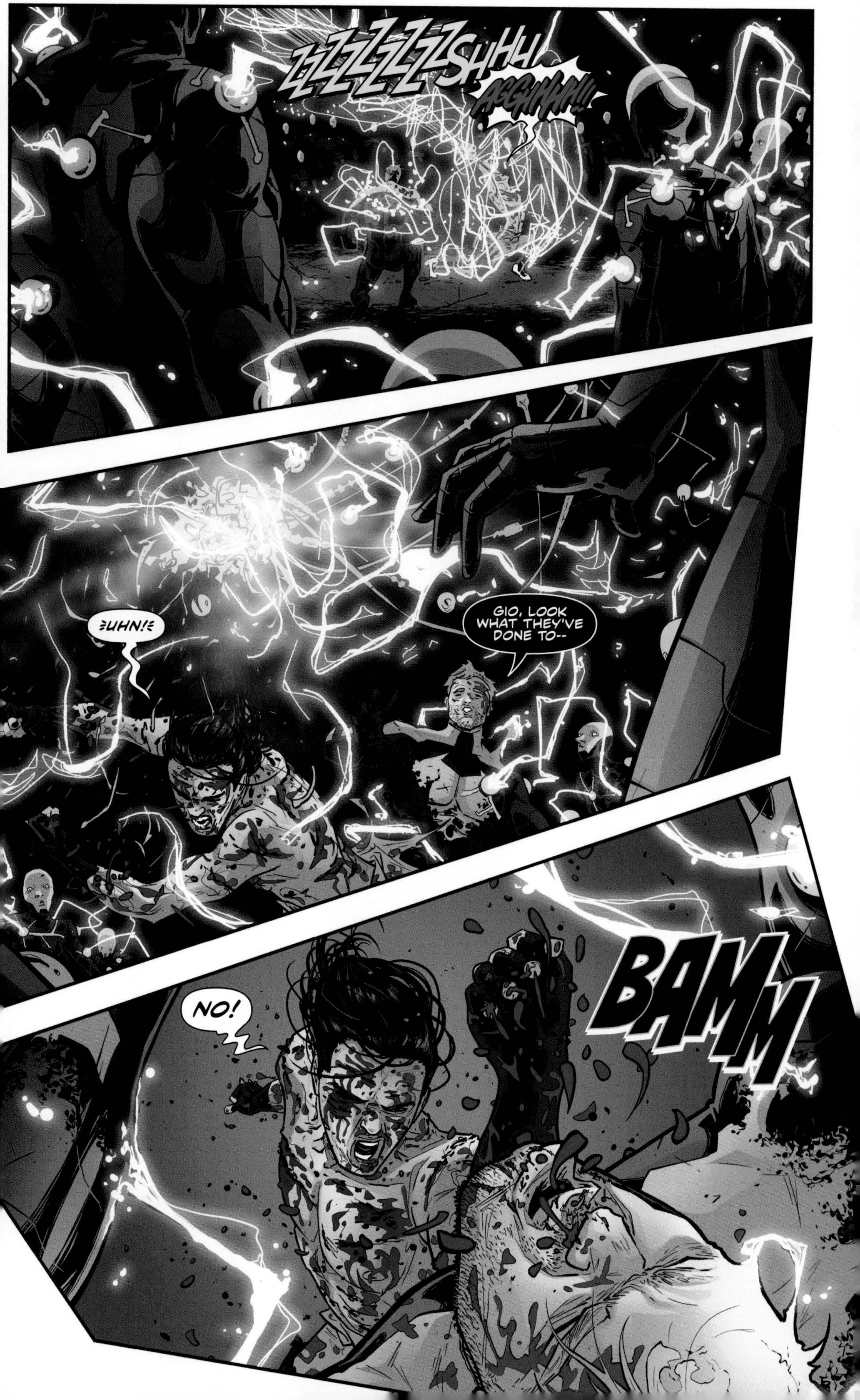
ZZZZZZZZSHHH
AGGHHH!!
UHN!
GIO, LOOK WHAT THEY'VE DONE TO--
NO!
BAMM

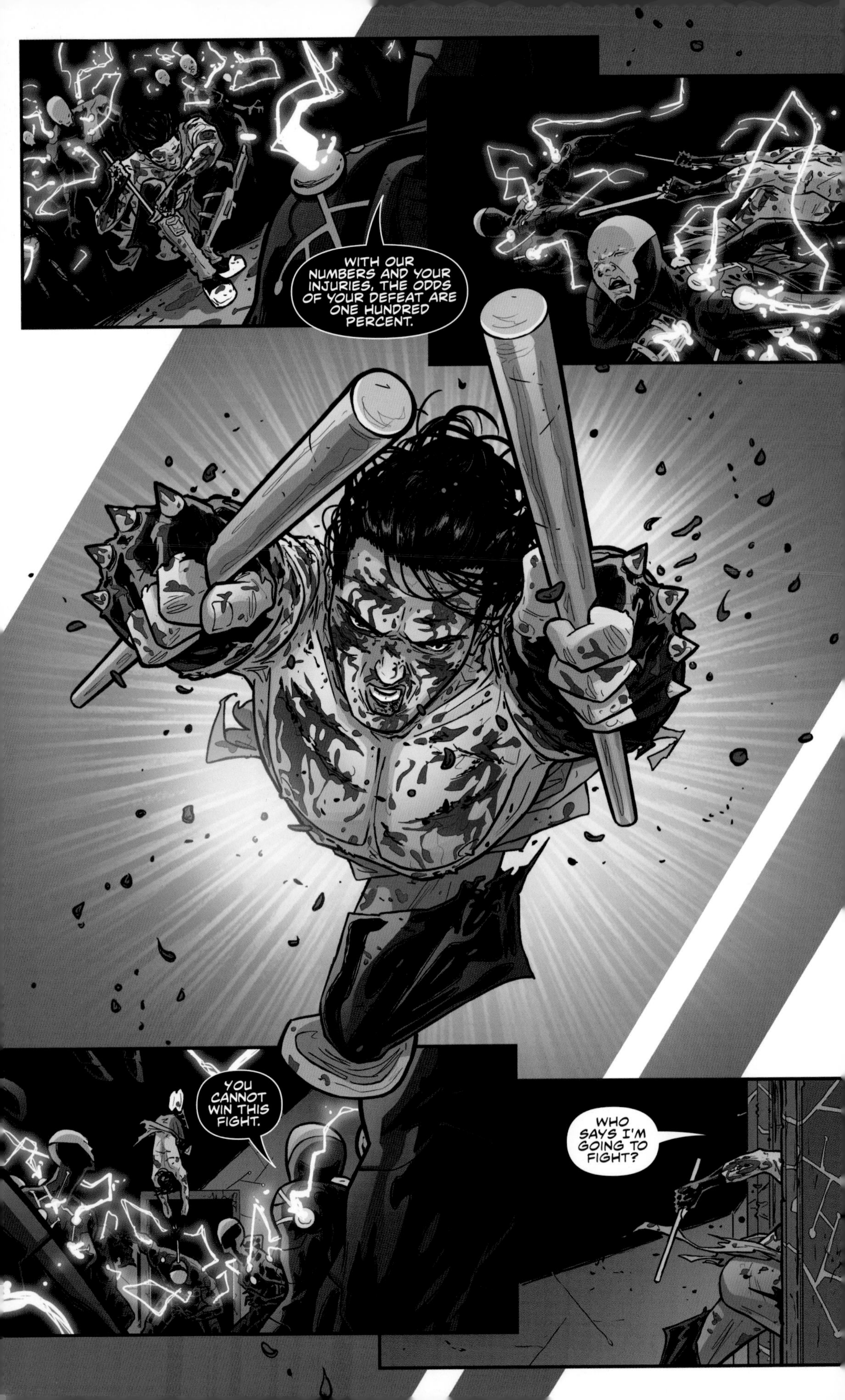
WITH OUR NUMBERS AND YOUR INJURIES, THE ODDS OF YOUR DEFEAT ARE ONE HUNDRED PERCENT.
YOU CANNOT WIN THIS FIGHT.
WHO SAYS I'M GOING TO FIGHT?

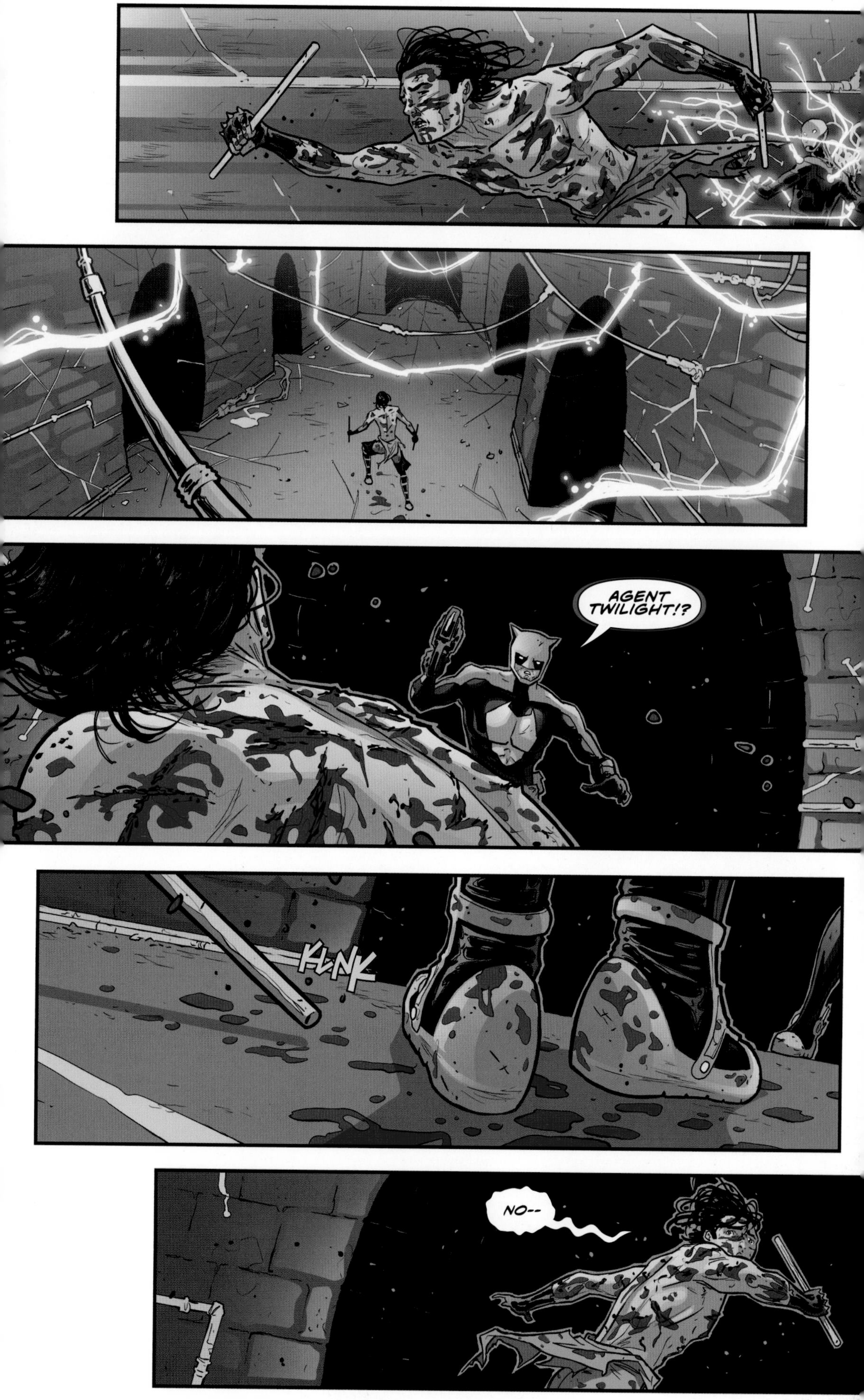
AGENT TWILIGHT!?
KLNK
NO--

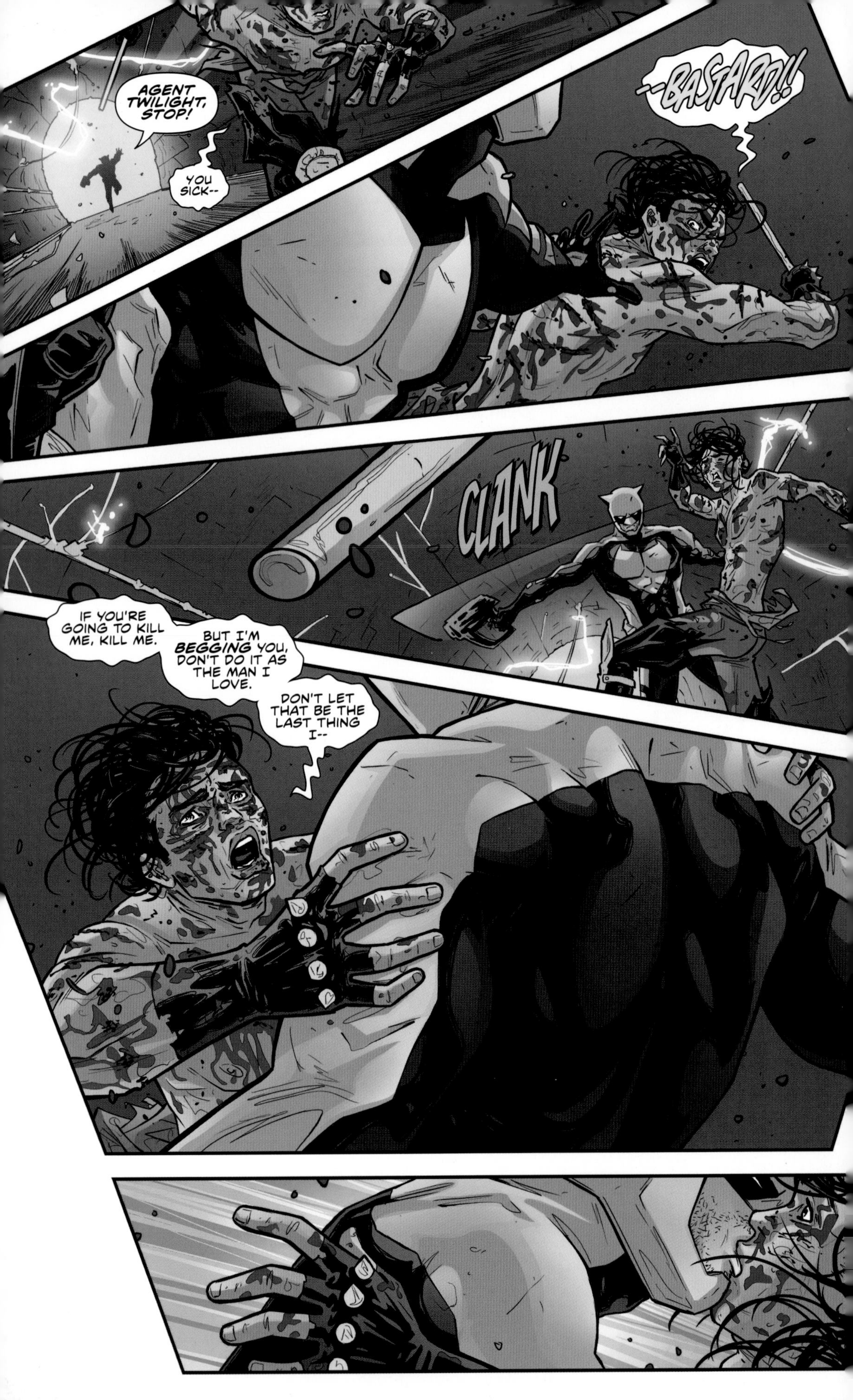
AGENT TWILIGHT, STOP!
YOU SICK--
--BASTARD!!
CLANK
IF YOU'RE GOING TO KILL ME, KILL ME.
BUT I'M BEGGING YOU, DON'T DO IT AS THE MAN I LOVE.
DON'T LET THAT BE THE LAST THING I--

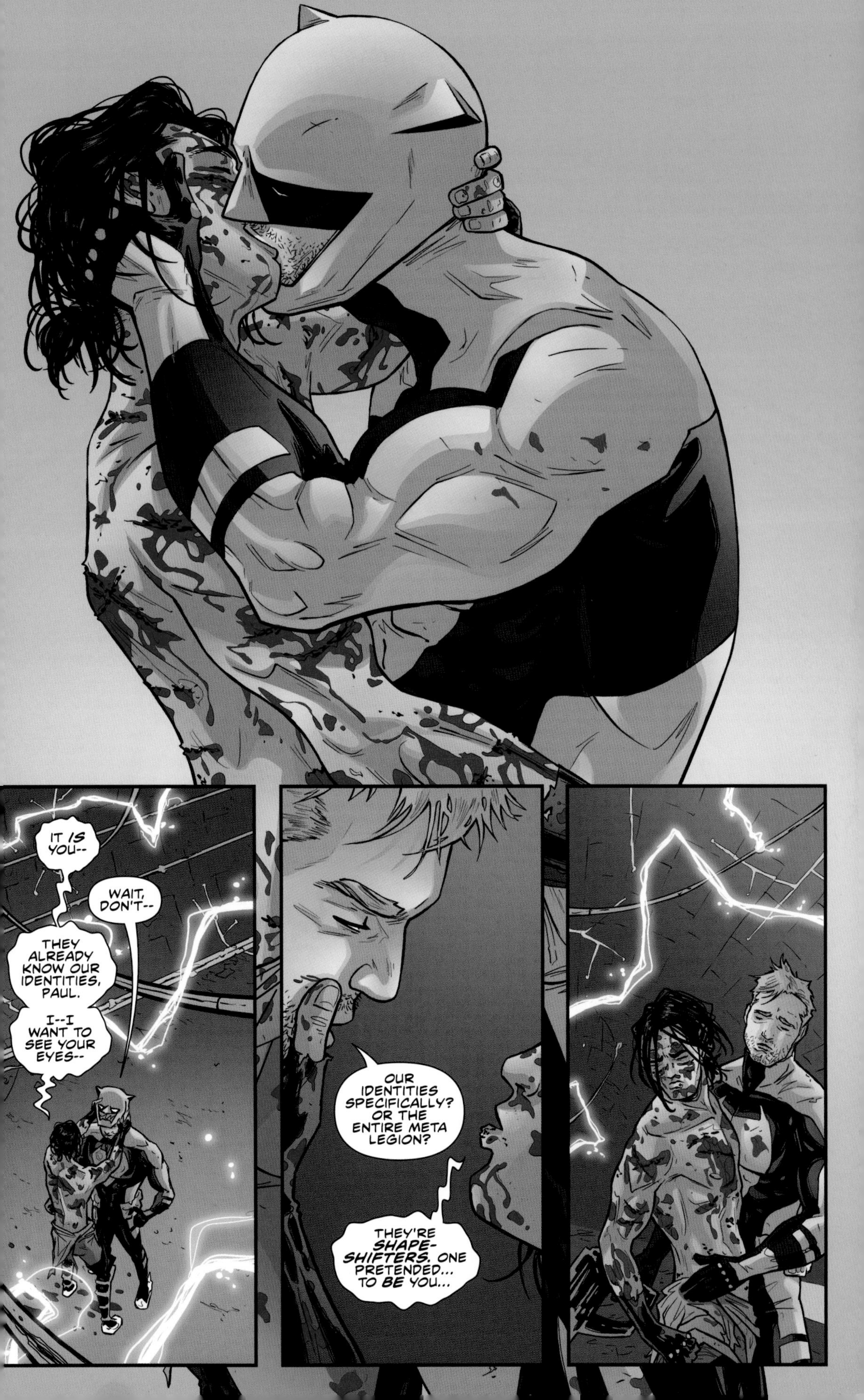
IT IS YOU--
WAIT, DON'T--
THEY ALREADY KNOW OUR IDENTITIES, PAUL.
I--I WANT TO SEE YOUR EYES--
OUR IDENTITIES SPECIFICALLY? OR THE ENTIRE META LEGION?
THEY'RE SHAPE-SHIFTERS. ONE PRETENDED... TO BE YOU...

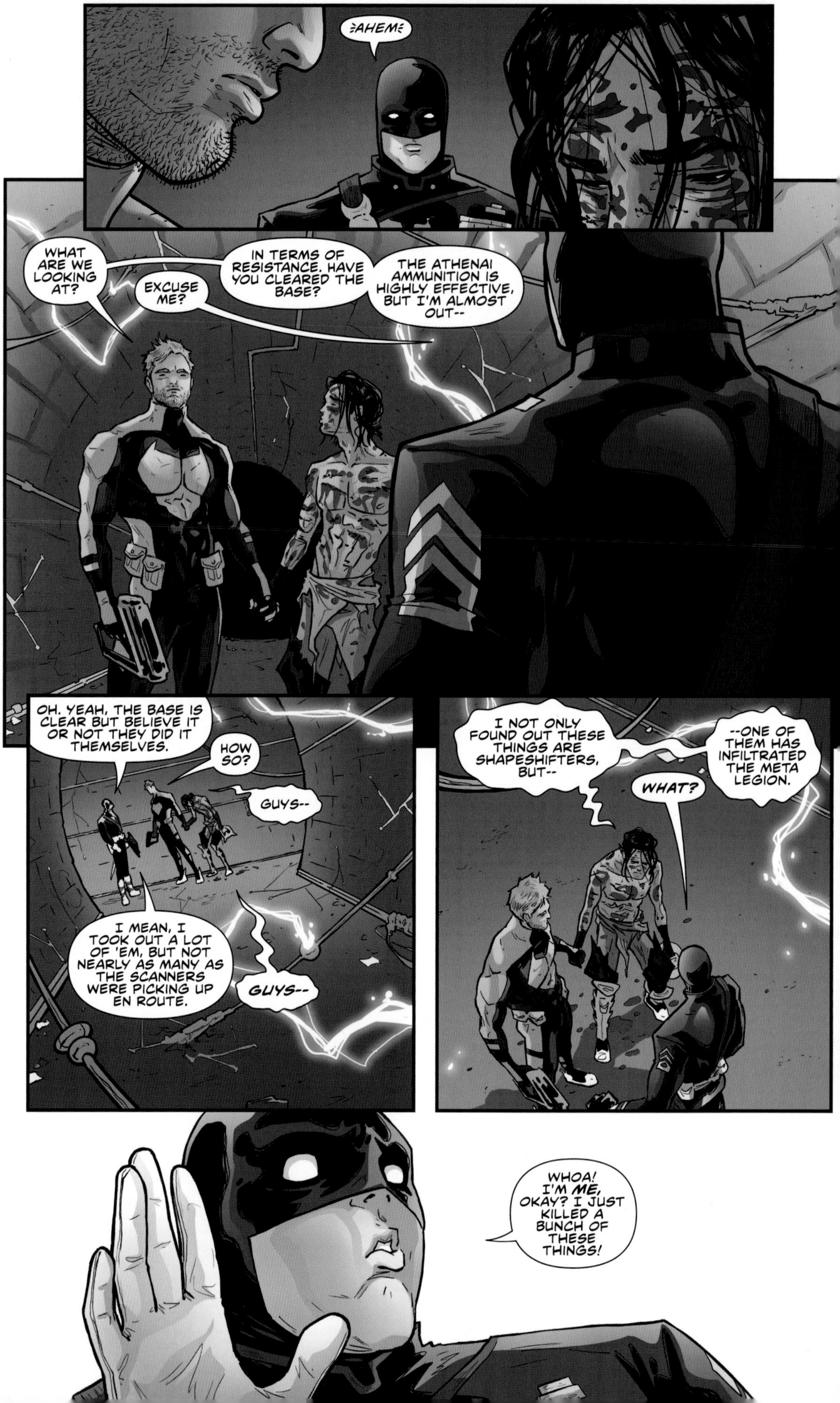
AHEM
WHAT ARE WE LOOKING AT?
EXCUSE ME?
IN TERMS OF RESISTANCE. HAVE YOU CLEARED THE BASE?
THE ATHENAI AMMUNITION IS HIGHLY EFFECTIVE, BUT I'M ALMOST OUT--
OH. YEAH, THE BASE IS CLEAR BUT BELIEVE IT OR NOT THEY DID IT THEMSELVES.
HOW SO?
GUYS--
I MEAN, I TOOK OUT A LOT OF 'EM, BUT NOT NEARLY AS MANY AS THE SCANNERS WERE PICKING UP EN ROUTE.
GUYS--
I NOT ONLY FOUND OUT THESE THINGS ARE SHAPESHIFTERS, BUT--
--ONE OF THEM HAS INFILTRATED THE META LEGION.
WHAT?
WHOA! I'M ME, OKAY? I JUST KILLED A BUNCH OF THESE THINGS!

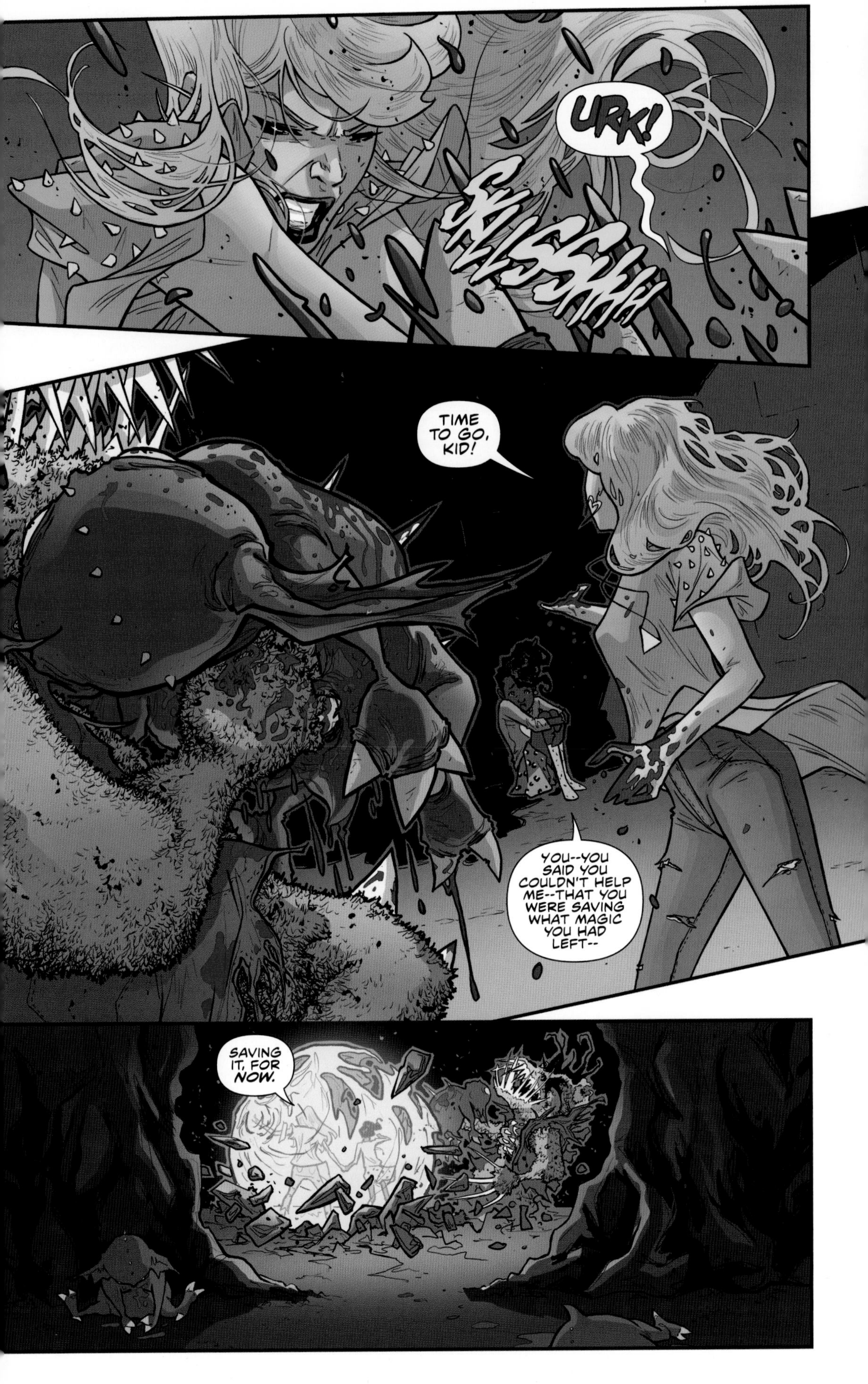
URK!
SKLISCHH!
TIME TO GO, KID!
YOU--YOU SAID YOU COULDN'T HELP ME--THAT YOU WERE SAVING WHAT MAGIC YOU HAD LEFT--
SAVING IT, FOR NOW.

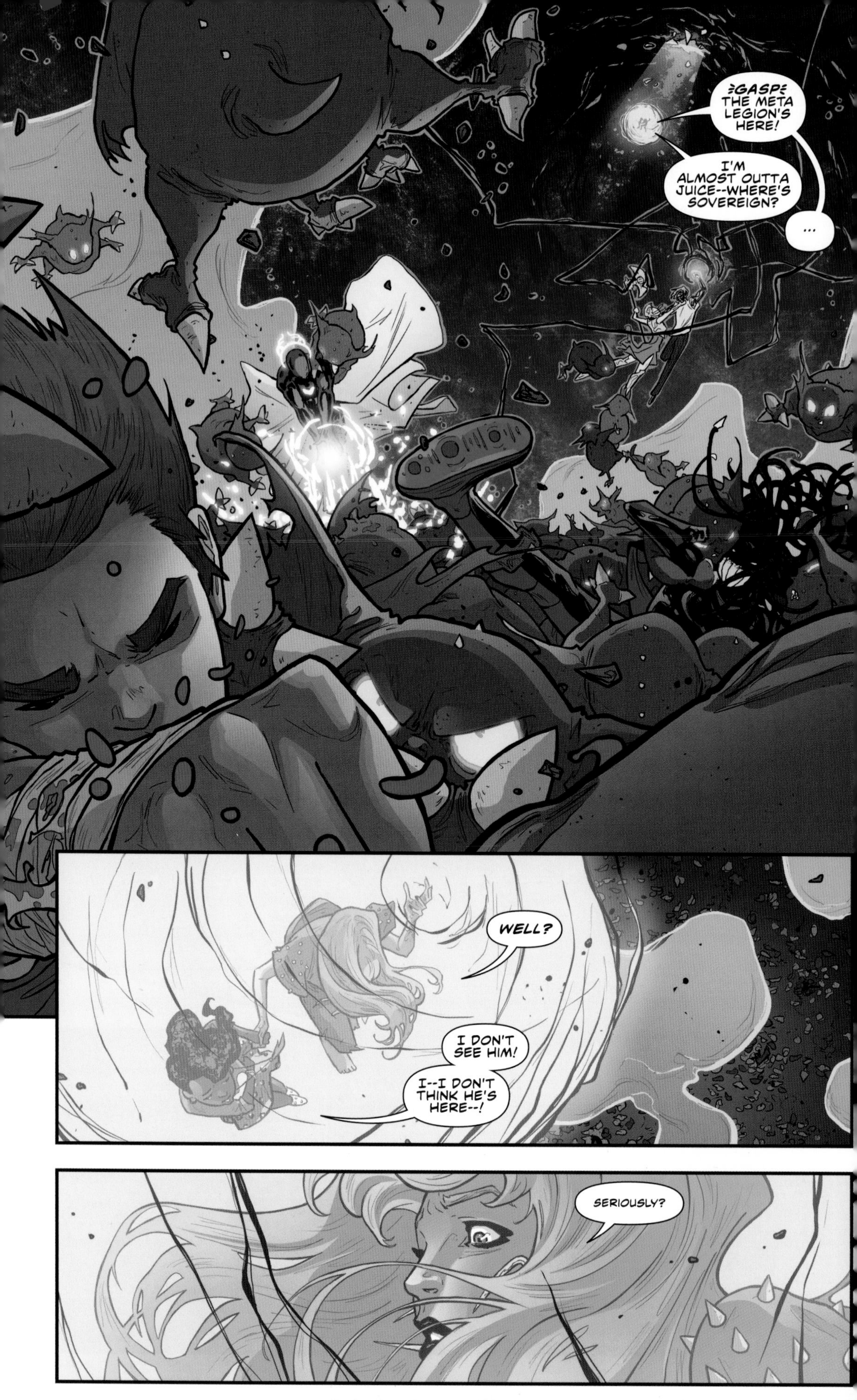

GASP THE META LEGION'S HERE!
I'M ALMOST OUTTA JUICE--WHERE'S SOVEREIGN?
...
WELL?
I DON'T SEE HIM!
I--I DON'T THINK HE'S HERE--!
SERIOUSLY?

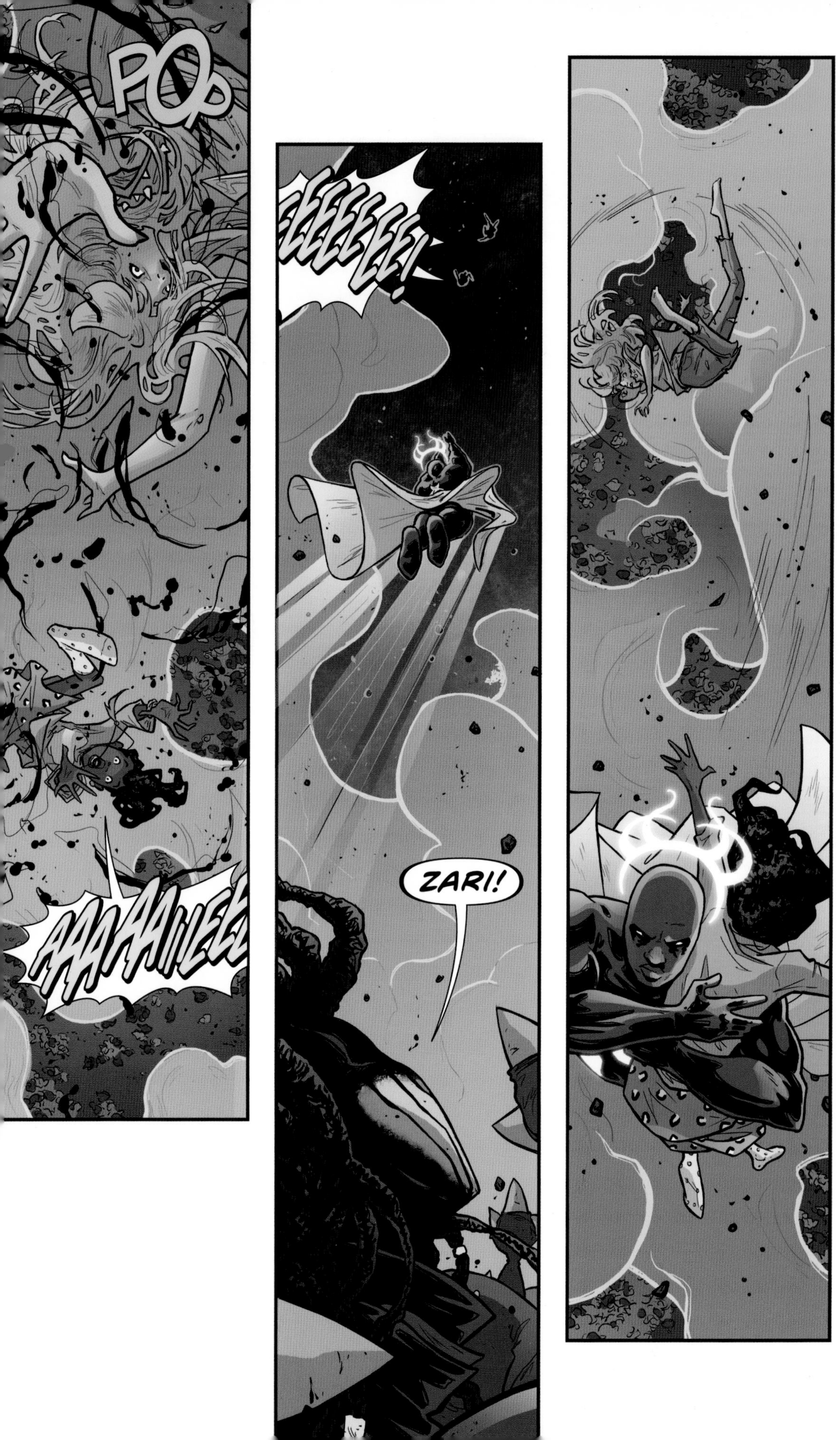
POP
AAAAAIEEE
EEEEEEEE!
ZARI!

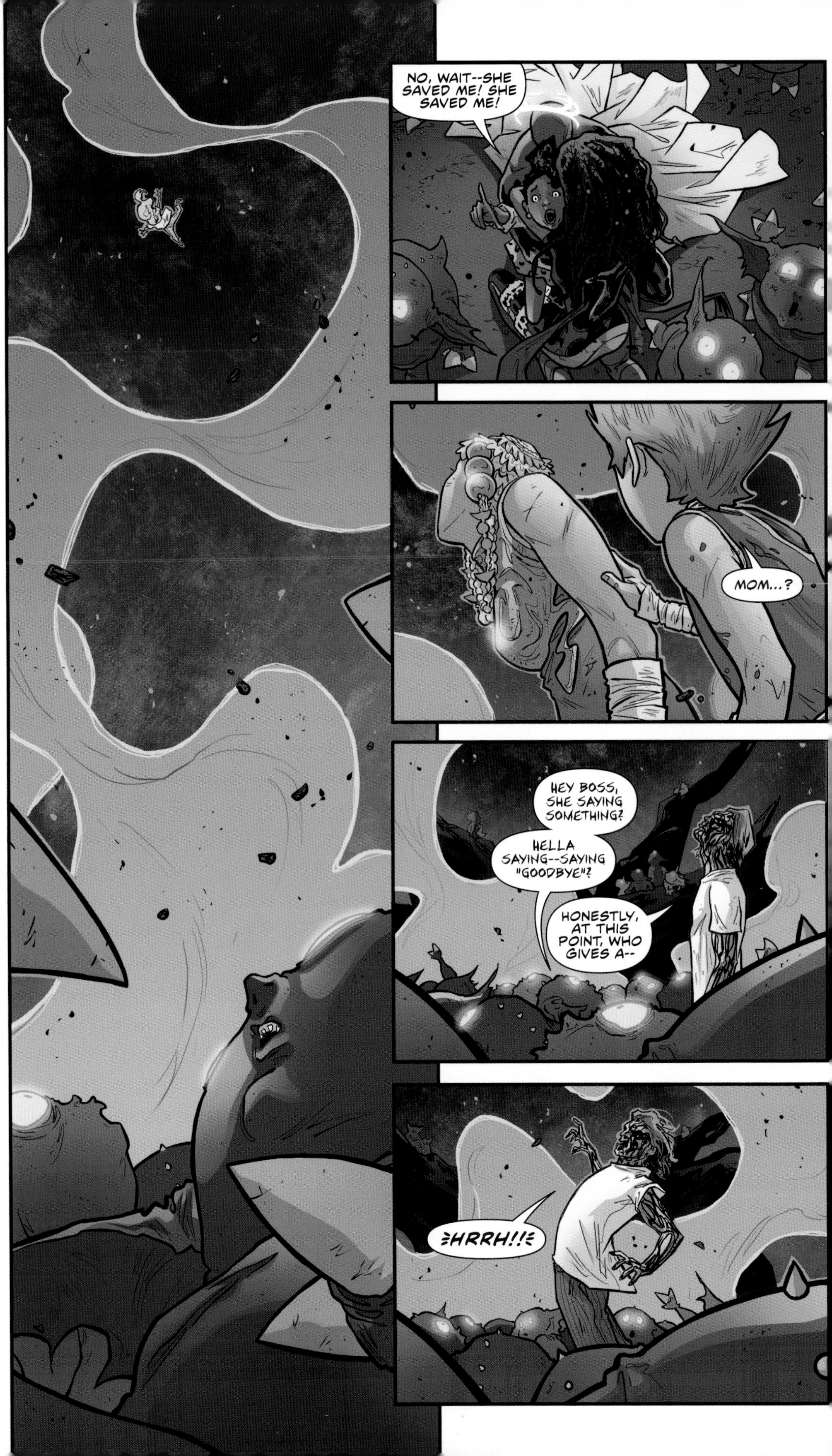
NO, WAIT--SHE SAVED ME! SHE SAVED ME!
MOM...?
HEY BOSS, SHE SAYING SOMETHING?
HELLA SAYING--SAYING "GOODBYE"?
HONESTLY, AT THIS POINT, WHO GIVES A--
HRRH!!

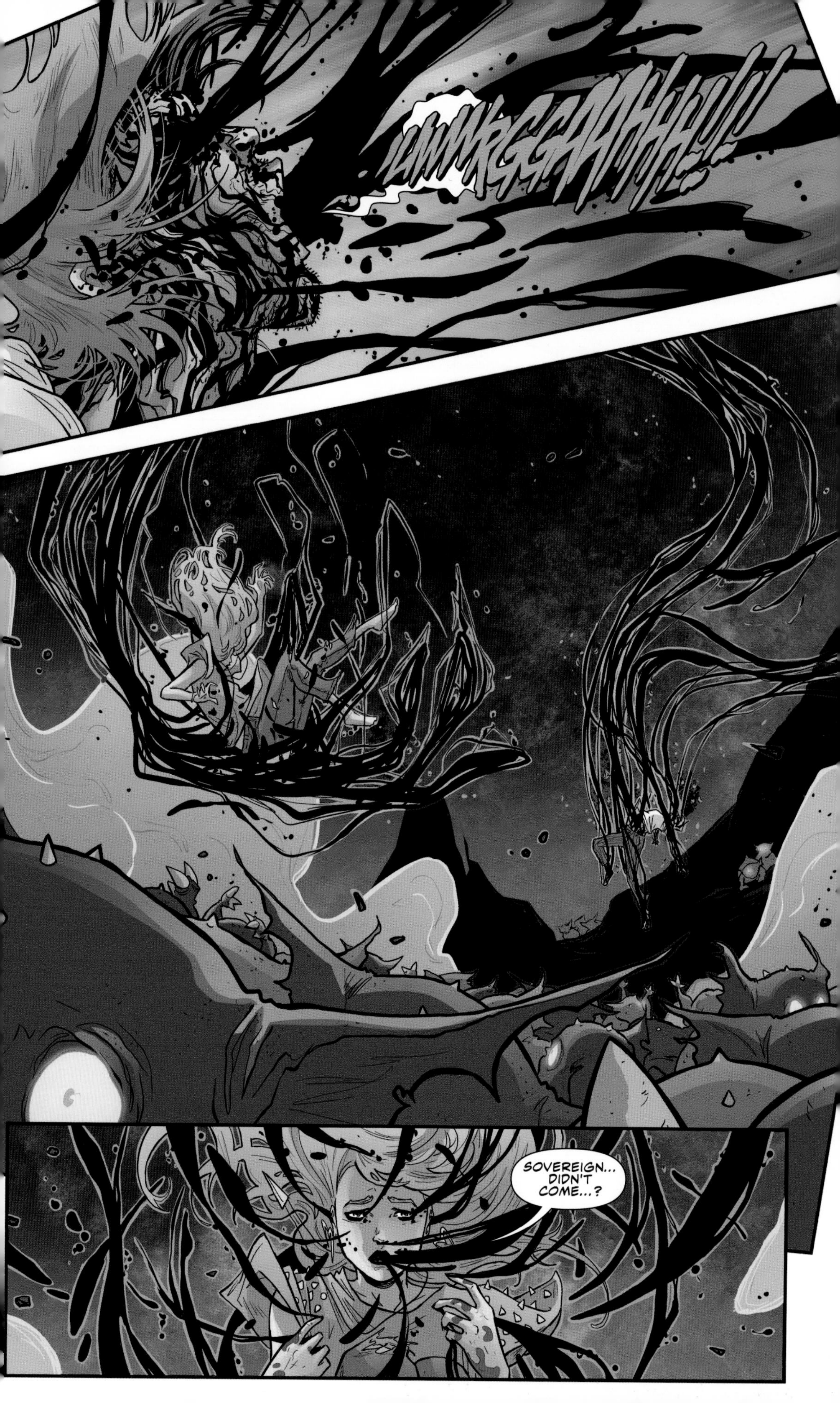
UWWRGGAAHHH!!!
SOVEREIGN... DIDN'T COME...?

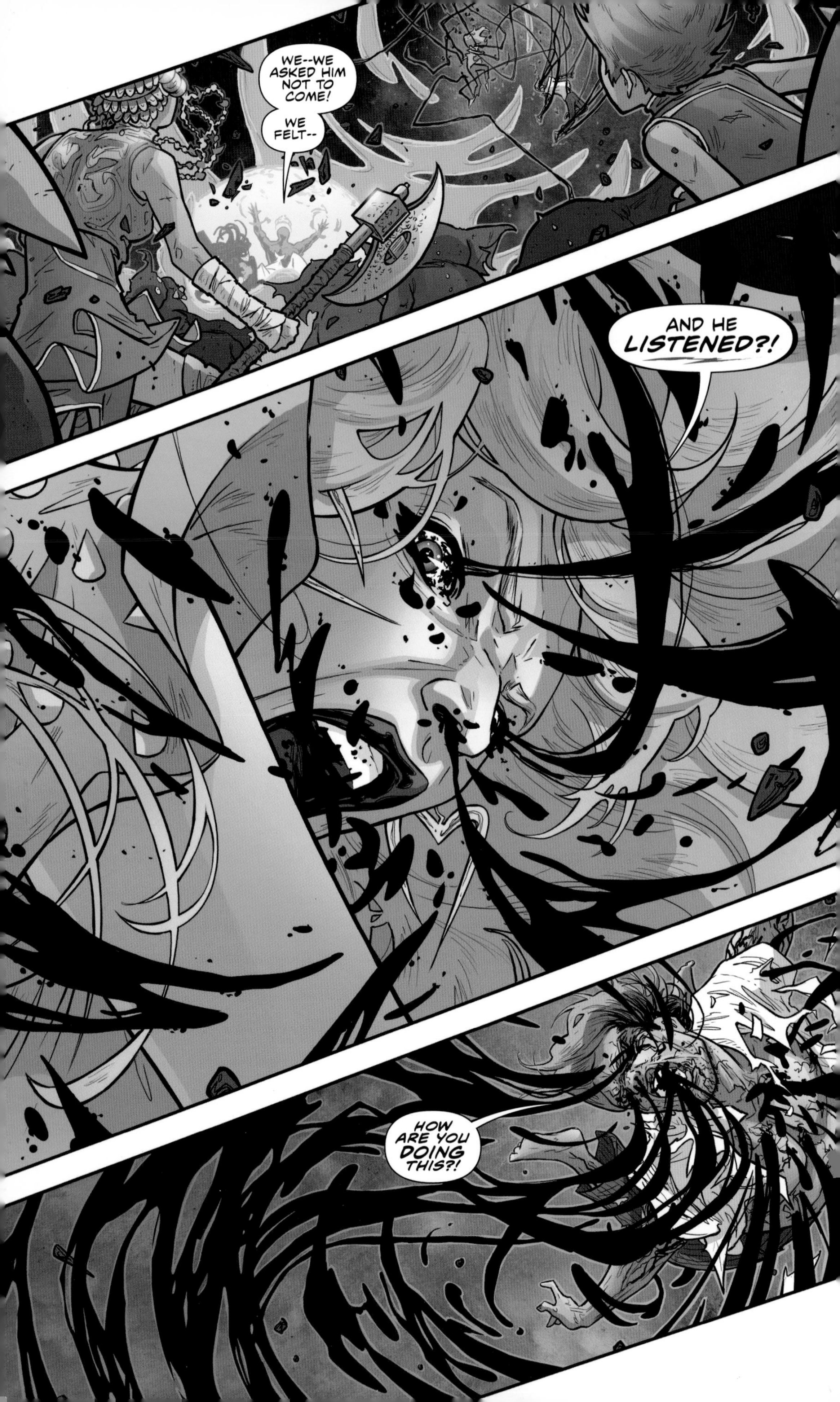
WE--WE ASKED HIM NOT TO COME!
WE FELT--
AND HE LISTENED?!
HOW ARE YOU DOING THIS?!

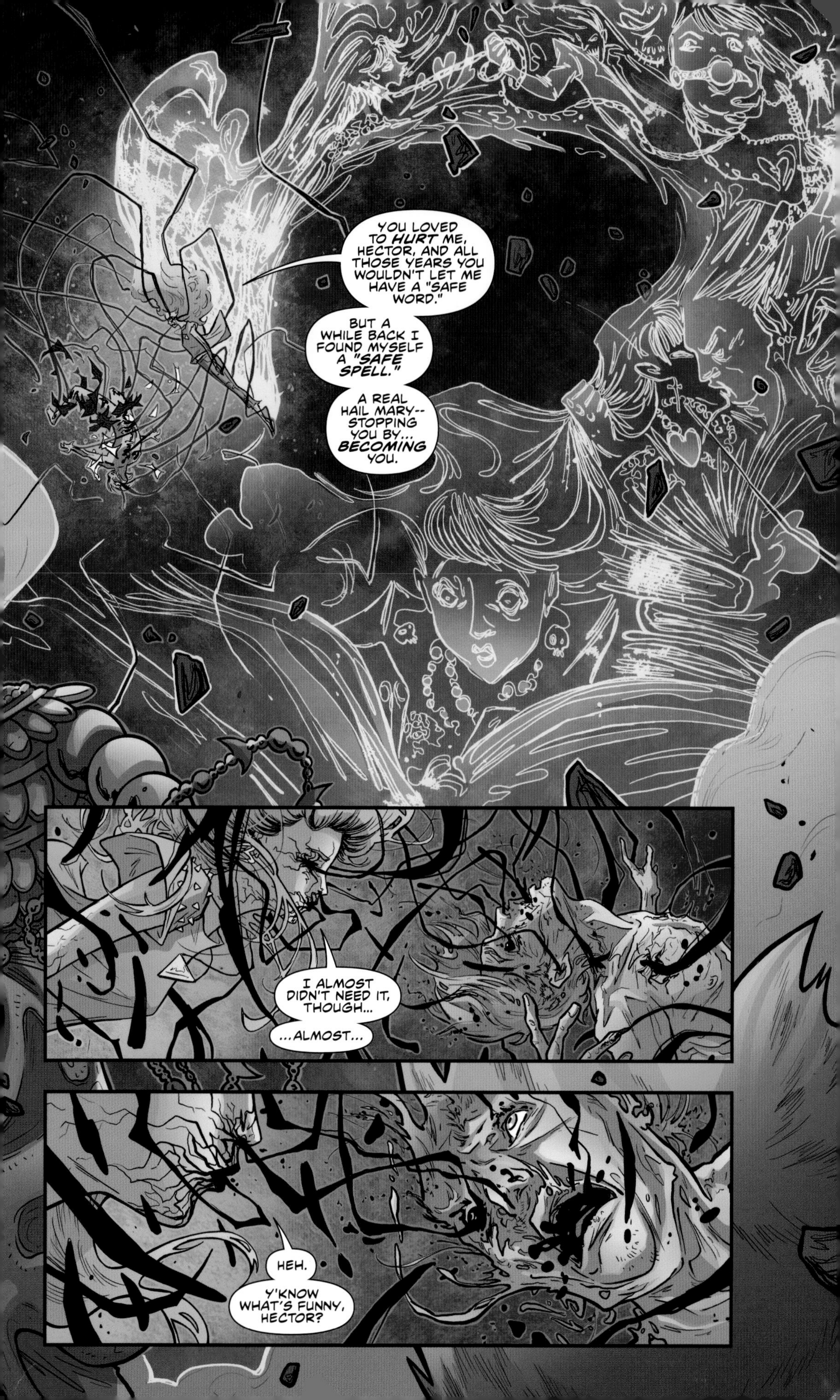
YOU LOVED TO HURT ME, HECTOR, AND ALL THOSE YEARS YOU WOULDN'T LET ME HAVE A "SAFE WORD."
BUT A WHILE BACK I FOUND MYSELF A "SAFE SPELL."
A REAL HAIL MARY-- STOPPING YOU BY... BECOMING YOU.
I ALMOST DIDN'T NEED IT, THOUGH...
...ALMOST...
HEH.
Y'KNOW WHAT'S FUNNY, HECTOR?

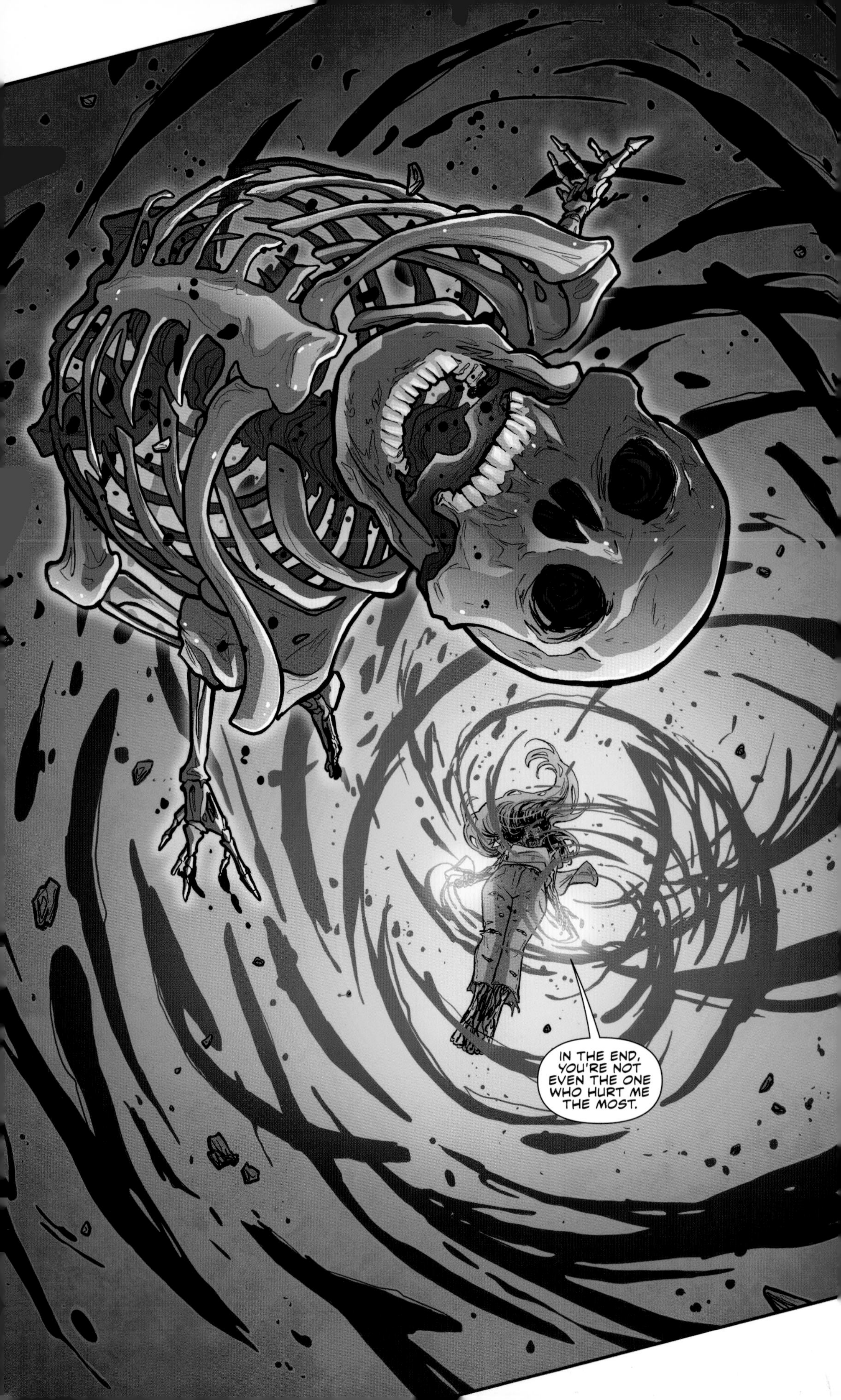
IN THE END, YOU'RE NOT EVEN THE ONE WHO HURT ME THE MOST.

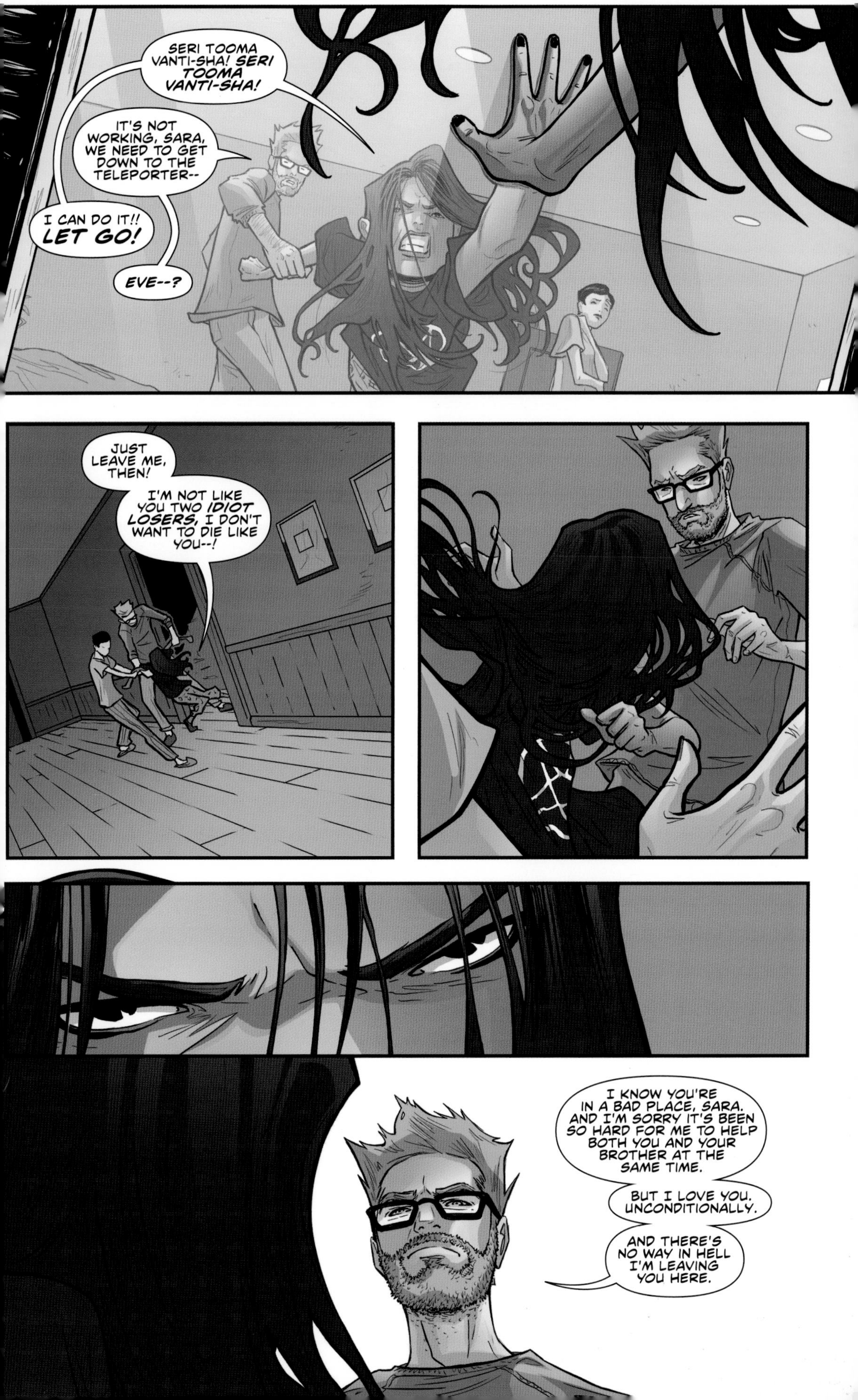

SERI TOOMA VANTI-SHA! SERI TOOMA VANTI-SHA!
IT'S NOT WORKING, SARA, WE NEED TO GET DOWN TO THE TELEPORTER--
I CAN DO IT!! LET GO!
EVE--?
JUST LEAVE ME, THEN!
I'M NOT LIKE YOU TWO IDIOT LOSERS, I DON'T WANT TO DIE LIKE YOU--!
I KNOW YOU'RE IN A BAD PLACE, SARA. AND I'M SORRY IT'S BEEN SO HARD FOR ME TO HELP BOTH YOU AND YOUR BROTHER AT THE SAME TIME.
BUT I LOVE YOU. UNCONDITIONALLY.
AND THERE'S NO WAY IN HELL I'M LEAVING YOU HERE.

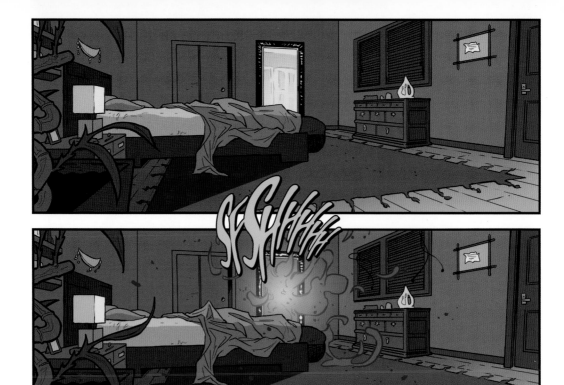

SFSHHHHH

SARA! ARE YOU OKAY?!

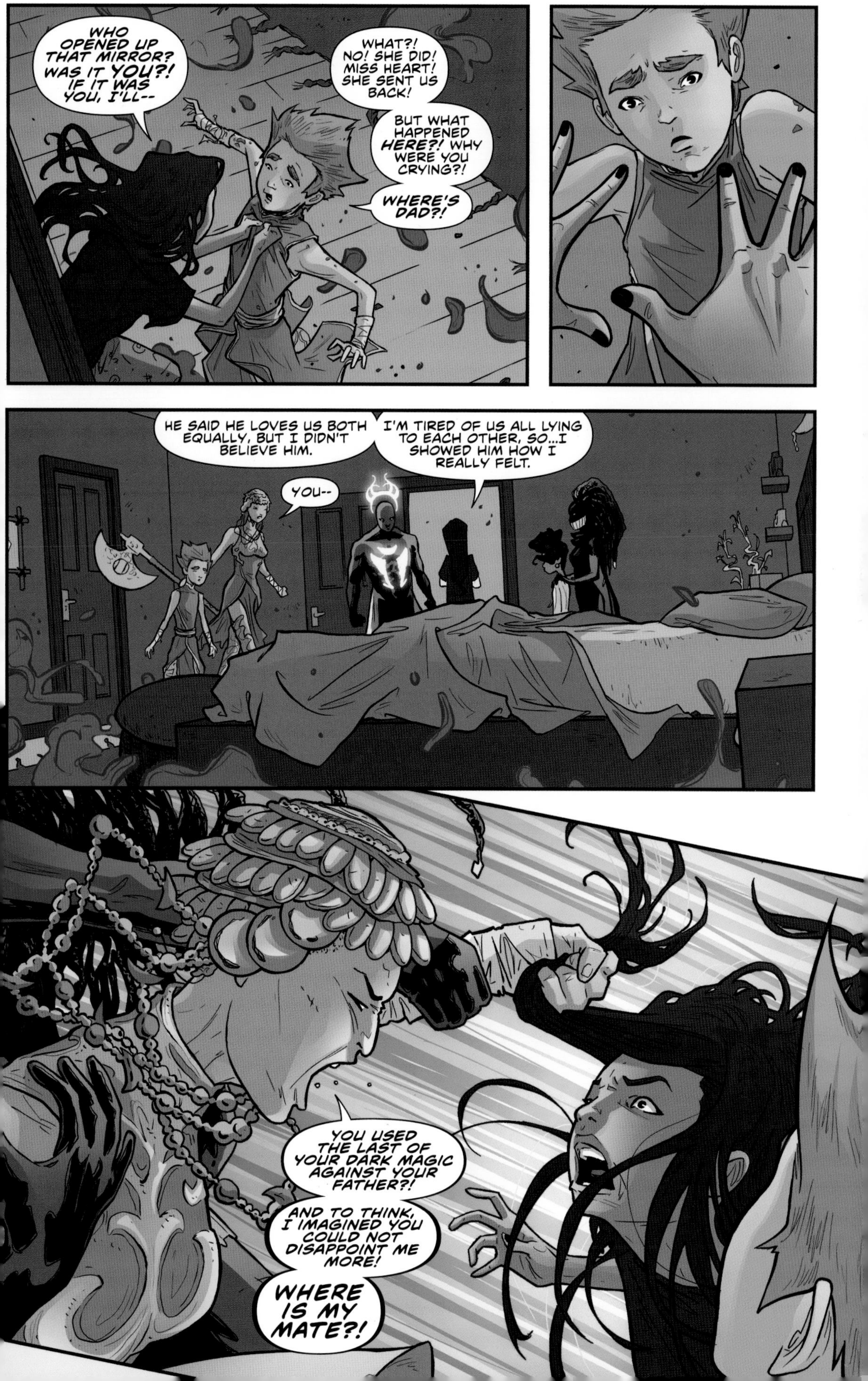
WHO OPENED UP THAT MIRROR? WAS IT YOU?! IF IT WAS YOU, I'LL--
WHAT?! NO! SHE DID! MISS HEART! SHE SENT US BACK!
BUT WHAT HAPPENED HERE?! WHY WERE YOU CRYING?!
WHERE'S DAD?!
HE SAID HE LOVES US BOTH EQUALLY, BUT I DIDN'T BELIEVE HIM.
I'M TIRED OF US ALL LYING TO EACH OTHER, SO...I SHOWED HIM HOW I REALLY FELT.
YOU--
YOU USED THE LAST OF YOUR DARK MAGIC AGAINST YOUR FATHER?!
AND TO THINK, I IMAGINED YOU COULD NOT DISAPPOINT ME MORE!
WHERE IS MY MATE?!

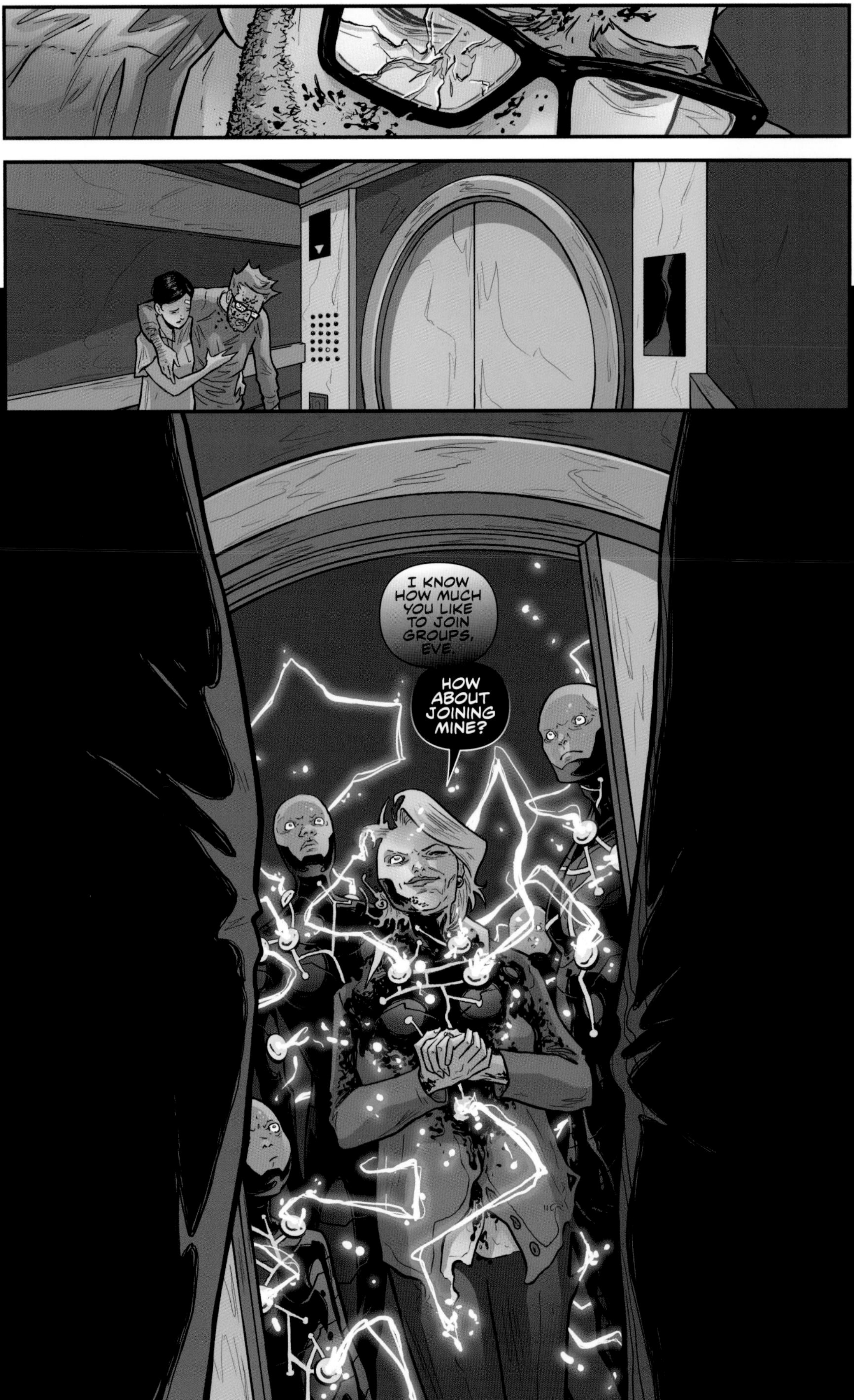
I KNOW HOW MUCH YOU LIKE TO JOIN GROUPS, EVE.
HOW ABOUT JOINING MINE?

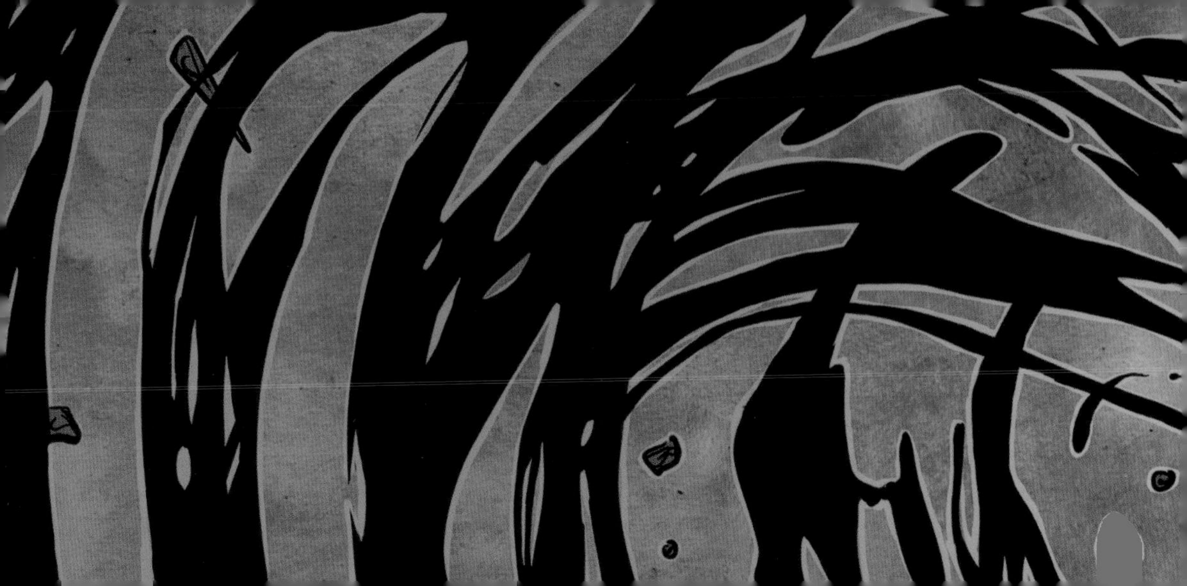

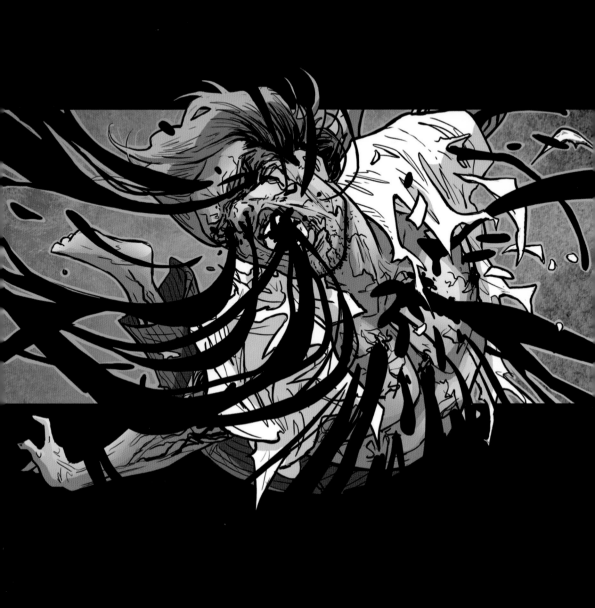

Chapter 12

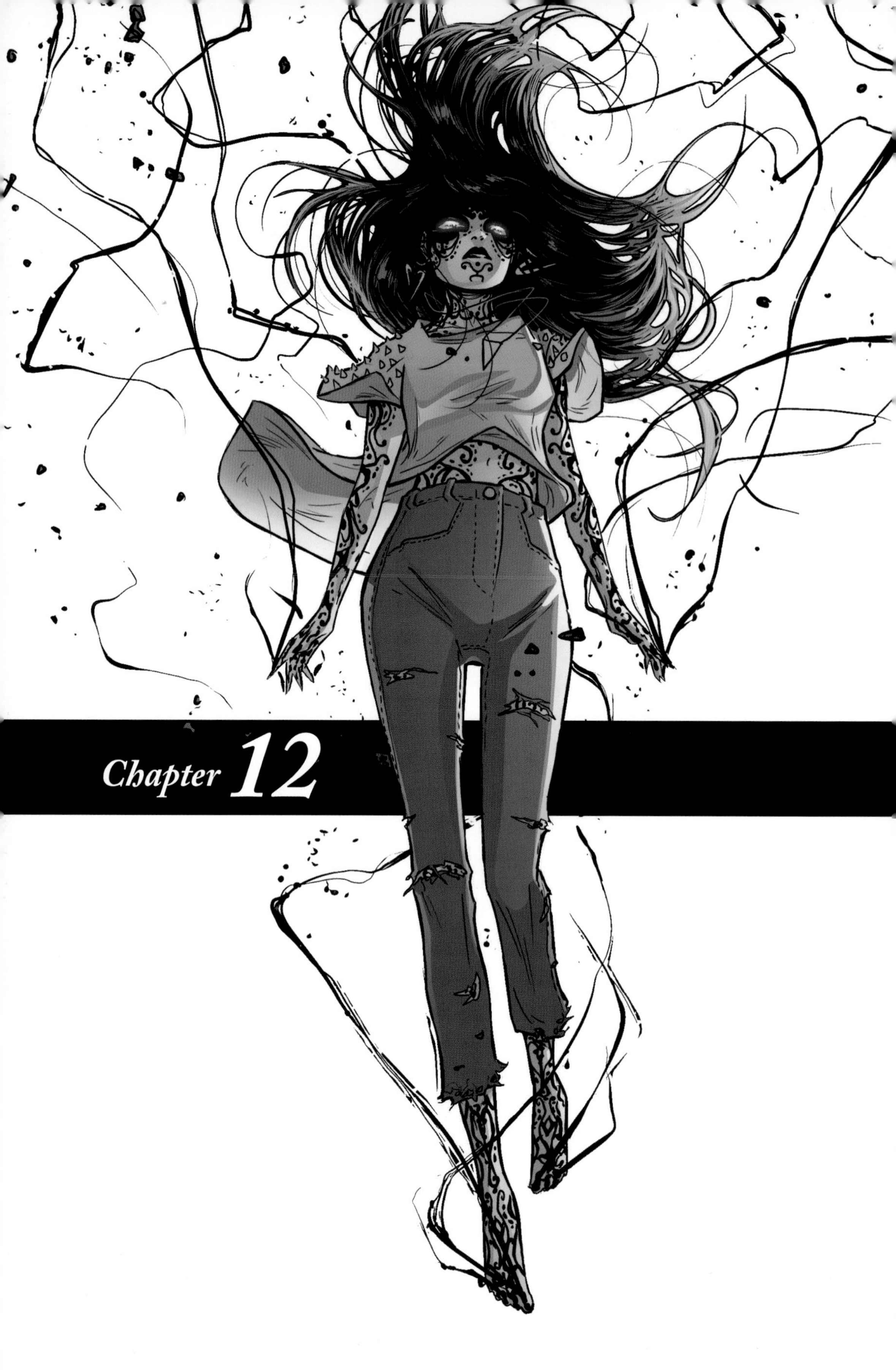

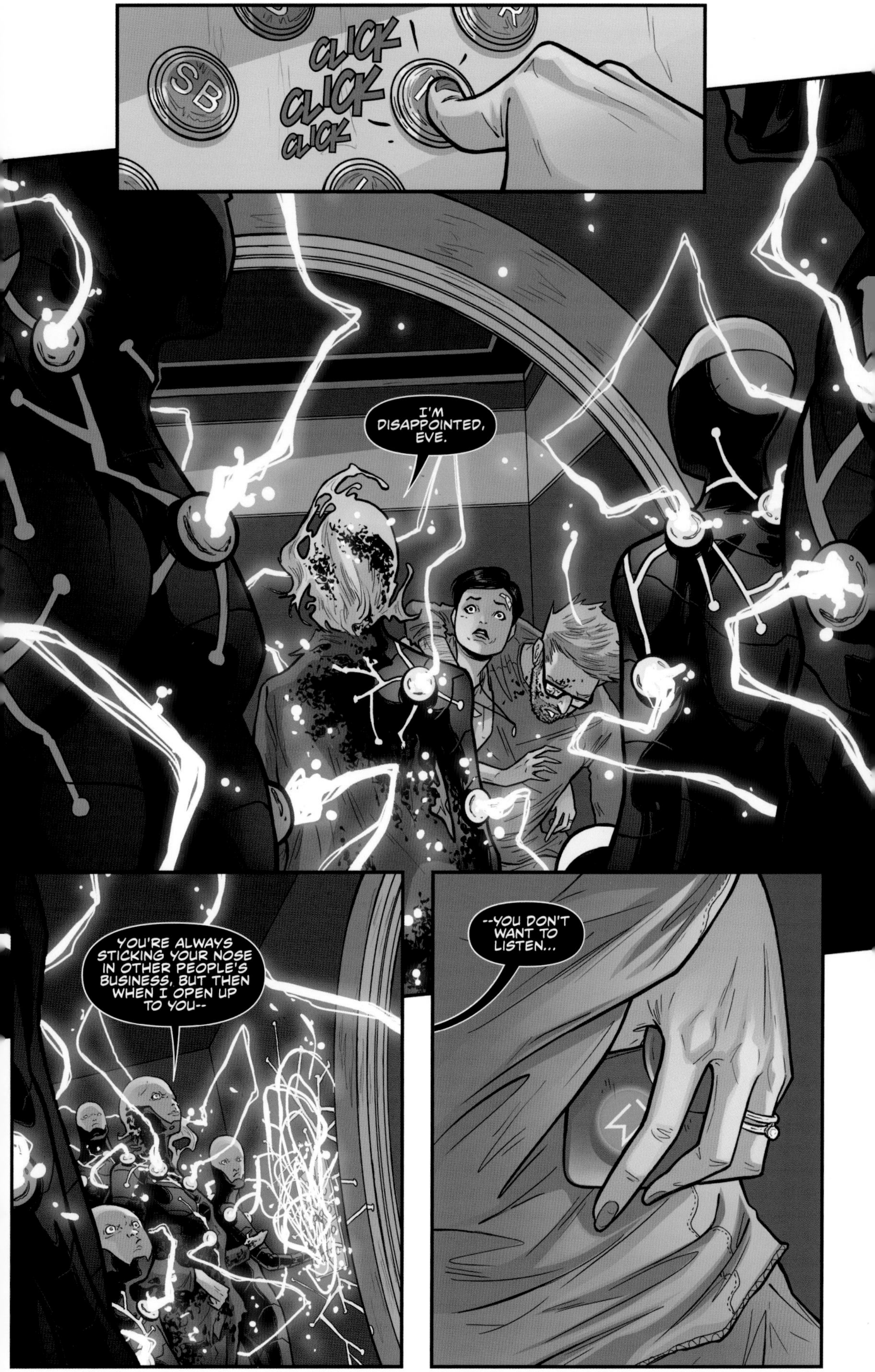
CLICK
CLICK
CLICK
I'M DISAPPOINTED, EVE.
YOU'RE ALWAYS STICKING YOUR NOSE IN OTHER PEOPLE'S BUSINESS, BUT THEN WHEN I OPEN UP TO YOU--
--YOU DON'T WANT TO LISTEN...

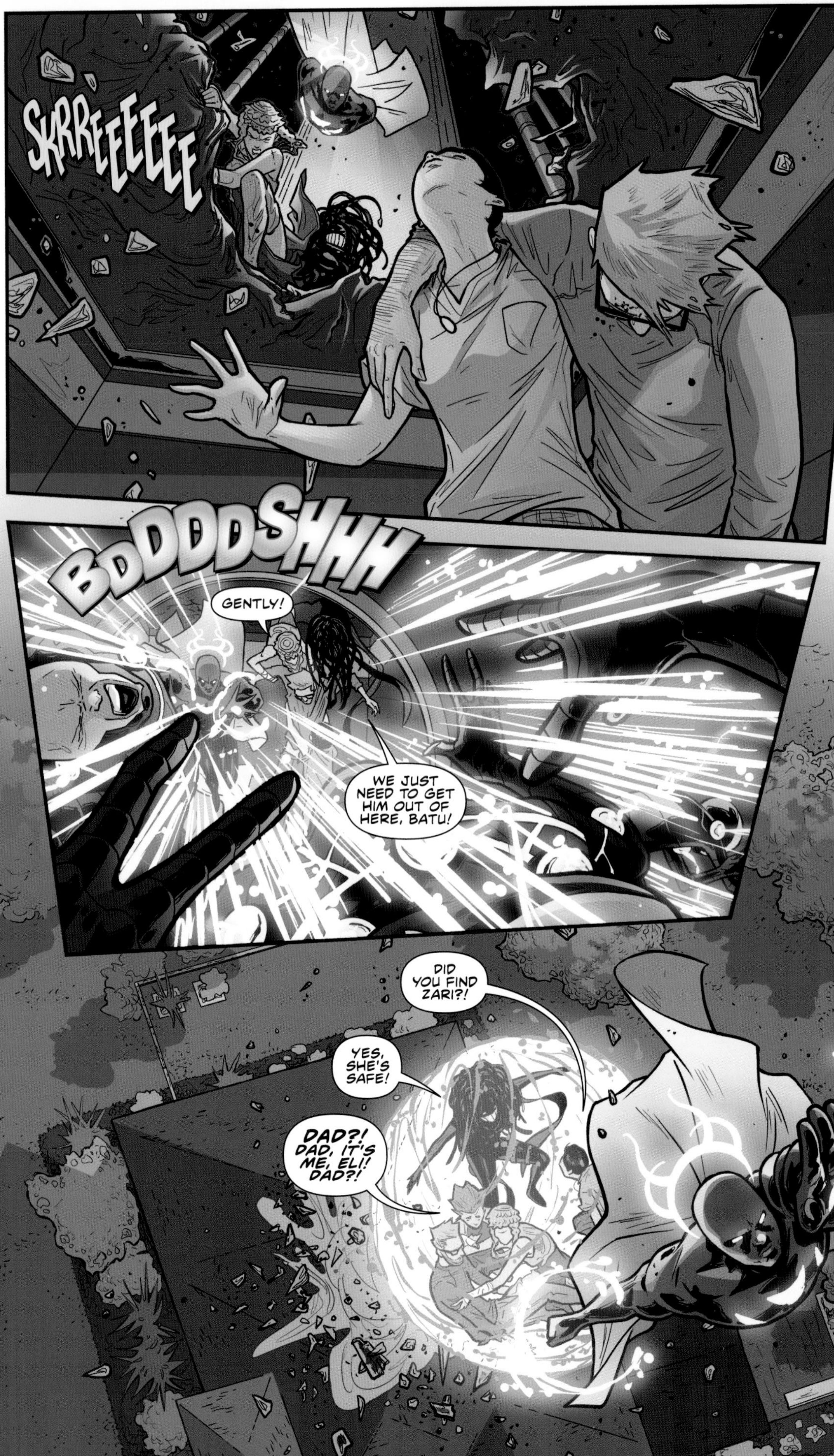

SKRREEEEEEE
BDDDDSHHH
GENTLY!
WE JUST NEED TO GET HIM OUT OF HERE, BATU!
DID YOU FIND ZARI?!
YES, SHE'S SAFE!
DAD?! DAD, IT'S ME, ELI! DAD?!

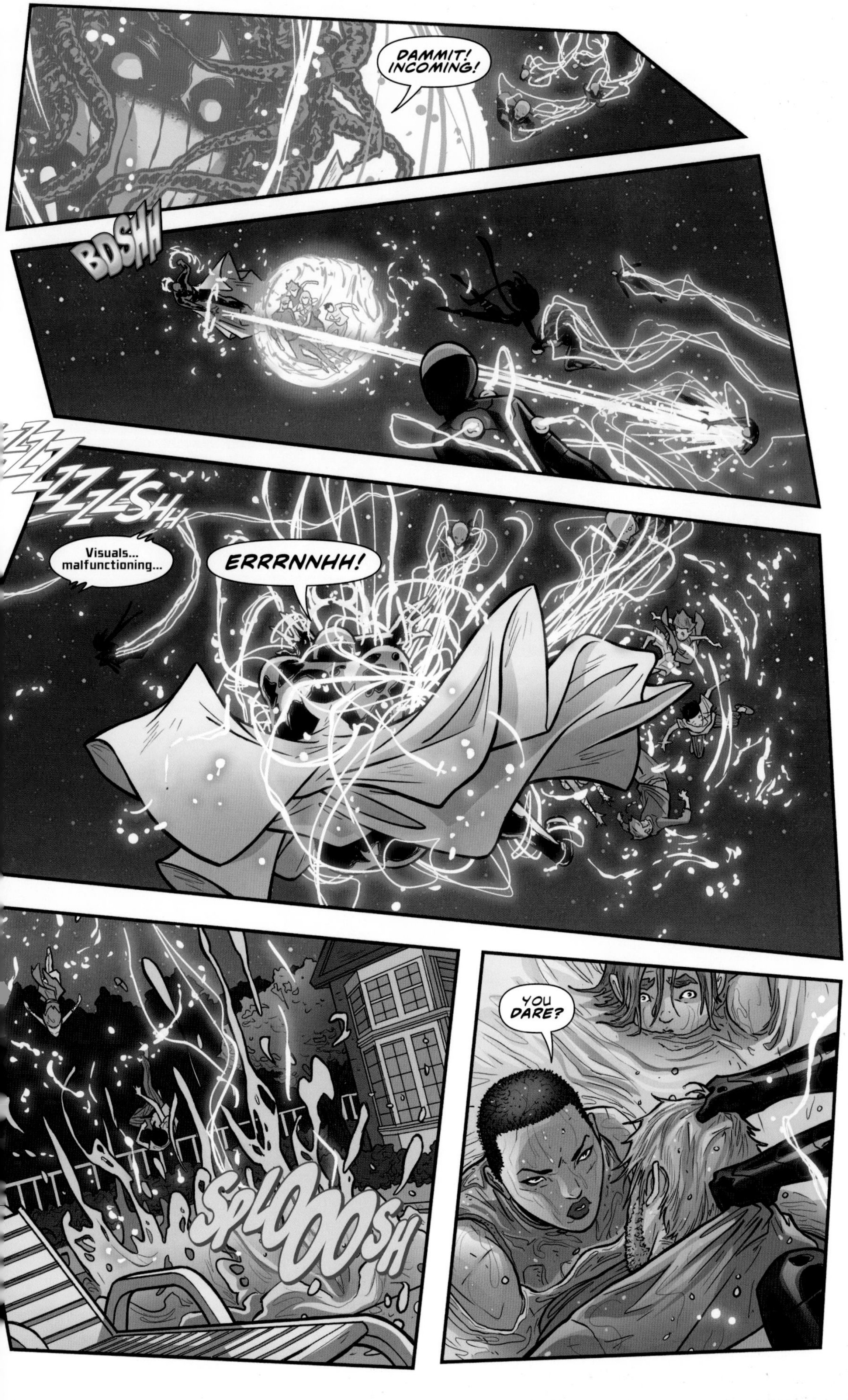
DAMMIT! INCOMING!
BDSHH
ZZZZZZZSHH
Visuals... malfunctioning...
ERRRNNHH!
SPLOOOSH
YOU DARE?

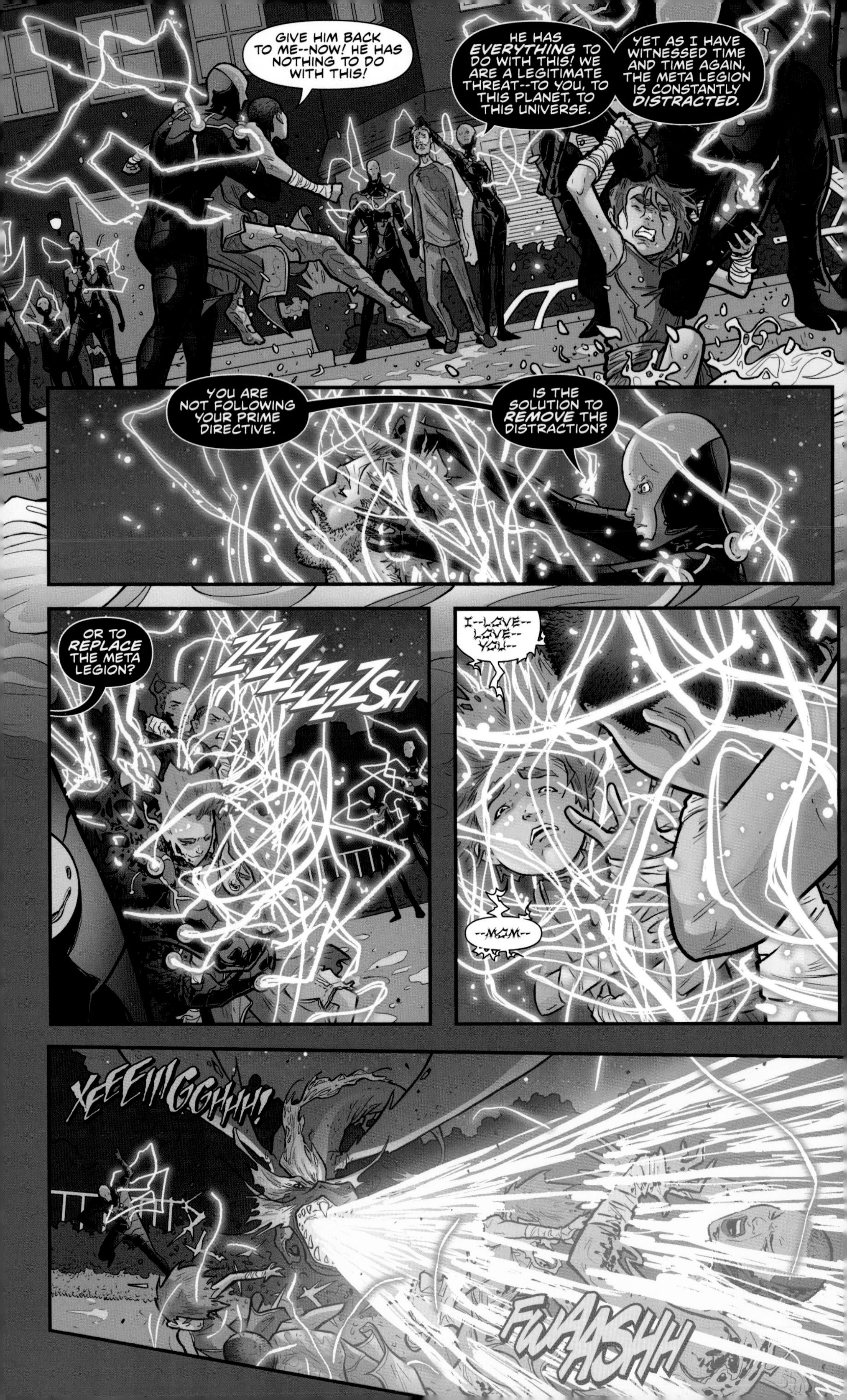
GIVE HIM BACK TO ME--NOW! HE HAS NOTHING TO DO WITH THIS!
HE HAS EVERYTHING TO DO WITH THIS! WE ARE A LEGITIMATE THREAT--TO YOU, TO THIS PLANET, TO THIS UNIVERSE.
YET AS I HAVE WITNESSED TIME AND TIME AGAIN, THE META LEGION IS CONSTANTLY DISTRACTED.
YOU ARE NOT FOLLOWING YOUR PRIME DIRECTIVE.
IS THE SOLUTION TO REMOVE THE DISTRACTION?
OR TO REPLACE THE META LEGION?
ZZZZZZZZSH
I--LOVE--LOVE--YOU--
--MOM--
XEEEIIIGGHHH!
FWAASHH

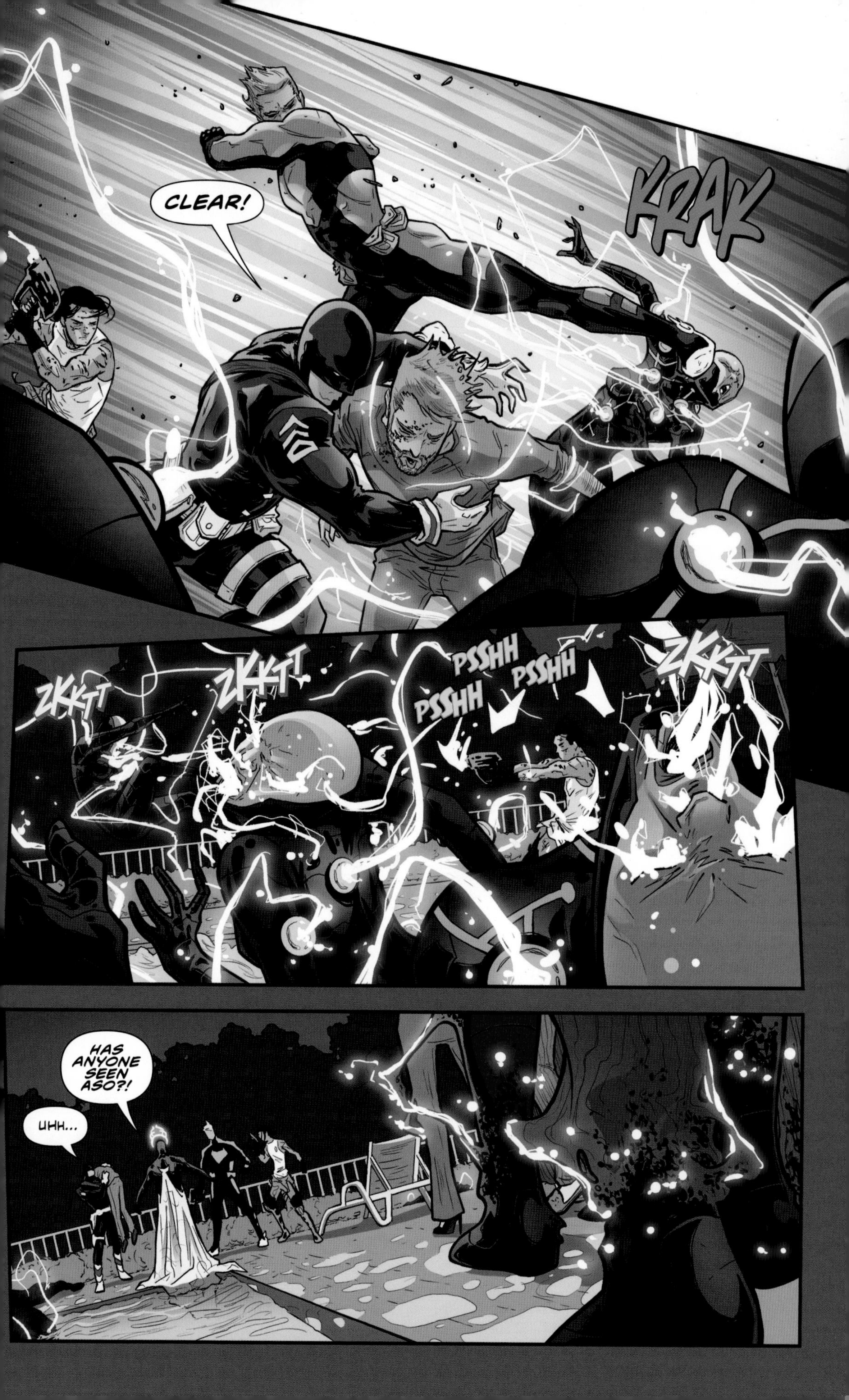
CLEAR!
KRAK
ZKKTT
ZKKTT
PSSHH
PSSHH
PSSHH
ZKKTT
HAS ANYONE SEEN ASO?!
UHH...

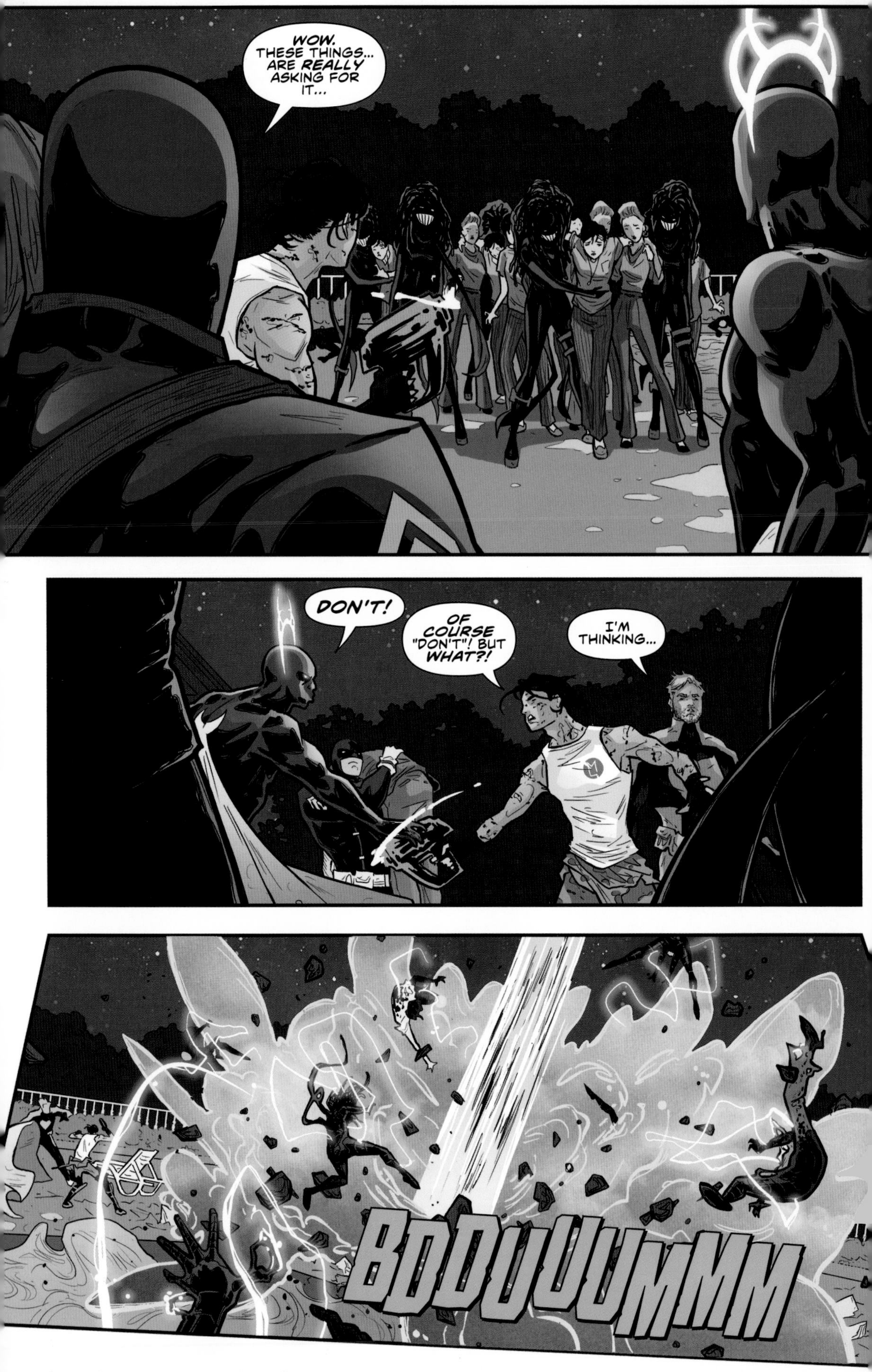
WOW. THESE THINGS... ARE REALLY ASKING FOR IT...
DON'T!
OF COURSE "DON'T"! BUT WHAT?!
I'M THINKING...
BDDUUUMMMM

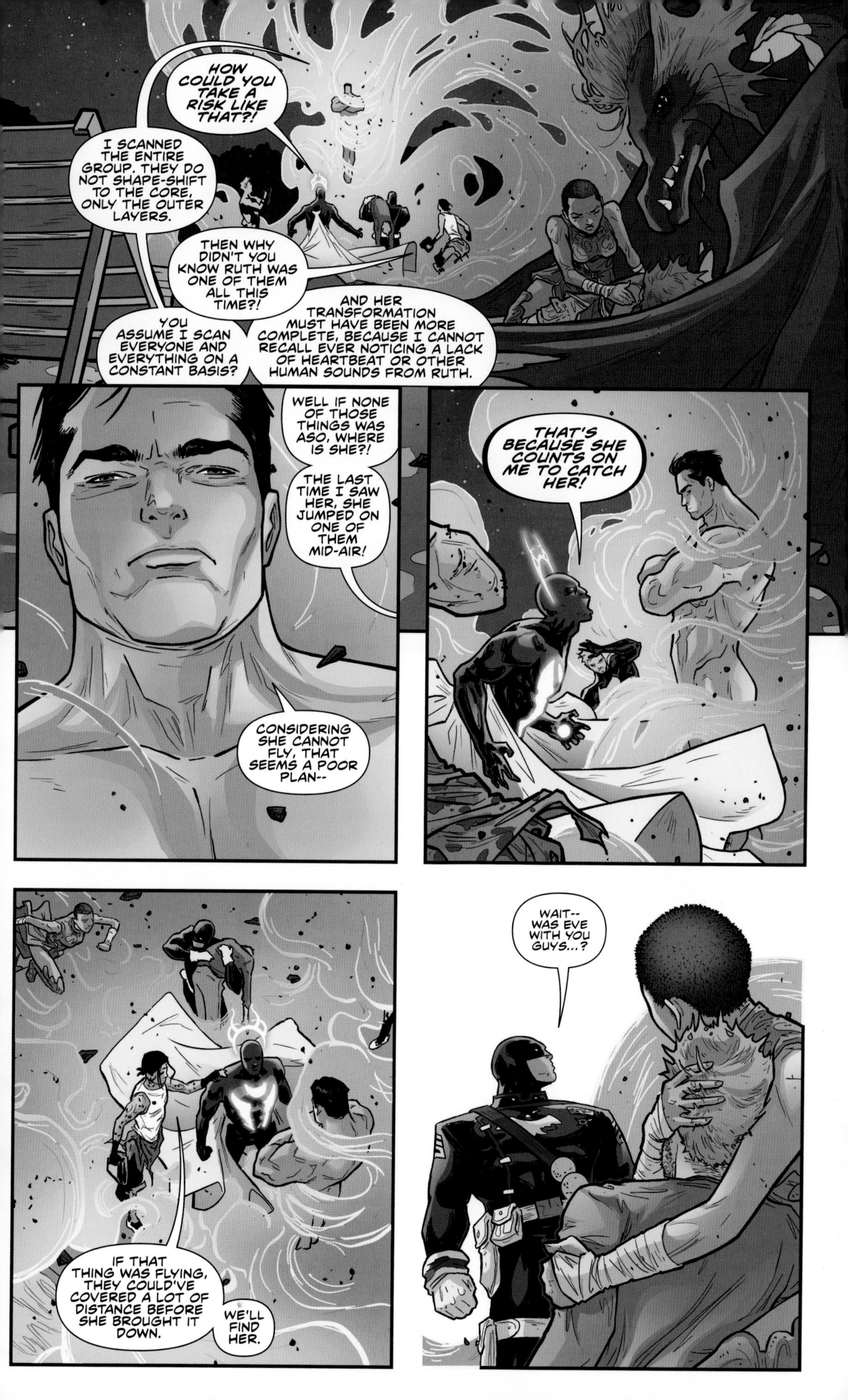
HOW COULD YOU TAKE A RISK LIKE THAT?!
I SCANNED THE ENTIRE GROUP. THEY DO NOT SHAPE-SHIFT TO THE CORE, ONLY THE OUTER LAYERS.
THEN WHY DIDN'T YOU KNOW RUTH WAS ONE OF THEM ALL THIS TIME?!
YOU ASSUME I SCAN EVERYONE AND EVERYTHING ON A CONSTANT BASIS?
AND HER TRANSFORMATION MUST HAVE BEEN MORE COMPLETE, BECAUSE I CANNOT RECALL EVER NOTICING A LACK OF HEARTBEAT OR OTHER HUMAN SOUNDS FROM RUTH.
WELL IF NONE OF THOSE THINGS WAS ASO, WHERE IS SHE?!
THE LAST TIME I SAW HER, SHE JUMPED ON ONE OF THEM MID-AIR!
CONSIDERING SHE CANNOT FLY, THAT SEEMS A POOR PLAN--
THAT'S BECAUSE SHE COUNTS ON ME TO CATCH HER!
IF THAT THING WAS FLYING, THEY COULD'VE COVERED A LOT OF DISTANCE BEFORE SHE BROUGHT IT DOWN.
WE'LL FIND HER.
WAIT-- WAS EVE WITH YOU GUYS...?

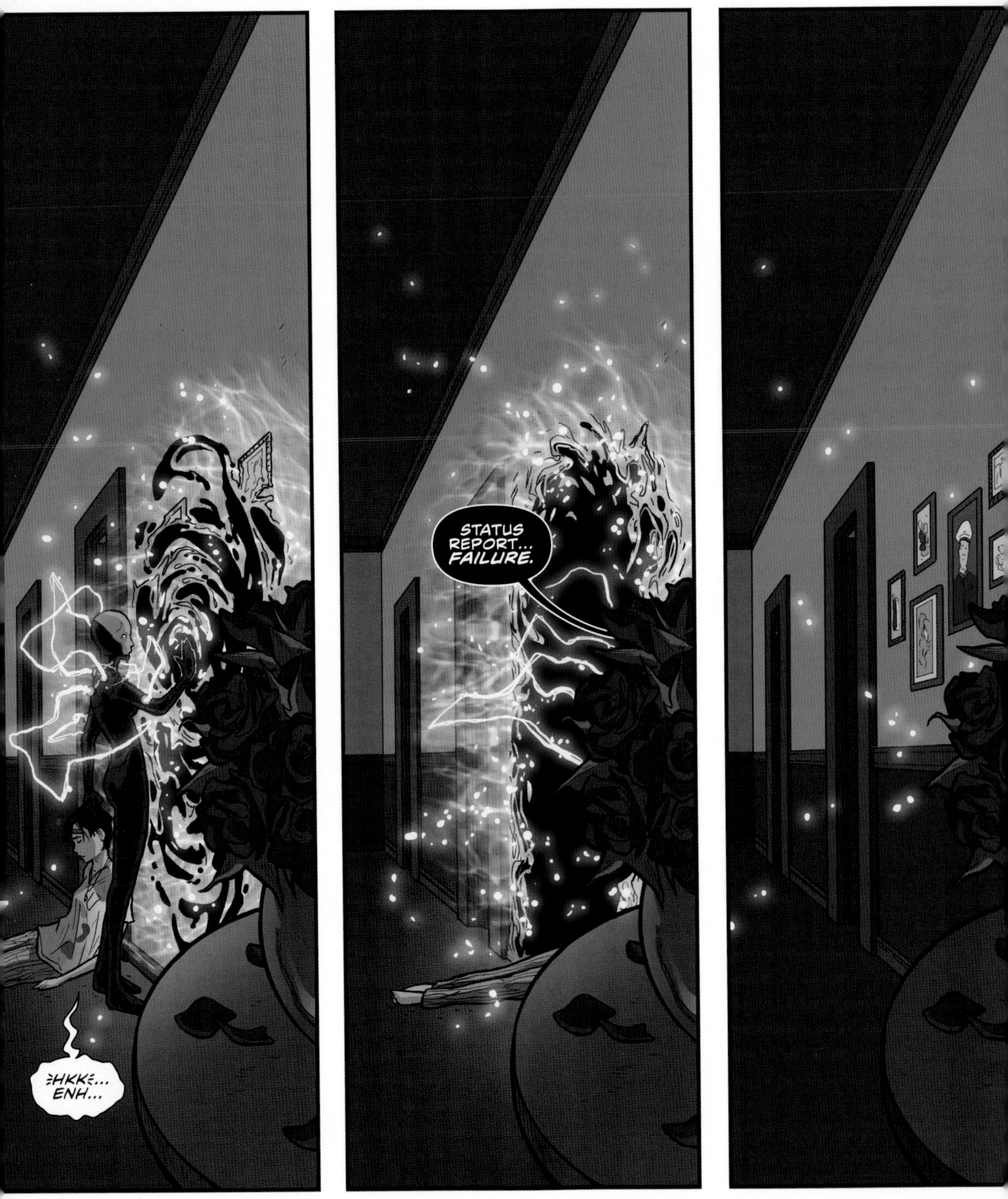
ƎHKKƐ... ENH...
STATUS REPORT... FAILURE.

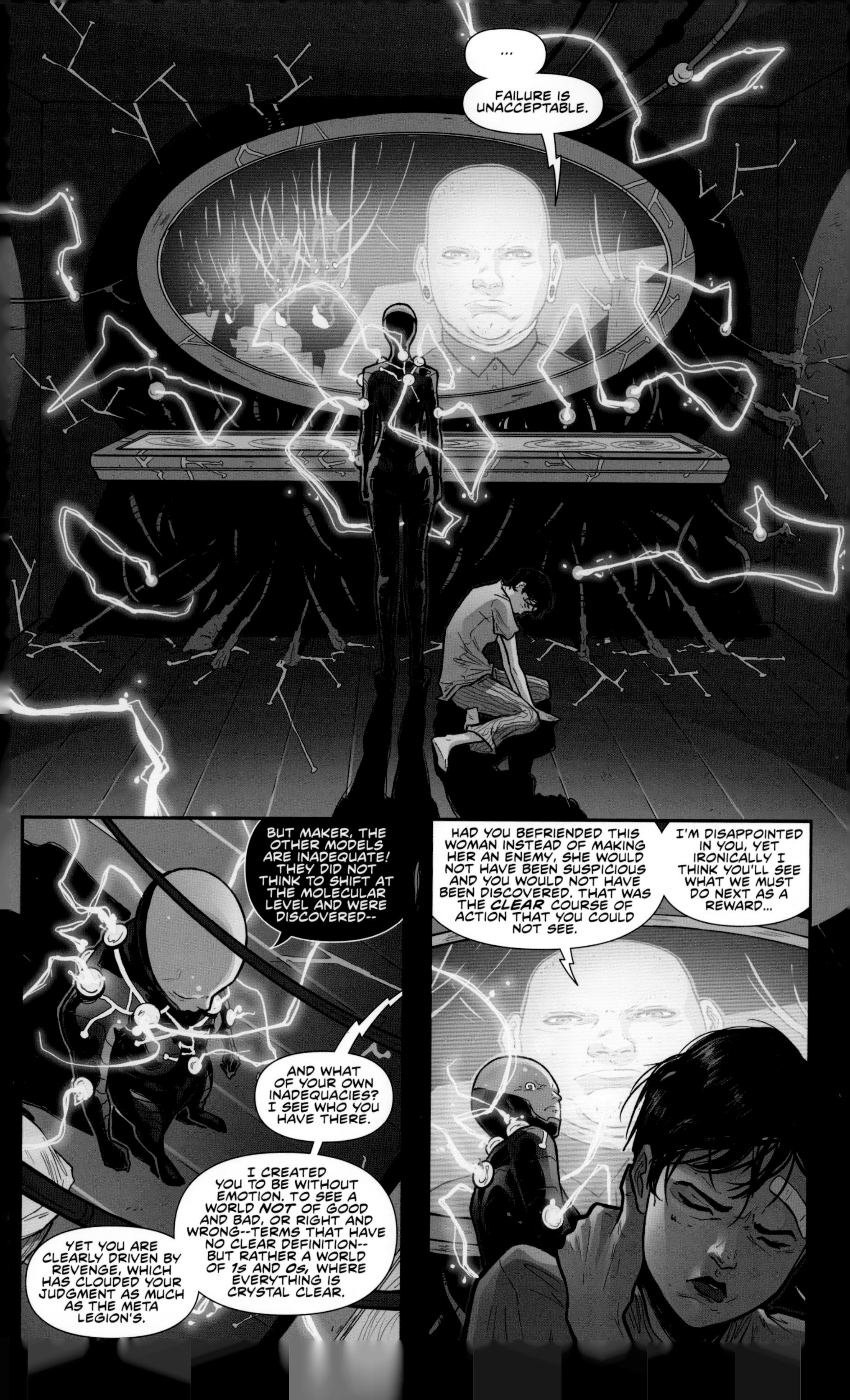
...
FAILURE IS UNACCEPTABLE.
BUT MAKER, THE OTHER MODELS ARE INADEQUATE! THEY DID NOT THINK TO SHIFT AT THE MOLECULAR LEVEL AND WERE DISCOVERED--
AND WHAT OF YOUR OWN INADEQUACIES? I SEE WHO YOU HAVE THERE.
I CREATED YOU TO BE WITHOUT EMOTION. TO SEE A WORLD NOT OF GOOD AND BAD, OR RIGHT AND WRONG--TERMS THAT HAVE NO CLEAR DEFINITION--BUT RATHER A WORLD OF 1s AND 0s, WHERE EVERYTHING IS CRYSTAL CLEAR.
YET YOU ARE CLEARLY DRIVEN BY REVENGE, WHICH HAS CLOUDED YOUR JUDGMENT AS MUCH AS THE META LEGION'S.
HAD YOU BEFRIENDED THIS WOMAN INSTEAD OF MAKING HER AN ENEMY, SHE WOULD NOT HAVE BEEN SUSPICIOUS AND YOU WOULD NOT HAVE BEEN DISCOVERED. THAT WAS THE CLEAR COURSE OF ACTION THAT YOU COULD NOT SEE.
I'M DISAPPOINTED IN YOU, YET IRONICALLY I THINK YOU'LL SEE WHAT WE MUST DO NEXT AS A REWARD...

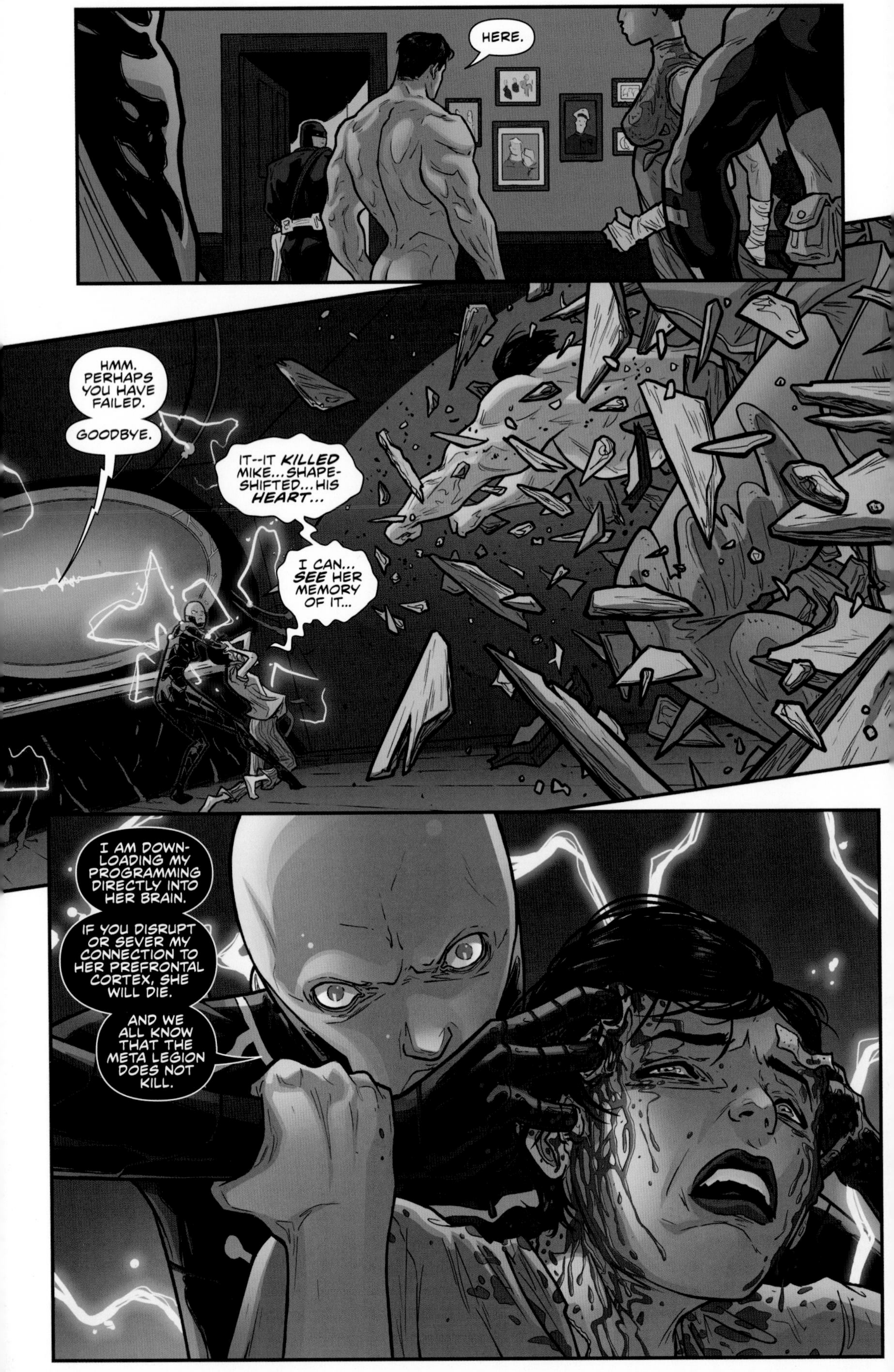
HERE.
HMM. PERHAPS YOU HAVE FAILED.
GOODBYE.
IT--IT KILLED MIKE... SHAPE-SHIFTED... HIS HEART...
I CAN... SEE HER MEMORY OF IT...
I AM DOWN-LOADING MY PROGRAMMING DIRECTLY INTO HER BRAIN.
IF YOU DISRUPT OR SEVER MY CONNECTION TO HER PREFRONTAL CORTEX, SHE WILL DIE.
AND WE ALL KNOW THAT THE META LEGION DOES NOT KILL.

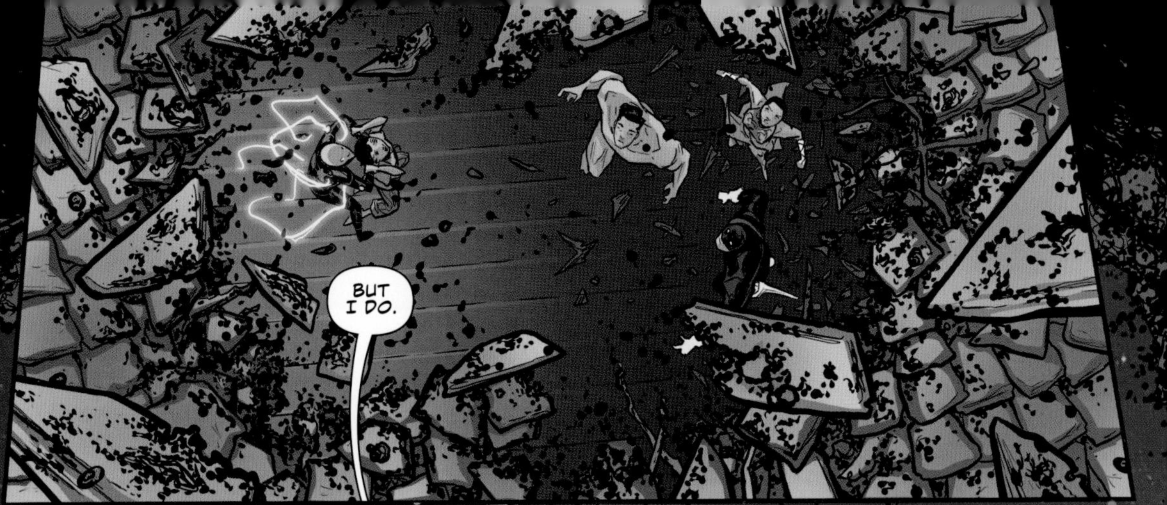
BUT I DO.

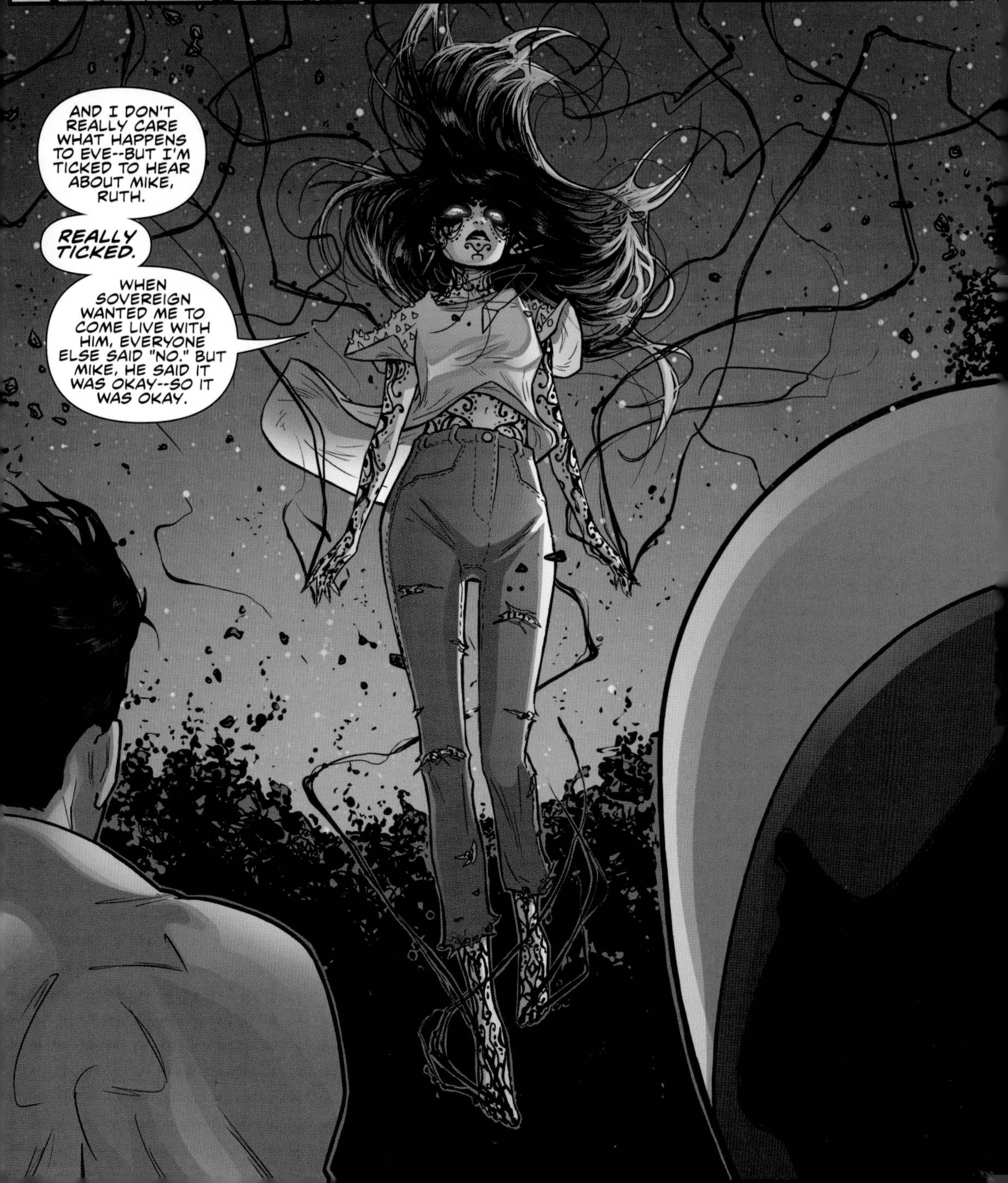
AND I DON'T REALLY CARE WHAT HAPPENS TO EVE--BUT I'M TICKED TO HEAR ABOUT MIKE, RUTH.
REALLY TICKED.
WHEN SOVEREIGN WANTED ME TO COME LIVE WITH HIM, EVERYONE ELSE SAID "NO." BUT MIKE, HE SAID IT WAS OKAY--SO IT WAS OKAY.

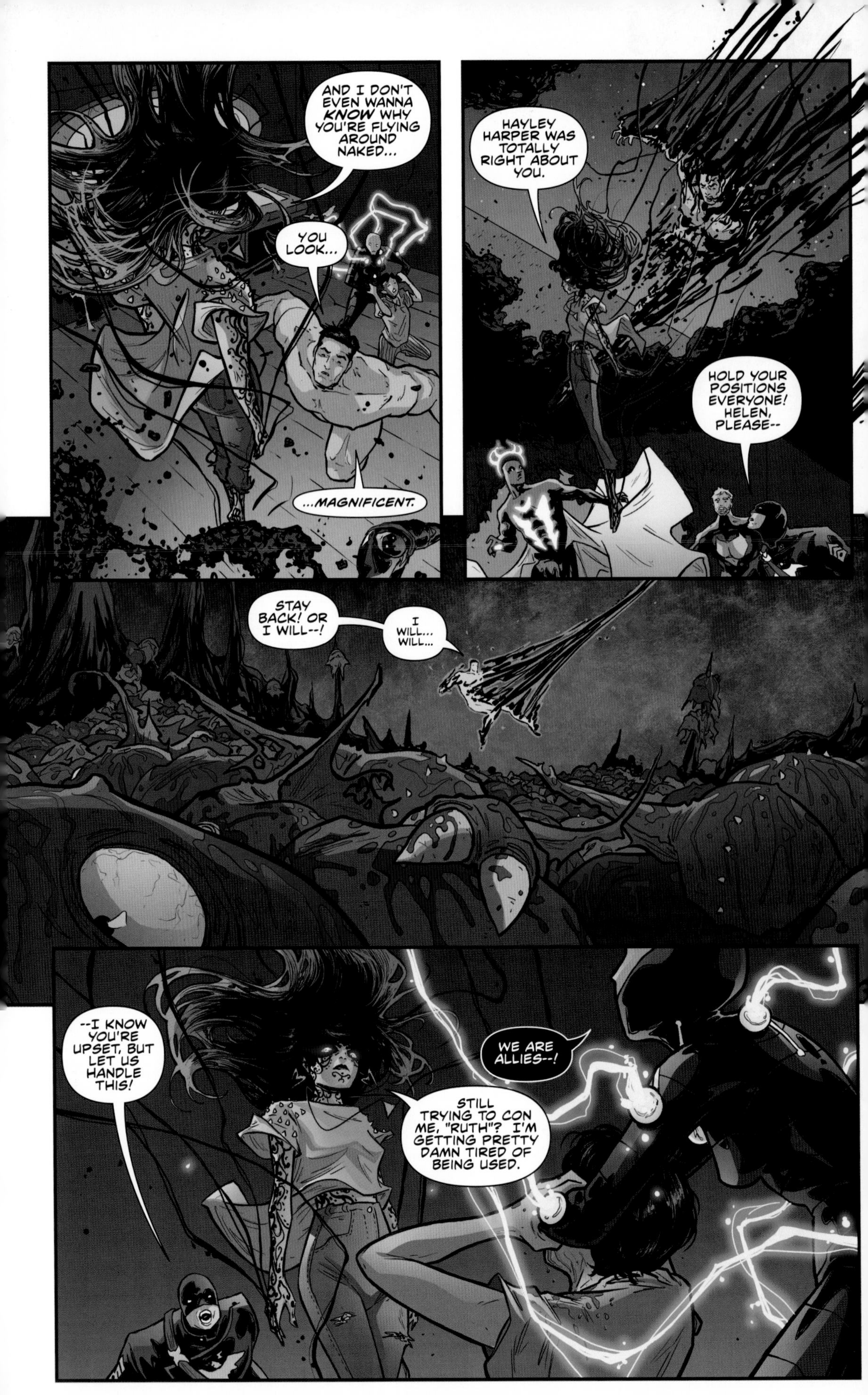
AND I DON'T EVEN WANNA *KNOW* WHY YOU'RE FLYING AROUND NAKED...
YOU LOOK...
...MAGNIFICENT.
HAYLEY HARPER WAS TOTALLY RIGHT ABOUT YOU.
HOLD YOUR POSITIONS EVERYONE! HELEN, PLEASE--
STAY BACK! OR I WILL--!
I WILL... WILL...
--I KNOW YOU'RE UPSET, BUT LET US HANDLE THIS!
WE ARE ALLIES--!
STILL TRYING TO CON ME, "RUTH"? I'M GETTING PRETTY DAMN TIRED OF BEING USED.

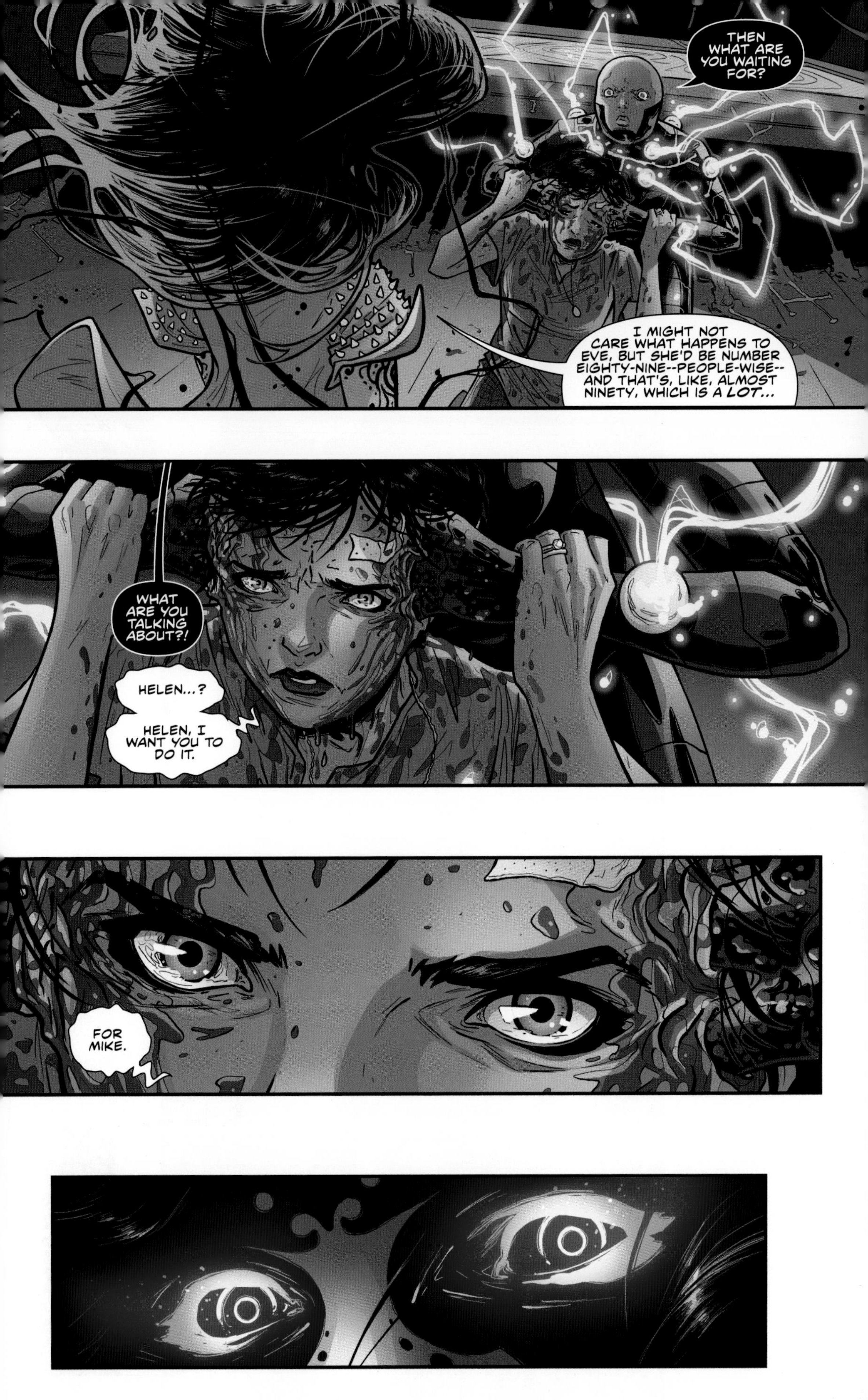
THEN WHAT ARE YOU WAITING FOR?
I MIGHT NOT CARE WHAT HAPPENS TO EVE, BUT SHE'D BE NUMBER EIGHTY-NINE--PEOPLE-WISE--AND THAT'S, LIKE, ALMOST NINETY, WHICH IS A LOT...
WHAT ARE YOU TALKING ABOUT?!
HELEN...?
HELEN, I WANT YOU TO DO IT.
FOR MIKE.

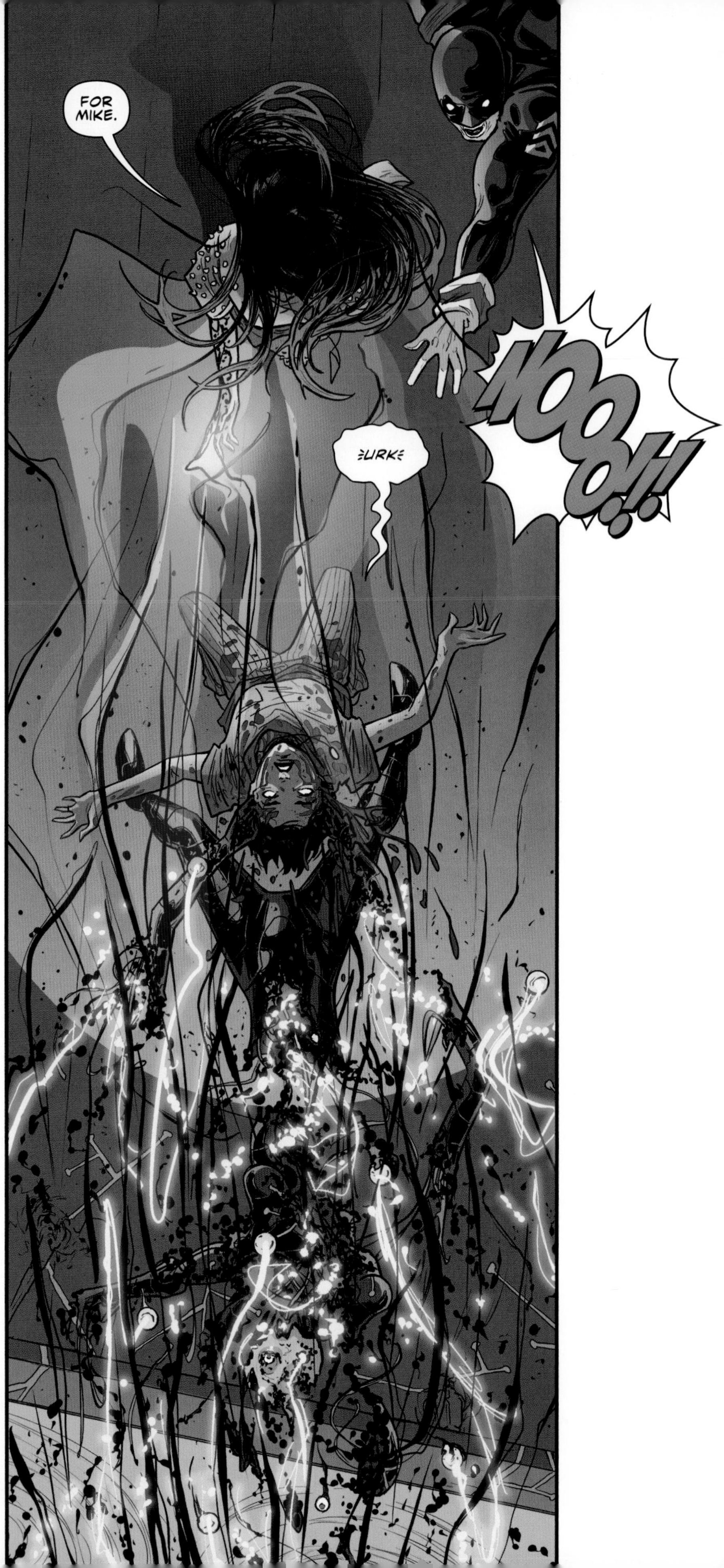
FOR MIKE.
URK
NOOO..!!!

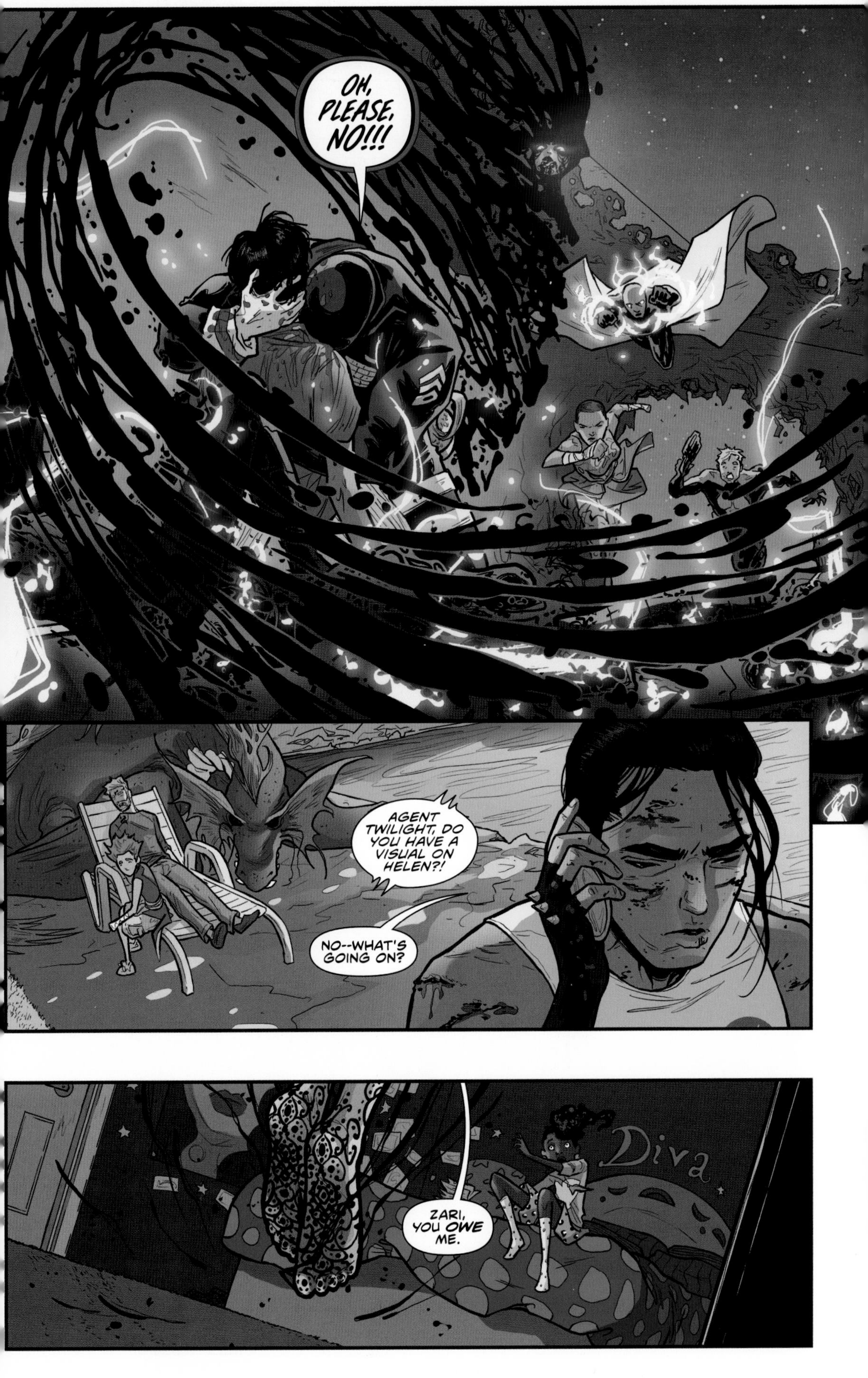
OH, PLEASE, NO!!!
AGENT TWILIGHT, DO YOU HAVE A VISUAL ON HELEN?!
NO--WHAT'S GOING ON?
Diva
ZARI, YOU OWE ME.

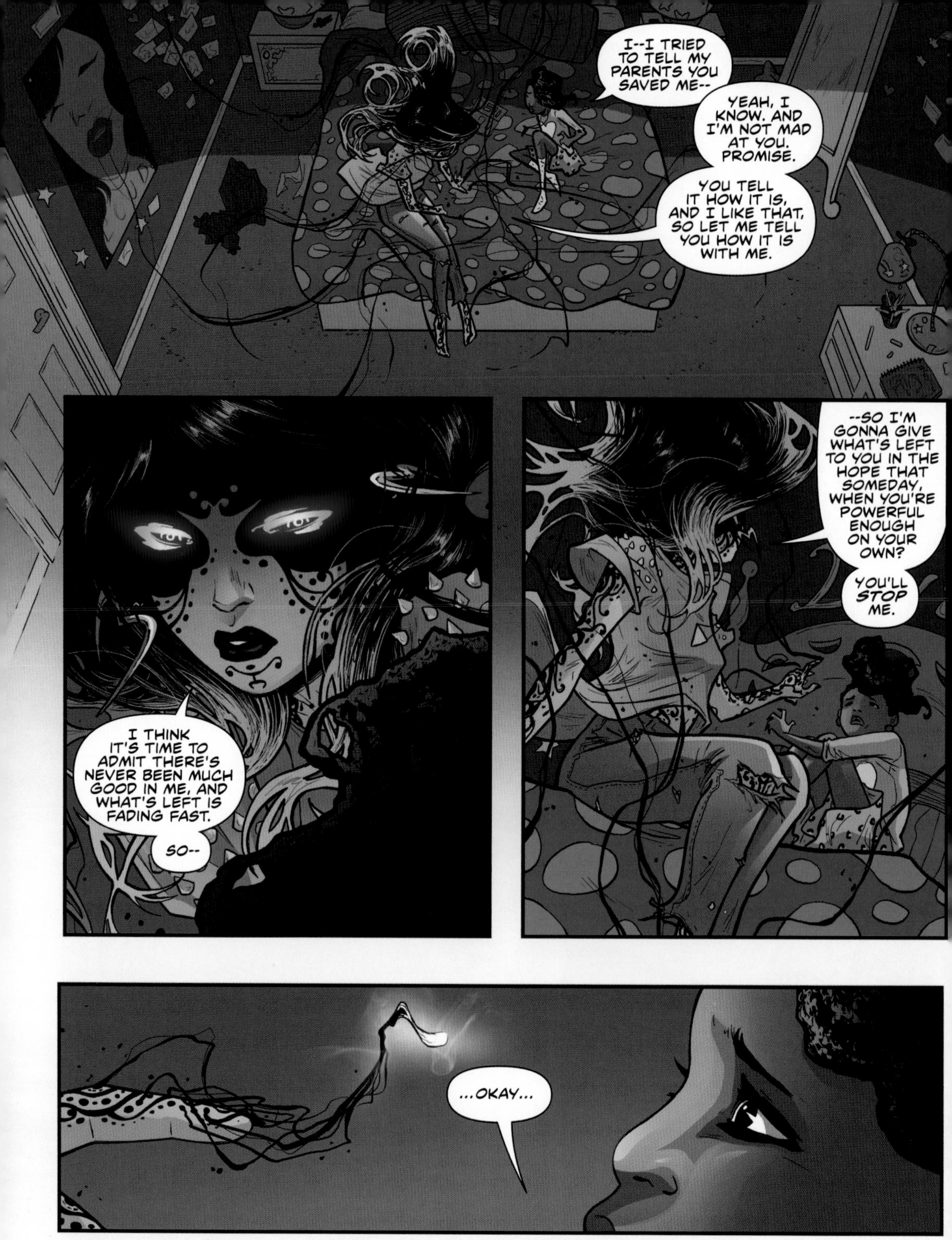
I--I TRIED TO TELL MY PARENTS YOU SAVED ME--
YEAH, I KNOW. AND I'M NOT MAD AT YOU. PROMISE.
YOU TELL IT HOW IT IS, AND I LIKE THAT, SO LET ME TELL YOU HOW IT IS WITH ME.
I THINK IT'S TIME TO ADMIT THERE'S NEVER BEEN MUCH GOOD IN ME, AND WHAT'S LEFT IS FADING FAST.
SO--
--SO I'M GONNA GIVE WHAT'S LEFT TO YOU IN THE HOPE THAT SOMEDAY, WHEN YOU'RE POWERFUL ENOUGH ON YOUR OWN?
YOU'LL STOP ME.
...OKAY...

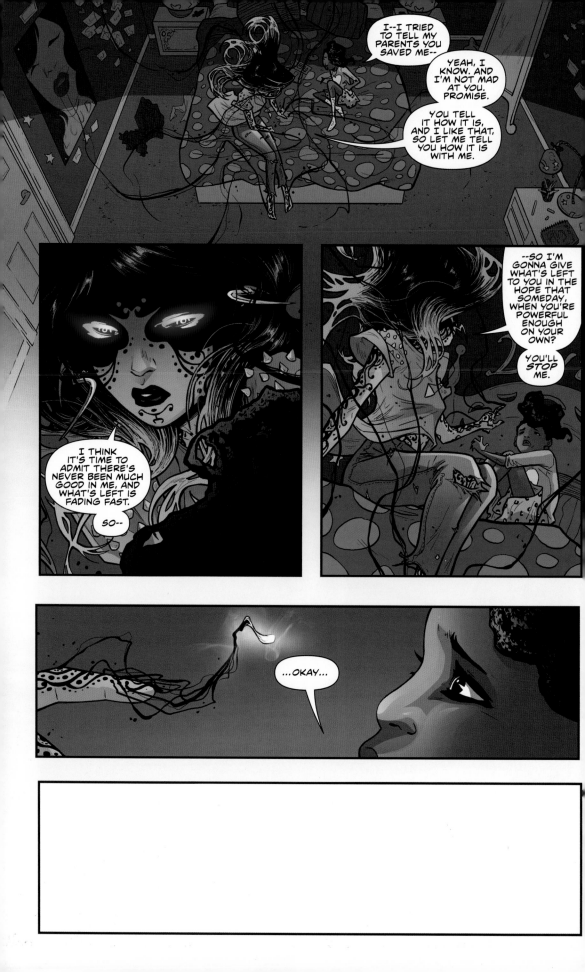

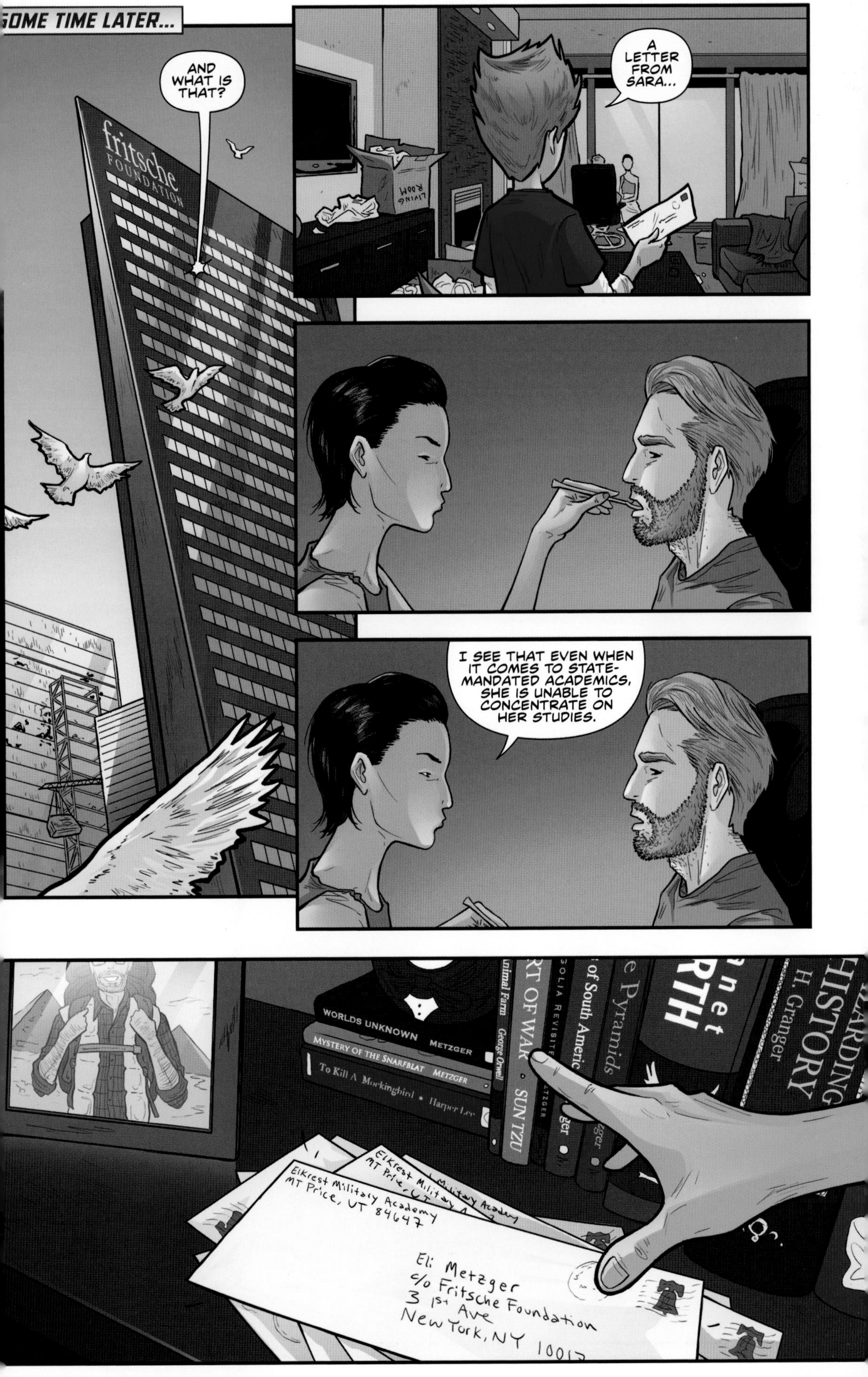
SOME TIME LATER...
AND WHAT IS THAT?
fritsche FOUNDATION
A LETTER FROM SARA...
I SEE THAT EVEN WHEN IT COMES TO STATE-MANDATED ACADEMICS, SHE IS UNABLE TO CONCENTRATE ON HER STUDIES.
WORLDS UNKNOWN METZGER
MYSTERY OF THE SNARFBLAT METZGER
To Kill A Mockingbird • Harper Lee
Animal Farm George Orwell
ART OF WAR SUN TZU
of South America
Pyramids
H. Granger
HISTORY
Elkrest Military Academy
MT Price, UT 84647
Eli Metzger
c/o Fritsche Foundation
3 1st Ave
New York, NY 10017

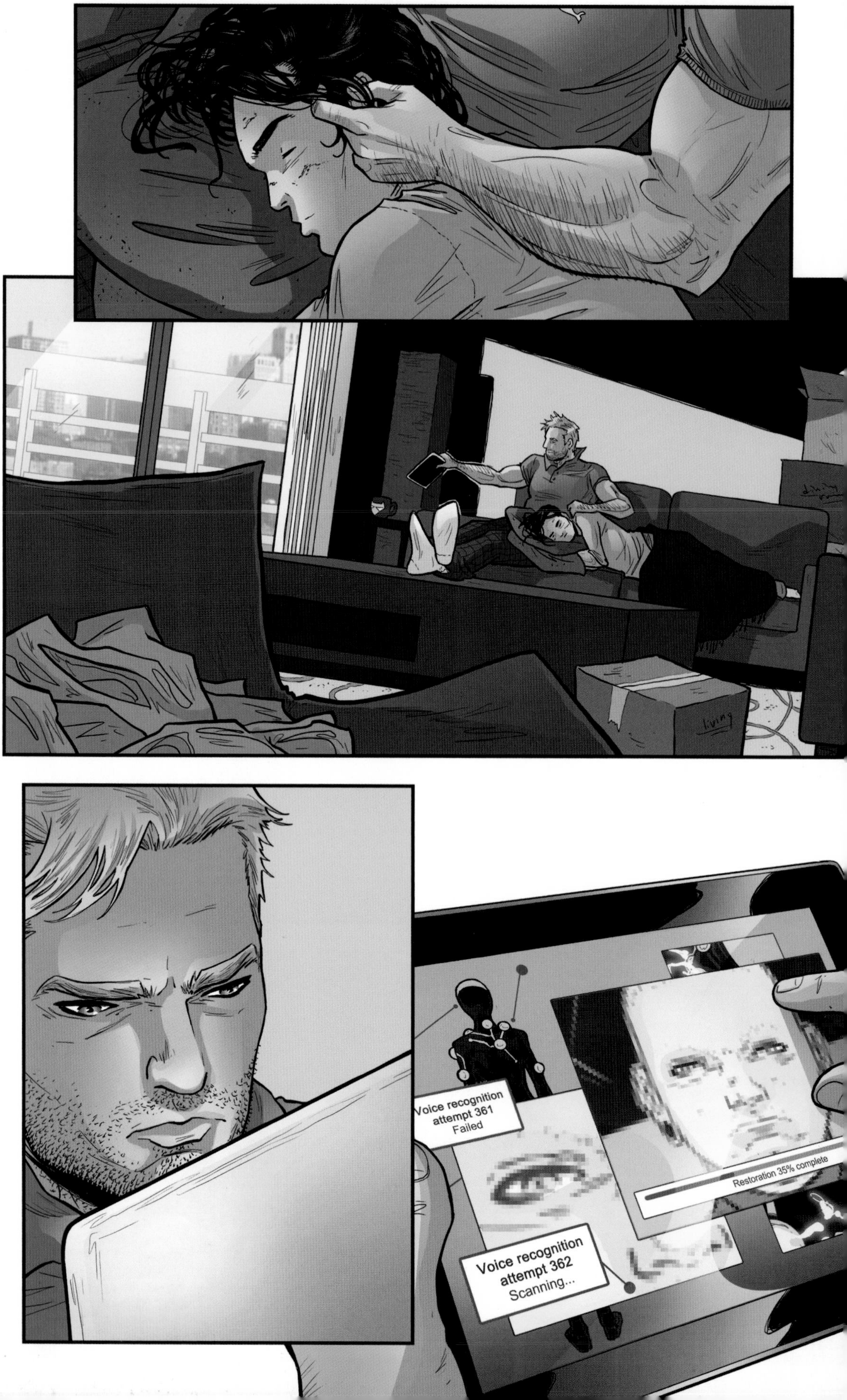
living
Voice recognition attempt 361 Failed
Restoration 35% complete
Voice recognition attempt 362 Scanning...

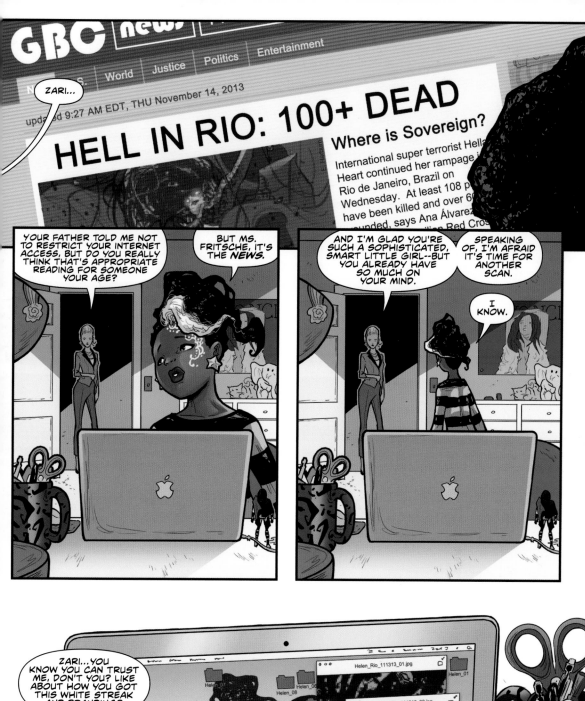

GBC news

N... | World | Justice | Politics | Entertainment

ZARI...

updated 9:27 AM EDT, THU November 14, 2013

HELL IN RIO: 100+ DEAD

Where is Sovereign?

International super terrorist Hella
Heart continued her rampage i.
Rio de Janeiro, Brazil on
Wednesday. At least 108 p
have been killed and over 60
...unded, says Ana Álvarez
...e Red Cros

YOUR FATHER TOLD ME NOT TO RESTRICT YOUR INTERNET ACCESS, BUT DO YOU REALLY THINK THAT'S APPROPRIATE READING FOR SOMEONE YOUR AGE?

BUT MS. FRITSCHE, IT'S THE *NEWS*.

AND I'M GLAD YOU'RE SUCH A SOPHISTICATED, SMART LITTLE GIRL--BUT YOU ALREADY HAVE SO MUCH ON YOUR MIND.

SPEAKING OF, I'M AFRAID IT'S TIME FOR ANOTHER SCAN.

I KNOW.

ZARI...YOU KNOW YOU CAN TRUST ME, DON'T YOU? LIKE ABOUT HOW YOU GOT THIS WHITE STREAK AND BRANDING?

I HATE HAVING TO KEEP PUTTING YOU THROUGH THESE EXAMINATIONS, ESPECIALLY IF THEY'RE UNNECESSARY...

MS. FRITSCHE, I PROMISE THAT IF I REMEMBER ANYTHING I THINK YOU SHOULD KNOW, I'LL BE SURE TO TELL YOU.

Helen_Rio_111313_01.jpg

Helen_Rio_111313_02.jpg

Helen_01

Helen_07

Helen_08

Helen_0

Helen_09

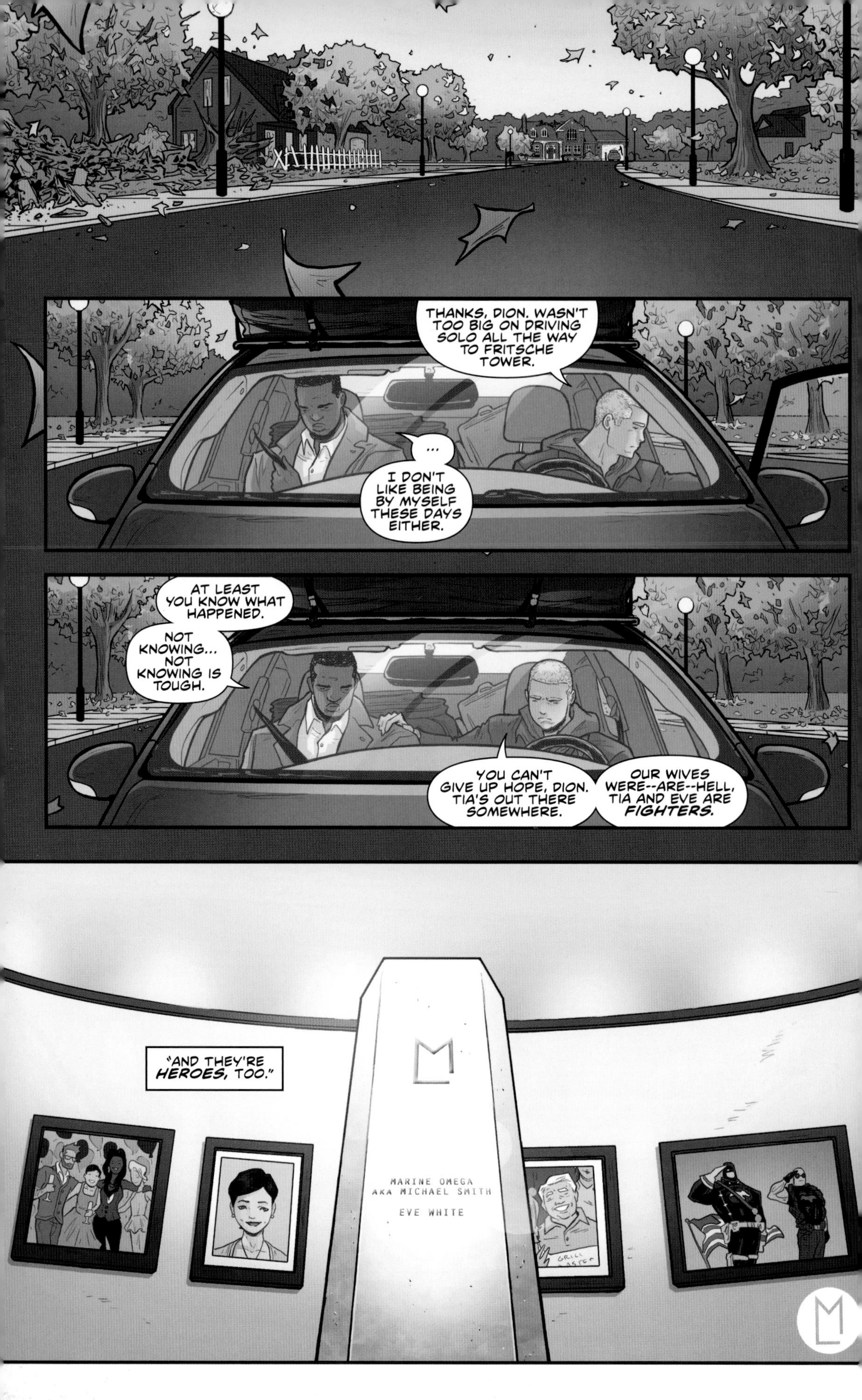
THANKS, DION. WASN'T TOO BIG ON DRIVING SOLO ALL THE WAY TO FRITSCHE TOWER.
...
I DON'T LIKE BEING BY MYSELF THESE DAYS EITHER.
AT LEAST YOU KNOW WHAT HAPPENED.
NOT KNOWING... NOT KNOWING IS TOUGH.
YOU CAN'T GIVE UP HOPE, DION. TIA'S OUT THERE SOMEWHERE.
OUR WIVES WERE--ARE--HELL, TIA AND EVE ARE *FIGHTERS.*
"AND THEY'RE *HEROES,* TOO."
MARINE OMEGA
AKA MICHAEL SMITH
EVE WHITE

Cover Gallery

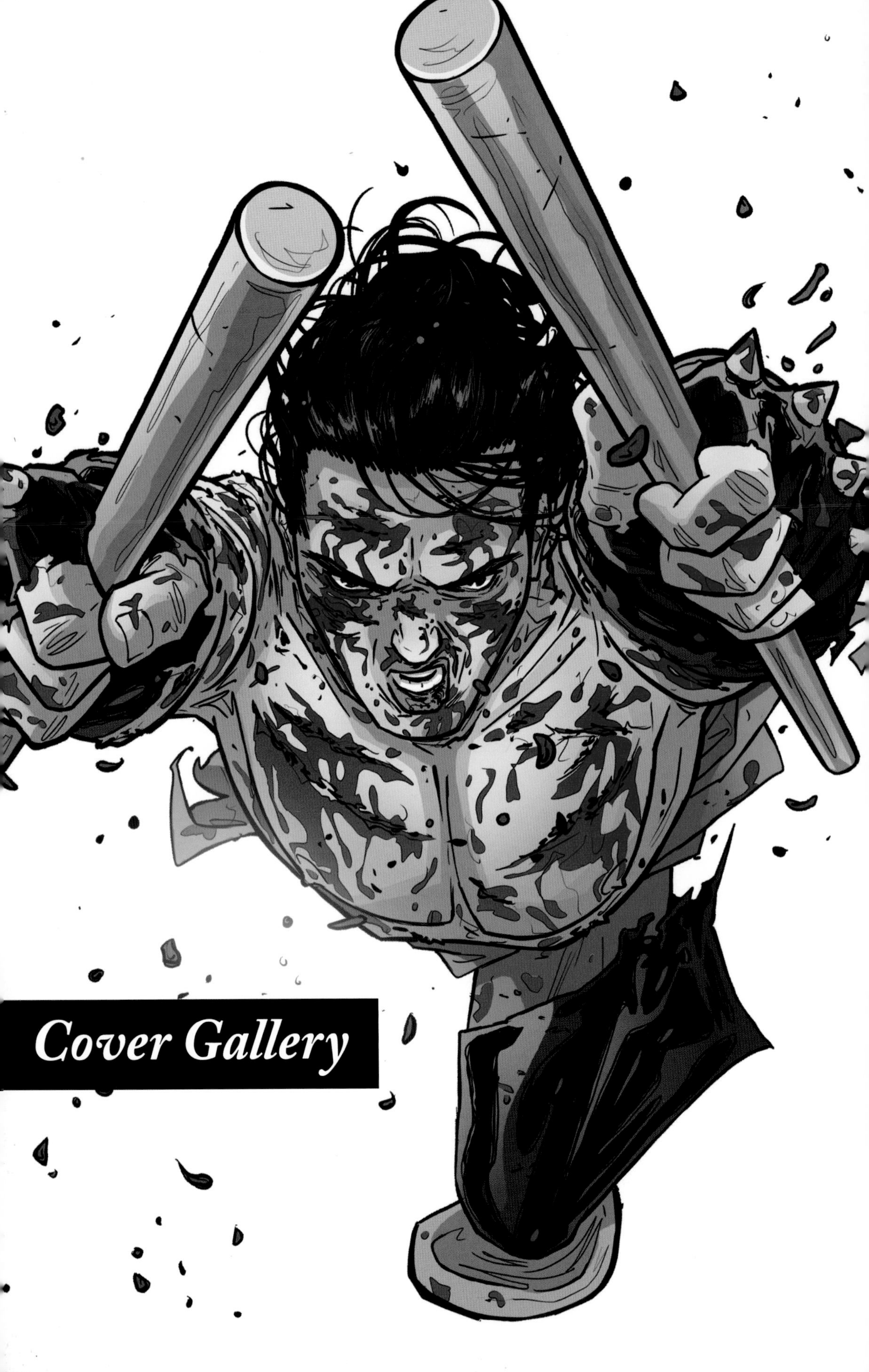

Issue Nine
Stephane Roux

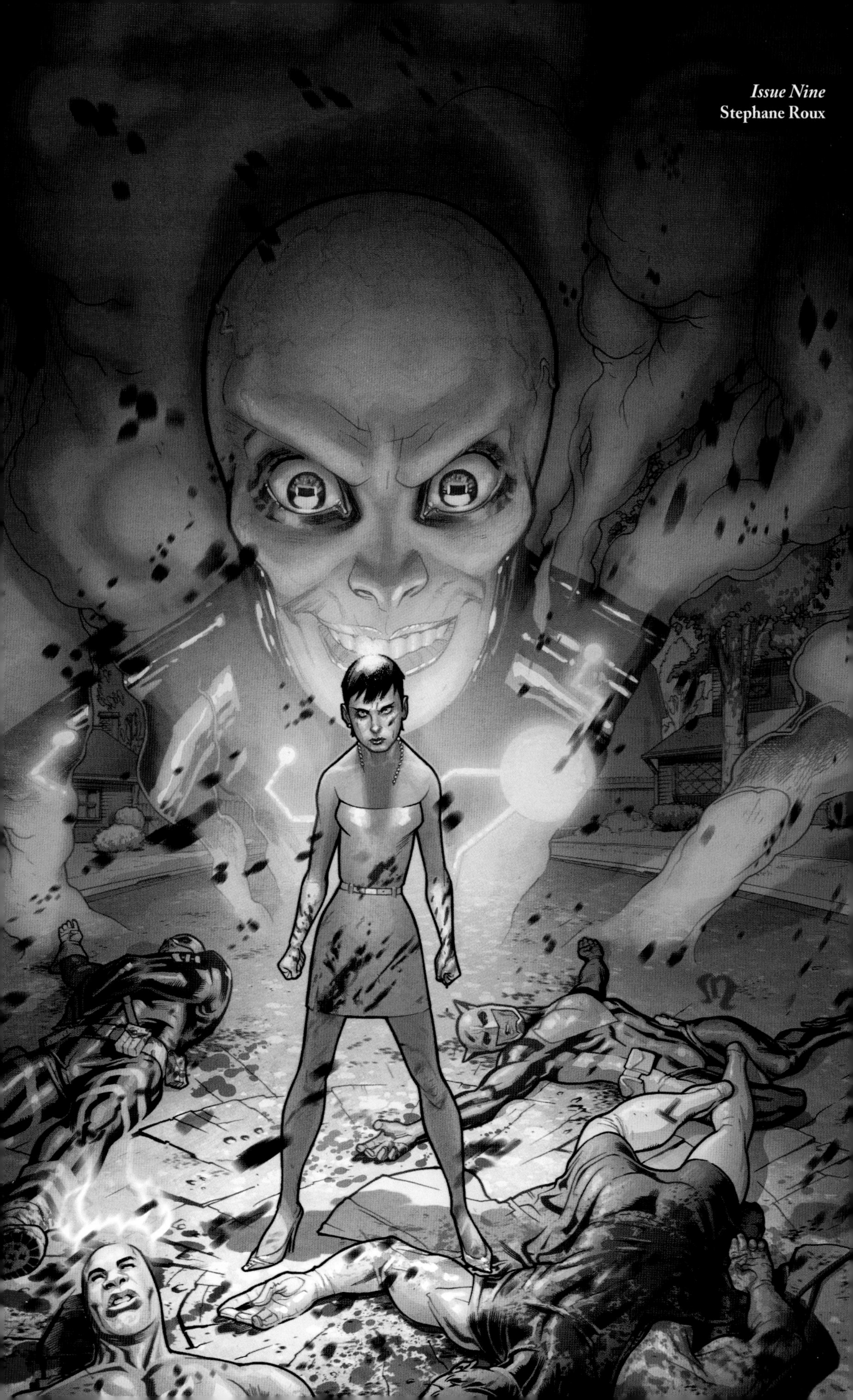

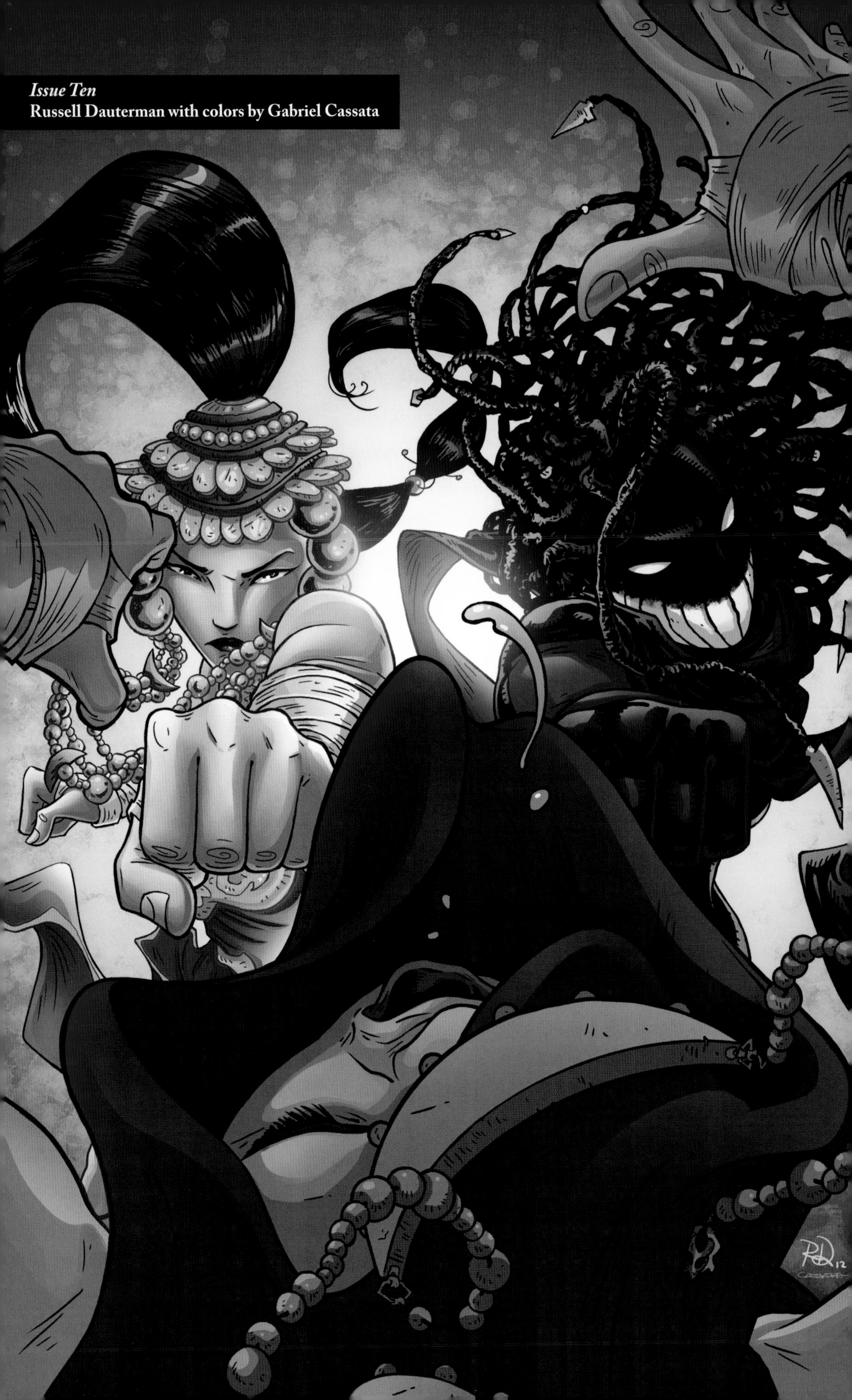

Issue Ten
Russell Dauterman with colors by Gabriel Cassata

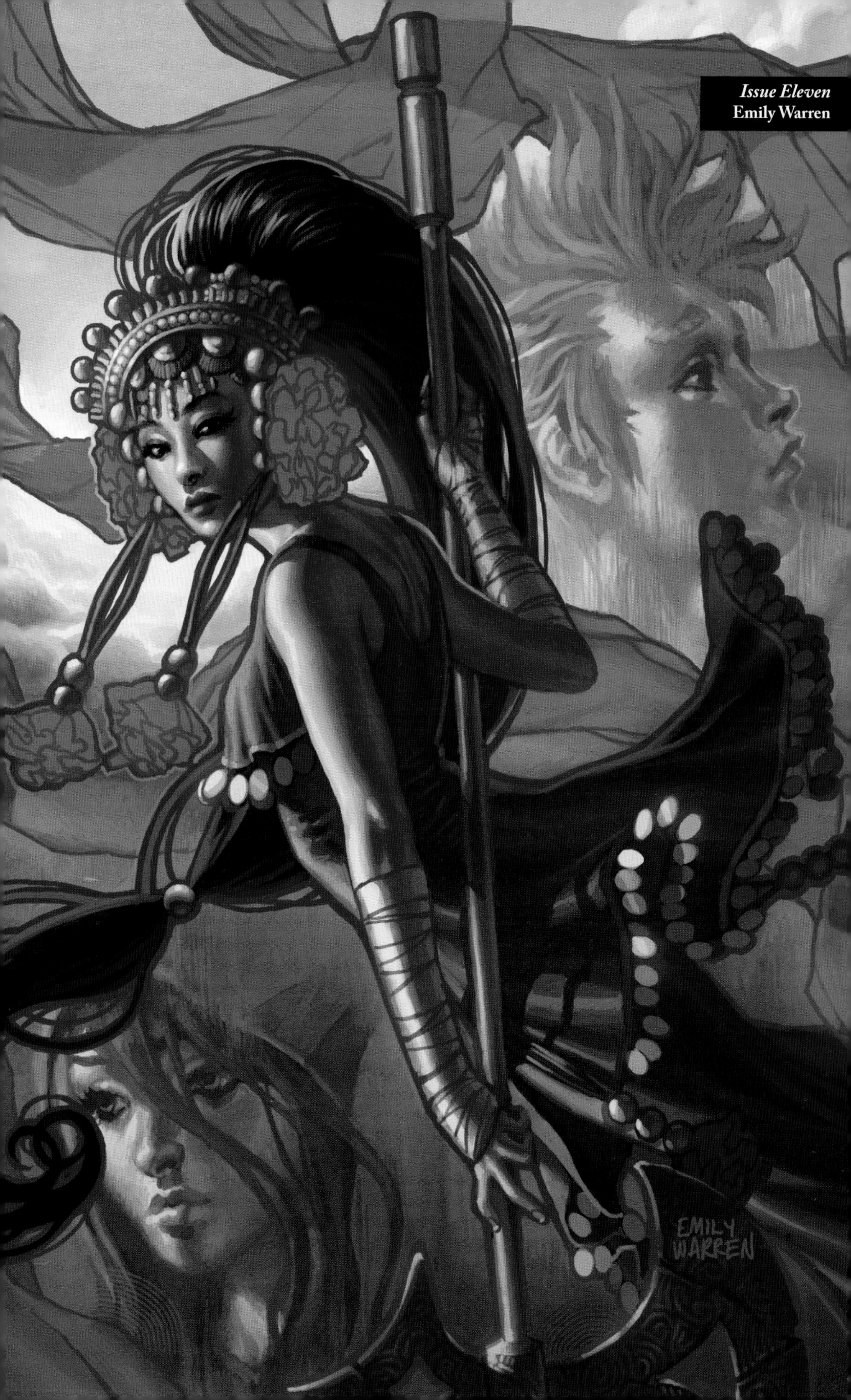
EMILY WARREN

Issue Eleven
Emily Warren

Issue Twelve
Russell Dauterman with colors by Gabriel Cassata

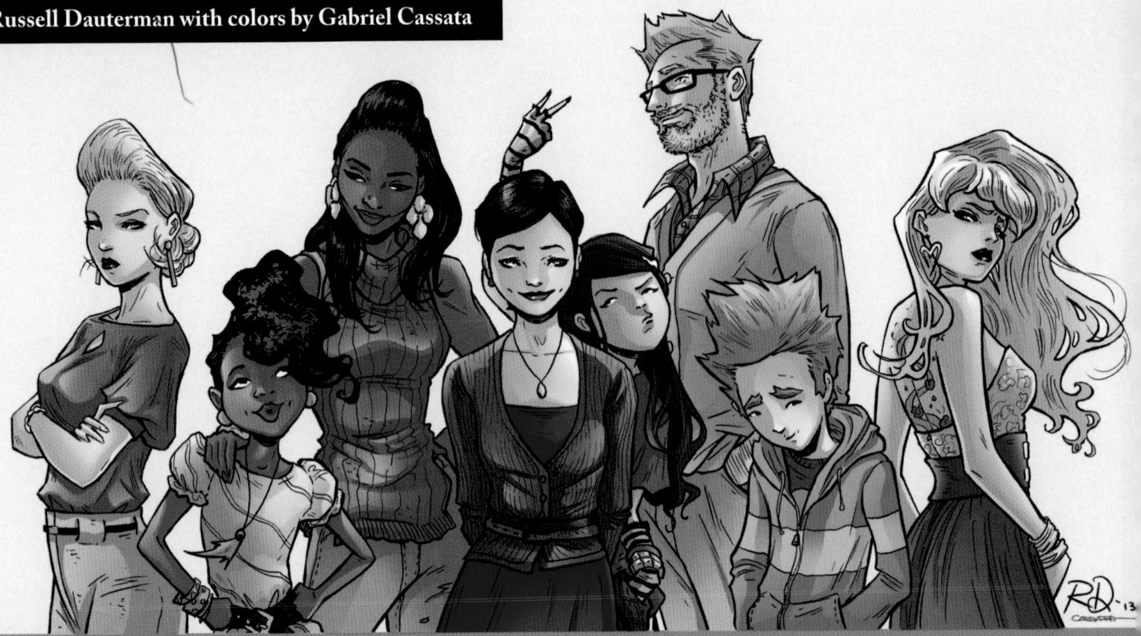

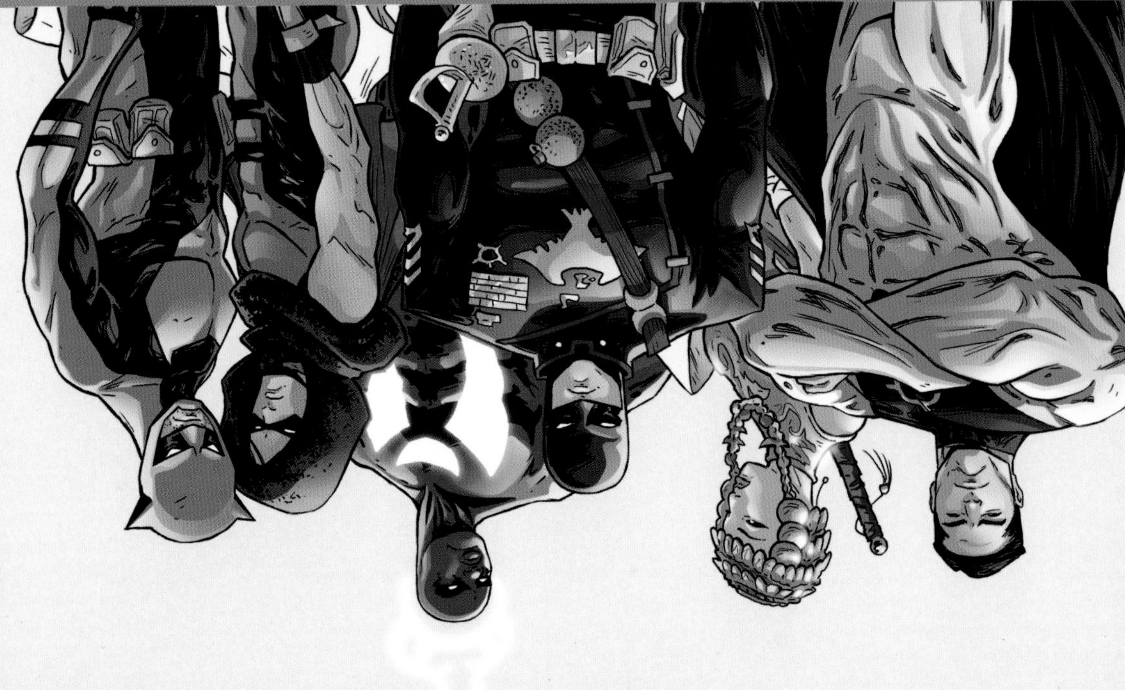

Author's Note

I wrote the comic I wanted to read.

On the one hand, like many women — and girls — who read comics, I just wanted to see more fully realized female characters on the page. Too often we get the same tired stereotypes we find in movies and TV, exploring the same tired stereotypical problems. In real life, women are just as complex as men, and deal with equally complex problems.

Of course I understand that men and women are different, but I think a lot of men would be surprised to learn we're not THAT different.

But beyond simply wanting to depict the female perspective, I've always been interested in supporting characters — both male and female. Lois Lane, Jim Gordon, Alfred Pennyworth, Agent Coulson.

Their relationship with iconic superheroes like Superman, Batman, and the Avengers not only reflects on them, but back on the superheroes as well. And when the heroes fly or swing off, these "regular people" don't go back into some box but continue to live their lives — in shadow of those heroes, intimately so.

This was a dynamic I wanted to explore.

On that note, you might wonder how I decided who would end up with who. Maybe someday I'll get to tell you exactly how Sovereign met Helen, Batu met Jeremy, Paul met Gio, etc. But I want you to know that I tried to make each pairing as realistic as possible. When choosing a romantic partner, we don't get to choose from everyone in existence but the people we happen across as dictated by our life choices.

If you think it's hard for people in Hollywood to get a date, imagine superheroes! But then, I think it can be hard for all of us to find the soulmate we imagine we deserve. And some of us never do, which means we find ourselves in imperfect relationships.

That's also something I wanted to explore.

So I hope you enjoyed all this exploring, where ordinary problems are seen through the superhero lens and superhero problems are seen through the ordinary lens.

*— **Grace Randolph***
New York, 2014

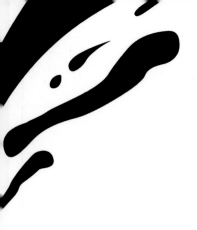

Cover Process

by Russell Dauterman

Issue Twelve Cover
Rough Concepts

Book SUPURBIA vol. 2 Issue 12

GRACE RANDOLPH'S
SUPURBIA
BOOM!

1

GRACE RANDOLPH'S
SUPURBIA

2

GRACE RANDOLPH'S
SUPURBIA
BOOM!

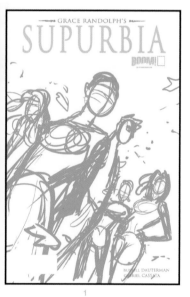

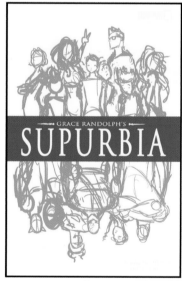

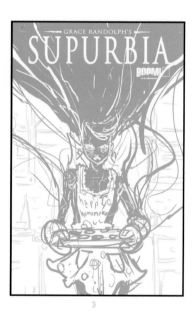

3

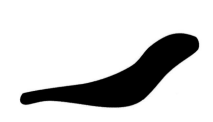

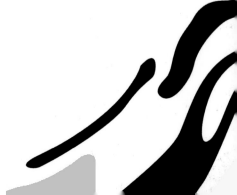

Book SUPURBIA vol. 2 Issue 12 Page # cover Artist(s) Russell Dauterman

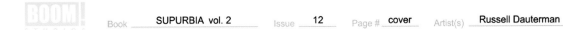

Issue Twelve Cover
Pencils

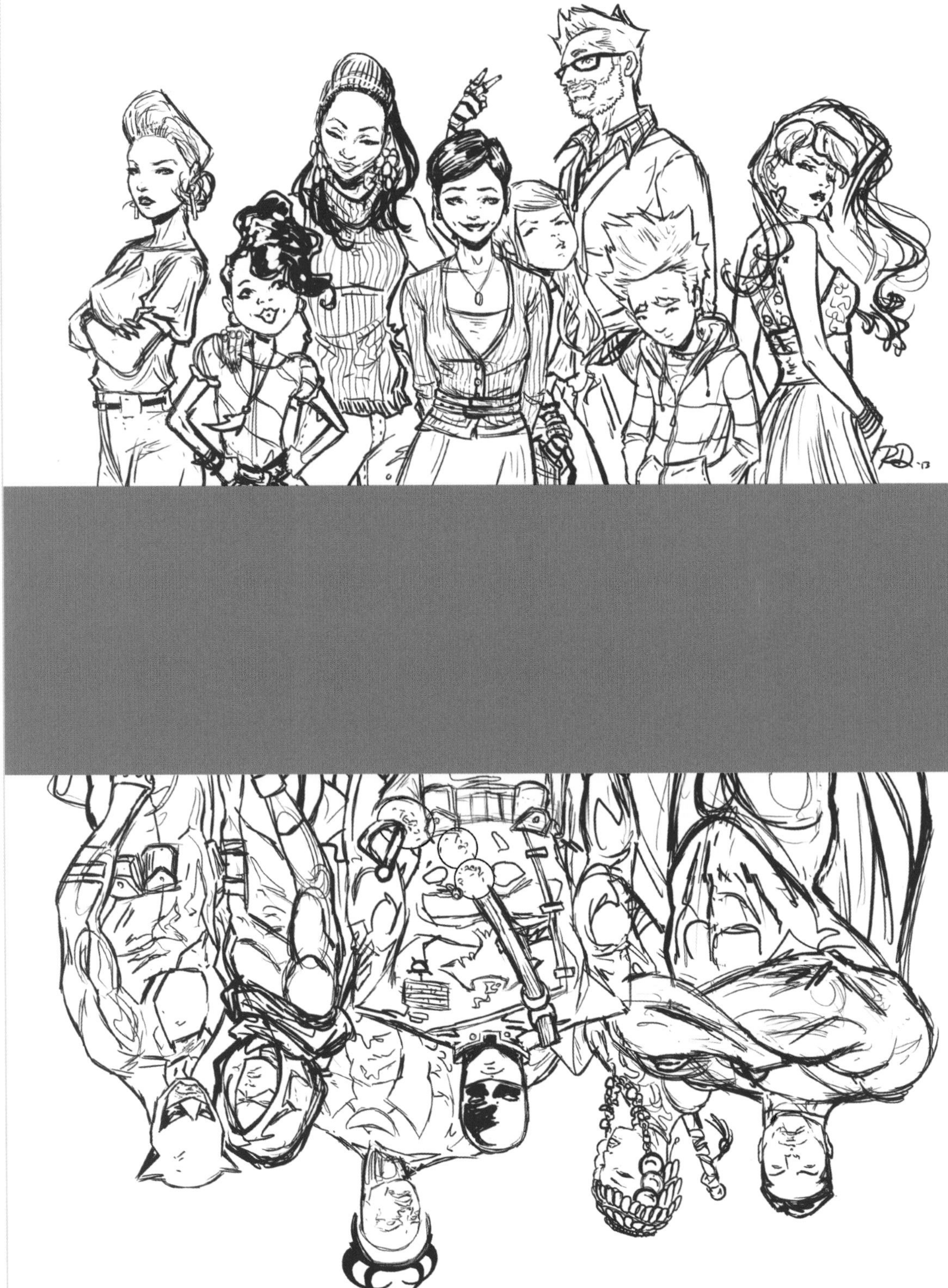

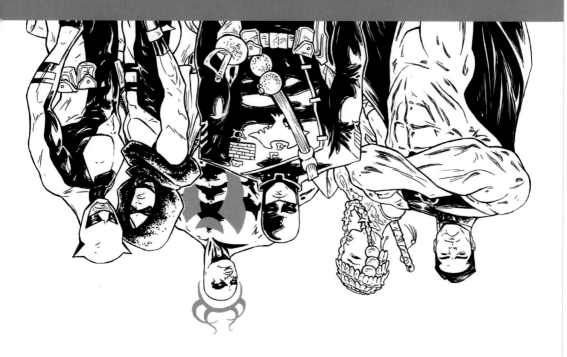

Dark Hella

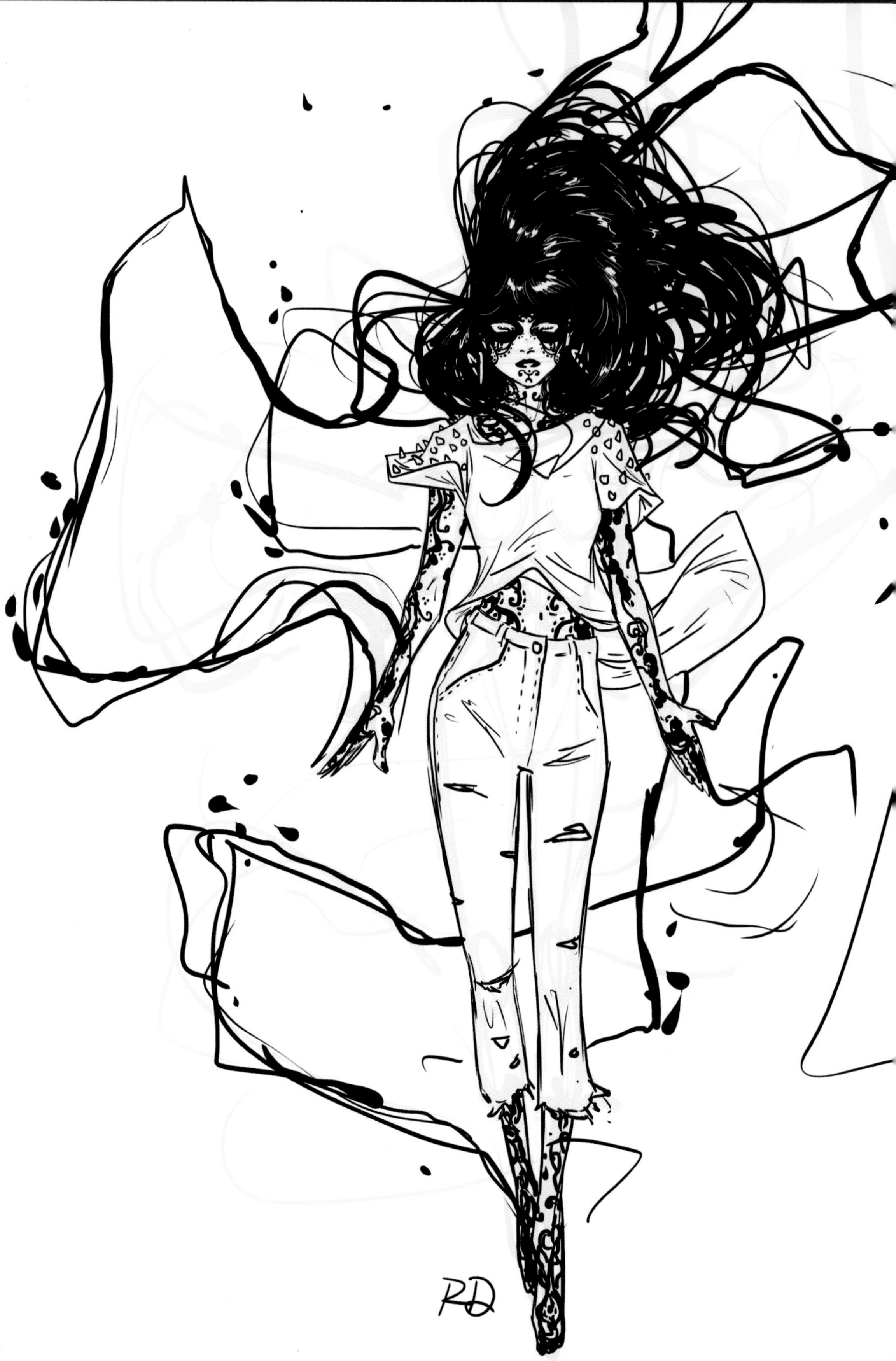
RD

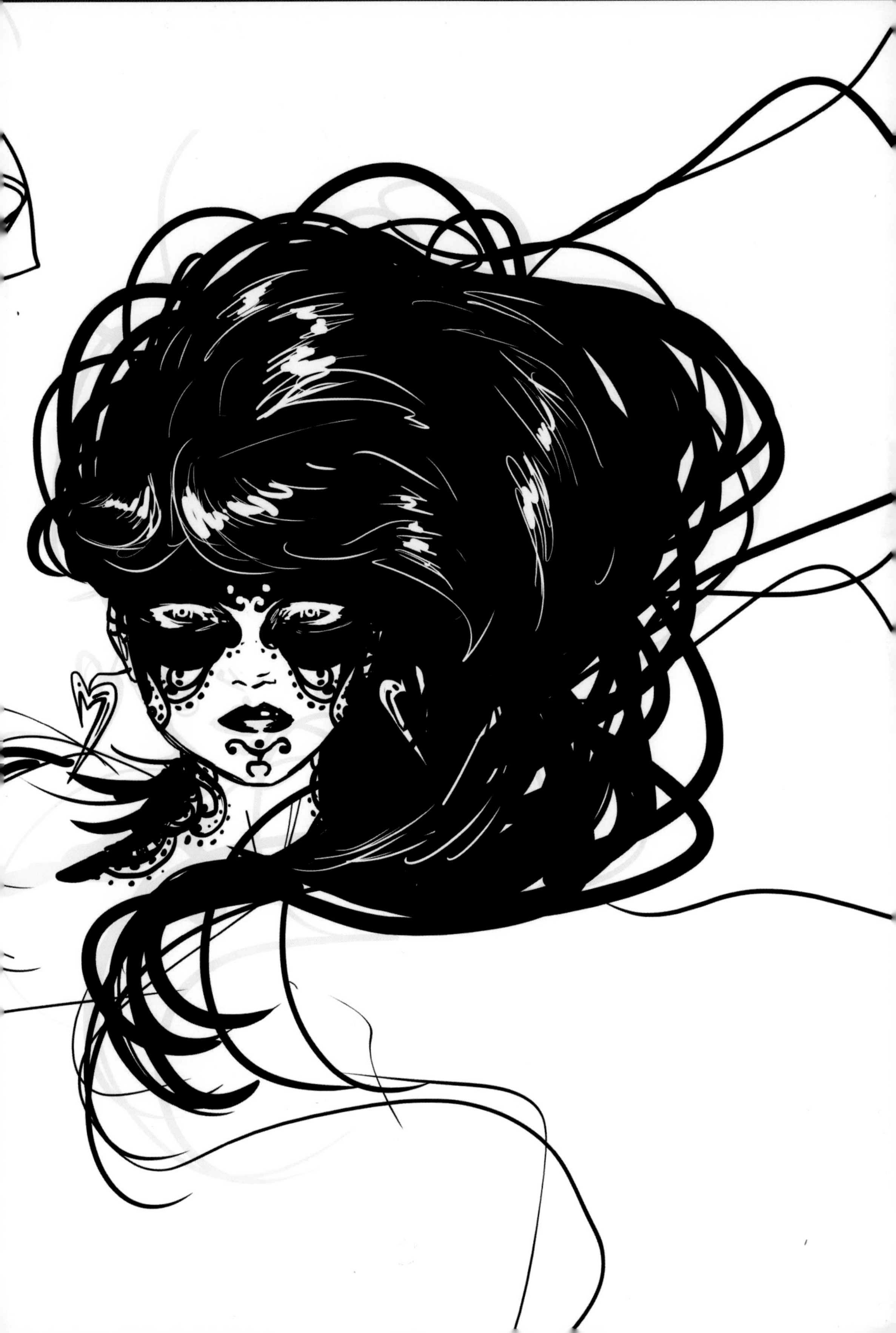